American Botanical Prints

of Two Centuries

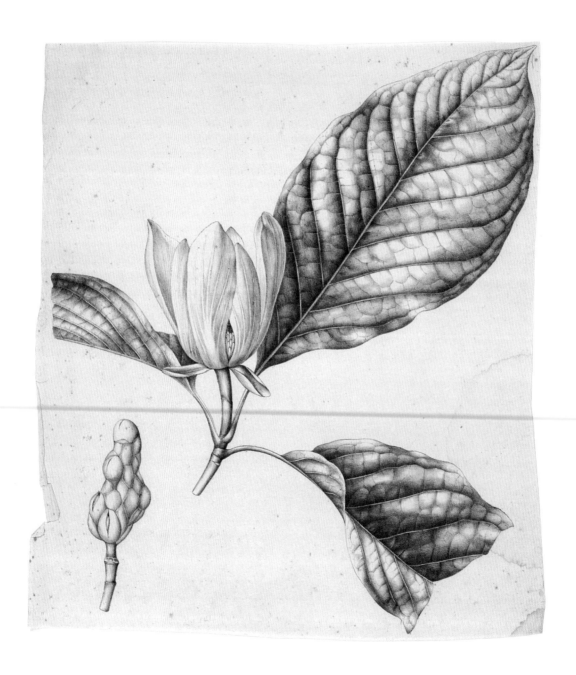

86. Lithograph of *Magnolia auriculata*, Ear-lobed umbrella tree from a drawing by Isaac Sprague.

American Botanical Prints

of Two Centuries

Catalogue of an exhibition

27 April–31 July 2003

Gavin D. R. Bridson

James J. White

Lugene B. Bruno

Hunt Institute for Botanical Documentation

Carnegie Mellon University

Pittsburgh, Pennsylvania

2003

Cover illustrations
Top:
14. Wood engraving of Passion-flower for Hermon
Bourne's *Flores Poetici: The Florist's Manual ... with*
More Than Eighty Beautifully-Coloured Engravings
of Poetic Flowers, 1833.
Bottom:
30. Lithograph, British Queen *[Laeliocattleya]*, by
Ralph Griswold, ca.1931.

Composed on Apple Macintosh using
    Microsoft Word and Adobe PageMaker
Set in Adobe ITC Bookman Standard Light
Printed offset on 80 pound Sterling Ultra Dull
    and bound by Allen Press, Inc., Lawrence Kansas
Reproduction photography with Nikon D1X camera by
    Frank A. Reynolds
Designed by Lugene B. Bruno

ISBN 0-913196-75-4

Preface

Surveys of printmaking are not unusual but are non-existent when restricted to American *and* to botanical subjects. This exhibition and catalogue present a sampling of two centuries of American botanical printmaking from utilitarian to creative, beginning with a Charleston intaglio print of 1806 and culminating in a digital print of 2000. In between are examples of woodcuts, engravings, etchings, lithographs, chromolithographs, linocuts, serigraphs and nature printing—virtually all from the Hunt Institute's extensive collections.

The 19th century in America was one of practical botanical printmaking. From the lowliest school textbook to the grandest exploration report, images of plants were required as illustrative extensions to the text and ranged in size from tiny text figures to large folio plates. Various printmaking processes were employed that required the manual skills of artists, engravers, lithographers, colorists, etc. By the end of the century, photography and photomechanical processes had been developed that could entirely eliminate the need for hand-worked printmaking methods in the production of utilitarian botanical illustrations. The 20th century saw artists indulging in printmaking purely for art's sake, and the flower and plant portrait provided a rewarding inspiration for many. In consequence of this rather fundamental difference between the two centuries, the section for the 19th century is composed mostly of books, and the section for the 20th is composed of hanging prints.

This catalogue complements our *Printmaking in the Service of Botany* (1986), a survey emphasizing printing *techniques* from herbals to photolithographs.

We gratefully acknowledge Hunt Institute editor Scarlett Townsend for diligent proofreading and graphics manager Frank Reynolds for his usually excellent photography.

— James J. White

6

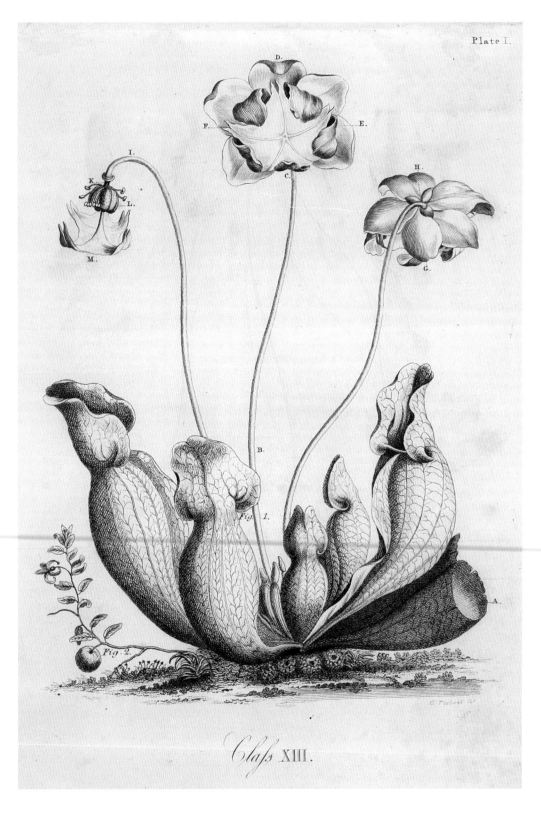

Engraving of *Sarracenia purpurea*, Purple Side-saddle flower for Benjamin Barton's
Elements of Botany, 1803.

The 19th century: Utilitarian printmaking

A ramble through some highways and byways of American botanical illustration

The earliest manufacture of surfaces for the production of multiple copies of plant images dates back to the 15th century. That procedure, which we generally call "printmaking," existed in two quite different forms in the earliest centuries, "engravings" that were printed from incised metal plates, and "woodcuts" that were literally cut with knives from a small plank of wood, the wood being cut away so that a linear image stood up in "relief." Each required quite different processes in order to create the printed pictures that illustrated the earliest botanical books. The details of these processes and some examples of the illustrations produced by their means are described and pictured in a previous Hunt Institute catalogue (Bridson and Wendel 1986). Printmaking in America commenced in the late 17th century, and its first century was characterized by highly varied levels of craftsmanship and creativity.[1] Woodcut craftsmanship had declined in Europe by this time, but incised printmaking processes—line engraving, etching, stipple engraving, aquatint, mezzotint—reached their peak by the end of the 18th century. American practitioners during this period ranged from crude, apparently self-taught, folk artists to highly trained and gifted emigré printmakers from Europe. American printmakers appear not to have made any botanical images before the last decade of the 18th century when a handful of unsigned plates were prepared for the Philadelphia publication of William Bartram's *Travels* in 1791,[2] etched copies of four French engravings were made for the American edition of Bernardin de Saint Pierre's *Studies of Nature* in 1797, and a single botanical plate was included in volume three of the *Transactions of the American Philosophical Society.*

Prints illustrating American botanical discoveries had, of course, already appeared in some quantity in the illustrated natural-history works of Catesby and others. Catesby's great *Natural History of Carolina* (1731–1743) and his *Hortus* (1737) were well known in their day, having been published in more than one edition, each illustrated with large, hand-colored plates, justly admired then and still highly prized by collectors. But the whole production of the book was a European affair. Catesby had taught himself the simple art of line etching and thus was able to prepare the copper plates himself, but the printing, hand-coloring, and publication were all done in London where a thriving book trade was well equipped to produce such results. America's population, though growing rapidly, was still comparatively sparse, and the primary concern with struggling to gain control of a seemingly endless continent left little room for the development of such peripheral activities as a book industry.

The second half of the 18th century saw the commencement of the "golden age" of botanical printmaking in Europe during which many of the botanical discoveries from the New World were incorporated into lavishly produced iconographic books. European botanical printmakers were eager to depict New World rarities and had a ready market for their images. The situation was nicely demonstrated by the illustrations reproduced in James Reveal's largely pictorial history of the botanical discovery of North America down to the 1870s (Reveal 1992). His illustrations were all of New World plant discoveries, and, significantly, all the earlier illustrations he provided, and many of the later ones also, were reproduced from contemporary European books. According to the estimate of Gordon Dunthorne (1961), the leading authority on the botanical prints of that period, "During the eighteenth and the first two decades of the nineteenth century, approximately thirty thousand flower prints were produced in England, France, Germany, Holland, Italy and Austria. Almost all of them in color." America entered the 19th century far, far behind in that field. American production of botanical prints, images that were created, engraved, and printed here, commenced in slight earnest in 1803 with Benjamin S. Barton's *Elements of Botany* published at Philadelphia, a city that was to feature prominently in the early annals of American natural-history publishing (Barnhill 1987).

Emergence of botanical printmaking in America

During the 18th century the beginnings of an engraving and copperplate printing branch of the book trade began to emerge. Largely confined to the great urban centers of Boston, New York and Philadelphia, their work was seen in early engraved maps, maritime charts, battle plans during the War of Independence, illustrated architectural books, some Bible illustrations, and so forth, some of considerable competence.[3] Real skills were developing but in a scattered pattern centered on a few successful printer/businessmen. In the late 18th century, with its newly acquired independence, America attracted ever growing numbers of European immigrants and with them a wide spectrum of trades, skills and talents, brought by people of all ages from runaway apprentices to senior masters in their professions. Engravers and copperplate printers were among them, and with this sudden influx of varied traditions, expertise and experience, the printing trades began to acquire a new breadth of proficiency and excellence. Between 1790 and 1797, Philadelphia printer Thomas Dobson produced the 18-volume third (first American) edition of the *Encyclopaedia* known as Encyclopaedia Britannica. Each volume ran to some 800 pages of letterpress and included 30 engraved plates. Lawrence Wroth, the learned historian of early American printing remarks

> it is a satisfaction to say ... that in these plates by such skilled craftsmen as Scot, Thackara, Vallance, Trenchard, Allardice, the Smithers, and Seymour one observes the coming of age of American book illustration. The whole work, illustrations, type of various sizes, and paper, even though somewhat drab in color, shows an achievement of professional craftsmen working together for an enlightened publisher. The first American book on anything like such a scale, Dobson's *Encyclopaedia* marks the end of printing in America as a household craft and the beginning of its factory stage of development (Wroth 1938, p. 294).

10

82. Line engraving of [variety of shapes and arrangements of leaves and parts of a flower] for John L. E. W. Shecut's *Flora Carolinaeensis*, 1806.

For the 30 plates in Barton's 1803 *Elements*, a similar team of eight Philadelphia engravers provided the necessary skill. William Bartram contributed competently appropriate drawings for nearly all the plates,

> his style was linear, and he did not use washes which would obscure details in his sketches. Even in the deeply shaded areas of the drawings, it is possible to understand the forms. Many of the engraved plates consist of details of plants—roots, flower parts, seeds, and so forth. Bartram provided the drawings, but he did not compose them on the plates—that was apparently the responsibility of the author. Some of the drawings do not, therefore, have a finished appearance (Barnhill 1987, p. 56).

American illustrated botanical literature made only slow progress. An American 1803 adaptation of Forsyth's *Treatise on ... Fruit Trees* had 13 plates; Shecut's 1806 *Flora Carolinaeensis* had only five; an 1811 American adaptation of Wakefield's *Introduction to Botany* had 12; and the American edition of Rees's *The Cyclopaedia*, which commenced in 1810, included a dozen botanical plates. In 1812 the second edition of B. S. Barton's *Elements* appeared. Its title page boasted that it was "illustrated by forty plates," making it the first substantially illustrated American botanical book. Nevertheless, major works on American botany were still being printed and published in Europe, such as A. Michaux's *Flora Boreali-Americana* (1803), the first flora of national scope, and F. A. Michaux's *Histoire des Arbres Forestiers de l'Amérique* (1810–1813), both produced in Paris with plates by Redouté and others. Over the next few years the American output increased only gradually in terms of numbers of new illustrated books, but the quality and quantity of plates produced increased significantly, in several instances matching European standards.

Despite America's technical progress in botanical illustration, its publications, with very few notable exceptions, never matched the grandeur of the greatest European flower books. As a new nation with a vast new continent to explore, America's botanical printmaking always had a more utilitarian goal. There was apparently no market, nor indeed enthusiasm, for a botanical equivalent of Audubon's giant *Birds of America* (1827–1837), printed in Britain and pitched at the most affluent of Europe's gentlemen book collectors. Botanical exploration was to continue right through the century; the last great American wilderness being explored by the Harriman Alaska Expedition in 1899. The essentially utilitarian nature of 19th-century American botanical printmaking is the characteristic that our exhibition seeks to emphasize.[4]

Picturing the New World flora

Almost the first need was to produce verbal and pictorial descriptions of the native flora of this great New World. Michaux's outstanding iconography of the great forest flora of eastern America, although published in French in Paris, acquired such an essential place in American botanical literature that an English language edition was published in 1841 at Philadelphia. Thomas Nuttall added a three-volume supplement in 1842–1849 with 122 new plates, all American productions. Meantime, in 1821–1823, again at Philadelphia, W. P. C. Barton, nephew of the previously mentioned B. S. Barton, had published *A Flora of North America* with 105 colored engravings. In 1846 Asa Strong produced *The American Flora* with 195 colored plates, a New York production for a change, and three years later Asa Gray's authoritative *Genera Florae Americae Boreali-Orientalis Illustrata* appeared, also in New York, with 186 plates by Isaac Sprague, one of America's great botanical illustrators. The late 1840s also saw the commencement of the great series of government funded illustrated expedition reports that hold such a major position in American botanical literature (to be mentioned later).

9. Hand-colored engraving of *Rudbeckia laciniata*, Jagged-leaved Rudbeckia from an illustration by William P. C. Barton for his *A Flora of North America*, 1821.

Anemone Pratensis

92. Chromolithograph of *Anemone pratensis*, Pasque flower for Asa B. Strong's
The American Flora, 1847.

Illustrating America's medico-botanical wealth

Alongside the great need to describe and illustrate American plants for scientific purposes was an interest in their practical value, medical botany being a major feature of their exploitation. Again, illustration was an important element since the correct identification of significant healing plants was crucial, mistakes perhaps proving fatal. W. P. C. Barton is again featured here with his 1817–1818 *Vegetable Materia Medica of the United States* published at Philadelphia that provided 60 fine colored plates. His publisher informed potential buyers that "the object of this work is to present the public with faithful representations of the many important medicinal plants of our country, most of which are as yet known only by name, to our physicians." At the same time in Boston Jacob Bigelow was publishing his elaborately illustrated *American Medical Botany* with 60 colored plates. These were undoubtedly expensive books that were available to relatively few of the public. The need to provide for less affluent purchasers was fulfilled by books such as Samuel Henry's *New and Complete American Medical Family Herbal*, published at New York in 1814 and illustrated with monochrome text figures,[5] and Constantine Rafinesque's *Medical Flora*, published at Philadelphia in 1828–1830 with 100 monochrome plates in a "pocket" format suitable for the field.[6] The 1840s saw a flurry of medical botanies: Mattson's *American Vegetable Practice* appeared in Boston in 1841 with 24 colored plates; in 1841 Rafinesque provided another modestly produced *Manual of the Medical Botany* with 52 plates; in 1845 Peter Good commenced his *Family Flora & Materia Medica Botanica*, which was to run to 98 colored plates over the next ten years; Carson's 1847 *Illustrations of Medical Botany* ran to 100 colored plates; and Griffith's *Medical Botany* added "upwards of three hundred illustrations" to the tally in 1847. Illustrations of medicinal plants were clearly a great requirement at the time.

16

MULLEN.

VERBASCUM.

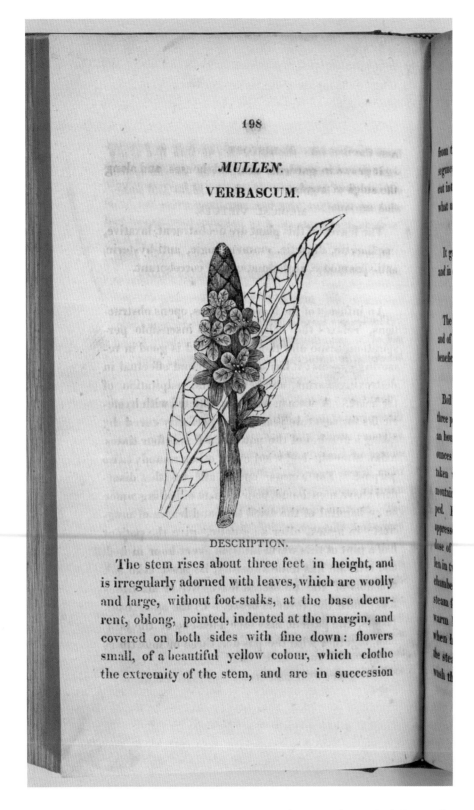

DESCRIPTION.

The stem rises about three feet in height, and is irregularly adorned with leaves, which are woolly and large, without foot-stalks, at the base decurrent, oblong, pointed, indented at the margin, and covered on both sides with fine down: flowers small, of a beautiful yellow colour, which clothe the extremity of the stem, and are in succession

35. Wood engraving of Mullen [Mullein], *Verbascum* for Samuel Henry's *A New and Complete American Medical Family Herbal*, 1814.

Pl. XIII.

Kalmia latifolia

10. Color line engraving of *Kalmia latifolia* for Jacob Bigelow's *American Medical Botany ... with Coloured Engravings*, 1817–1820.

Wild Red Raspberry.   Rubus Strigosus.

W Sharp del   Sharp, Michelin & Cᵒ 17 Tremont Row.

62. Chromolithograph of Wild red raspberry, *Rubus strigosus* for Morris Mattson's
*The American Vegetable Practice; or, A New and Improved Guide to Health Designed for the
Use of Families in Six Parts*, 1841.

Garden flowers and fruit portrayed

Another great field for plant exploitation was the rapidly burgeoning horticultural industry. Apart from the personal needs of American gardeners the creation of great urban centers stimulated immense attention on the identification, selection and production of plant resources for the dinner table, the parlor, the kitchen and the flower garden. Following many examples in Britain, France, Belgium, and elsewhere, America began to produce periodicals, usually in monthly issues, that included colored plates of notable novelties or varieties of flowers, fruit, and occasional vegetables. *Floral Magazine* appeared in Philadelphia from 1832 to 1834, the grand *Orchardists Companion* in Philadelphia from 1841 to 1843, *Monthly Flora* in New York in 1846, *The Horticulturist* (later *Gardener's Monthly And Horticulturist*) in Albany from 1846 onwards, *The Philadelphia Florist* (later *The Florist and Horticultural Journal*) in Philadelphia from 1852 to 1855, *The Gardener's Monthly and Horticultural Advertiser* in Philadelphia from 1859 onwards—all fall into this category. But colored plates were too expensive for the Massachusetts Horticultural Society. Their rather grand *Transactions* included 15 plates in the three numbers produced in 1847–1851, but the enterprise failed and was not revived on that scale again.

By midcentury, fruit became a highly important element in the horticulture industry, for, as one modern historian informs us,

> the rise of public interest in fruit-growing was hastened by the growth of cities and the building of the Erie Railroad. Fruit and vegetable production expanded dramatically, and New York was the market. In June, 1847, a single train delivered eighty thousand bushels of strawberries to New York. New Jersey became an important center for strawberry, apple, and peach growing. Railroads grew rapidly and special express trains were scheduled to rush quality fruits to New York mansions and hotels. Literature on fruit growing burgeoned (Pennsylvania Horticultural Society 1976, p. 85).

THE CEDAR OF LEBANON.

Full grown Tree at Foxley, planted by Sir Uvedale Price.
[Scale 1 in. to 12 feet.]

[Horticulturist, June, 1847.]

21. Wood engraving of The Cedar of Lebanon for Andrew Jackson Downing's *The Horticulturist and Journal of Rural Art and Rural Taste,* July 1846–June 1847.

In 1847–1856 C. M. Hovey published *The Fruits of America* in New York with over 90 plates, "The book of books in horticulture so far as size, color plates, and fine printing go. …" according to Hedrick (1950). The third volume of Ebenezer Emmons' *Agriculture of New York*, published at Albany in 1851, dealt with fruit, apples, pears, quince, peach, plum, etc., and provided 81 colored plates. *The Illustrated Pear Culturist*, an 1857 New York publication, included over 30 colored plates, but it was soon outclassed by the even more attractive W. D. Brincklé edition of *Hoffy's North American Pomologist* published at Philadelphia in 1860 with 60 remarkable colored plates described by McGrath (1966) as "almost good enough to eat."[7]

21

38. Wood engraving of The Concord Grape for Charles Mason Hovey's *The Magazine of Horticulture, Botany and All Useful Discoveries and Improvements in Rural Affairs,* 1854.

THE CONCORD GRAPE.
(FIG. 2.)

Attractive, even beautiful, though some of these horticultural plates were, they were generally produced in serviceably handy volumes, apparently with as much of an eye to practicality as towards visual appeal. Whereas in Europe, monographs on selected horticultural flowers and "pomonas"[8] had, since the 18th century, frequently been produced in stately folio tomes that were to be found in the libraries of gentlemen and connoisseurs, rather than practical horticulturists, America did not venture into such lavish and expensive publishing ventures, an odd exception being J. F. Allen's famous *Victoria Regia; or, The Great Water Lily of America*, with illustrations by William Sharp (Boston, 1854). The plates were truly enormous, of "European" proportions one might say, and permitted life-size illustration of this plant wonder but were limited to only six.[9]

Below:
81. William Sharp's color lithograph of *Victoria Regia [Victoria amazonica* (Poepp.) Sowerby] for John Fisk Allen's *Victoria Regia,* 1854.

Exploration, discovery, and scientific illustration

The 1850s saw the publication of a large number of illustrated expedition reports that included an impressive number of botanical contributions from John Torrey, Asa Gray, George Engelmann, William S. Sullivant and other leading botanists of the day. For over a decade these reports rolled off the presses, the standard of illustration reaching an excellence that could match that of comparable European publications. In midcentury acres of paper were consumed in America and Europe for plates that depicted new plant discoveries from around the world, and amongst the American artists who contributed to this surge were two who must be singled out for mention. By the mid 1840s Asa Gray was keenly feeling the need for a skilled botanical artist. The ever growing tide of plant collections from the field created a corresponding need to prepare and publish scientifically accurate illustrations of all these novelties. In 1845 Gray was introduced to Isaac Sprague, a Massachusetts artist in his 30s who had already proved his artistic skill at bird and flower painting and had worked in the field with Audubon in 1843—it was to be a fortuitous meeting. Hunter Dupree, Gray's biographer, commented

> during the rest of Gray's career Sprague's competent illustrations provided seldom-mentioned but oft-seen support. He was much more than a mere artist who did what was set before him, for he learned to make his own analyses of flowers. Thus his work was scientifically correct without requiring Gray to check constantly. Indeed he often made discoveries by his close observation (Dupree 1959).

A further asset came Gray's way in the person of Joseph Prestele, a highly skilled immigrant German lithographic artist with the added advantage that he had already worked for some leading European botanists and understood the specialized illustrative needs of the science when translating an artist's drawing onto stone.[10]

Tab. 4.

Gaillardia amblyodon.

84. Hand-colored lithograph by Joseph Prestele from Isaac Sprague's drawing of *Gaillardia amblyodon* for Asa Gray's *Chloris Boreali-Americana*, 1848.

Tab. 9.

Sprague del.

Thermopsis mollis.

85. Hand-colored lithograph by Joseph Prestele from Isaac Sprague's drawing of *Thermopsis mollis* for Asa Gray's *Chloris Boreali-Americana*, 1848.

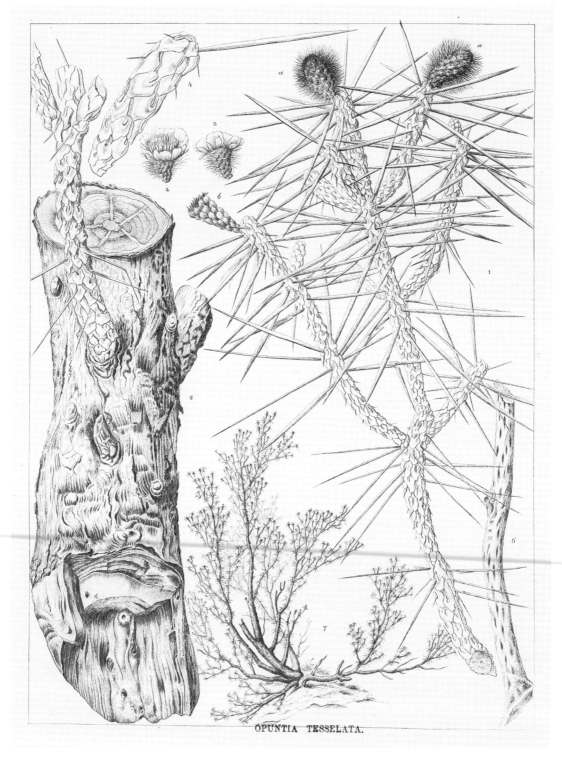

OPUNTIA TESSELATA.

74. Lithograph by Joseph Prestele from Paulus Roetter and Heinrich Balduin Möllhausen's drawing of *Opuntia tessellata* E. [as published] for George Engelmann and J. M. Bigelow's "Description of the cactaceae" in the *Reports of Explorations and Surveys, to Ascertain the Most Practicable and Economical Route for a Railroad from the Mississippi River to the Pacific Ocean*, 1856.

The plates that accompanied the United States Army's great western exploration reports of the 1840s to the 1870s were among the high points of American botanical illustration. These were generally published without coloring in quarto government-published tomes that were not well known to the general public. In consequence they have not acquired the same later attention and reputation as some of the more brightly colored contemporary plates of lesser botanical stature. The tally was considerable: over 350 scientific plates accompanied the official reports by John Torrey in 1848, 1852, and 1853 (2); George Engelmann in 1856; Torrey and Asa Gray in 1857 (2); Torrey in 1857, 1858 (2); Engelmann in 1859; Torrey in 1859; and Sereno Watson in 1871. They depicted plants collected in expeditions covering Missouri to Arkansas, the Great Salt Lake and the Rocky Mountains, the Zuni and Colorado Rivers, the Red River of Louisiana, the 35th parallel westward, the 32nd parallel from the Red River to the Rio Grande, the 40th, 38th and 39th parallels, the 35th parallel westward, the 35th and 32nd parallels in California, the Mexican Boundary Survey, the 40th parallel, and the exploration of parts of Nevada, Utah, California, New Mexico and Arizona, many of them newly discovered or described species. A particularly noteworthy example of this output are the 24 engravings of Cactaceae collected near the 35th parallel on Whipple's 1853–1854 railroad exploration that illustrated Englemann's 1856 botanical report. They are breathtaking in the precision of their technical execution—illustrations of austere beauty indeed. But perhaps most impressive of all the expedition plates were those of the tall folio atlases depicting the scientific results of Lt. Charles Wilkes' United States Exploring Expedition that crisscrossed the Pacific from 1838 to 1842. The mishandling of the collections brought back from this voyage, the troubled history of the preparation of the printed reports, the occurrence of a disastrous fire that destroyed vital materials and finished publications, make up one of the unhappy tales of 19th-century American natural history. In the end 200 botanical plates were produced that demonstrate the best qualities of scientific printmaking at this period, each one the collaborative effort of botanist, artist, editor, and printmaker. Though exquisitely detailed, and aesthetically pleasing as plants are to the botanist and plant enthusiast, the plates remain rigidly academic in their presentation—models of scientific illustration. The reports were published by William Brackenridge in 1855, Asa Gray in 1857, William Sullivant in 1862, and John Torrey in 1874.

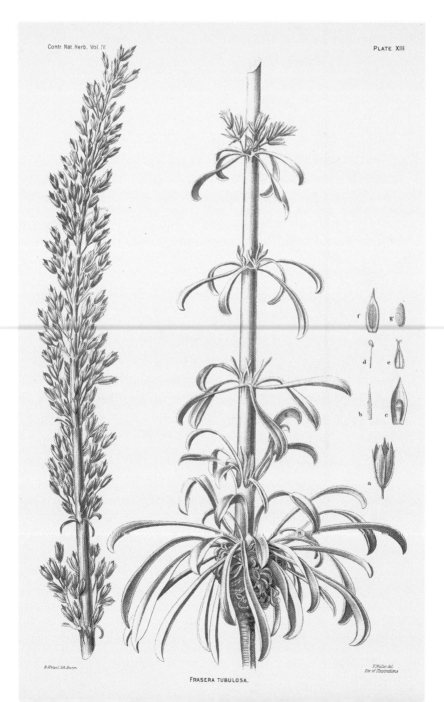

66. Lithograph of *Frasera tubulosa* Coville from a drawing by Frank Muller for Frederick V. Coville's "Botany of the Death Valley Expedition" in *Contributions from the United States National Herbarium,* 1893.

A CACTUS GROVE, ARIZONA (SPECIES—CEREUS GIGANTEUS)

77. Chromolithograph from H. J. Morgan's 1871 painting of A cactus grove, Arizona (species–*Cereus giganteus*) *[Carnegiea gigantea* (Engelm.) Britt. et Rose] for Joseph Trimble Rothrock's *Report upon United States Geographical Surveys West of the One Hundredth Meridian ...,* 1878.

Text-figures for teaching botany

What we have been describing, the production of "plate" books in the first half of the 19th century, is only part of the story of printmaking in the service of American botany for this period. One of the most basic needs for the emerging American nation was the provision of cheap educational manuals that would instruct school and junior college students in the rudiments of the sciences, botany amongst them. By the 19th century it had become an established convention that introductory textbooks should provide pictorial sketches of the basic structures and shapes of plants and their parts. Extensive verbal descriptions were always provided, but, on the basis that a picture is worth a thousand words, authors virtually always provided sketches or diagrams, however tiny, either crowded onto a few explanatory plates or in the form of "figures" dotted about the text pages. However humble, they still required the services of printmaking specialists to produce them. Barton's 1803 *Elements* (mentioned above) was the first and was followed by popular works such as Priscilla Wakefield's *Introduction* in 1811, Barton's second edition in 1812, Sir James E. Smith's *Introduction* in 1814, Robert J. Thornton's *Grammar* in 1818, John Locke's *Outlines* in 1819, George Sumner's *Compendium* in 1820, Christopher Irving's *Catechism* in 1822, Sir James E. Smith's *Grammar* in 1822, Barton's third edition in 1827, Thomas Nuttall's *Introduction* in 1827, Almira Phelps' *Familiar Lectures* in 1829, and Jane Marcet's *Conversations* in 1830. These earlier educational books had their sketches and diagrams grouped on a few engraved copperplates. From about 1832 onwards, with the universal adoption of wood engraving for such work, text figures became the norm. There was a constant stream of such books for the rest of the century. Mrs. Phelps (or Lincoln) published a second edition of *Familiar Lectures* in 1831 and continued for more than 25 editions down to ca.1860, and her *Botany for Beginners*, first published in 1833, continued for about 14 editions down to ca.1848. Asa Gray published his first *Elements of Botany* in 1836, *Botanical Text-Book* in 1842, *First Lessons in Botany* in 1857, *Botany for Young People*

83. Lithograph of Table III (Fig. 41. Stamens and pistil of *Ulex europaeus, Furze;* 42. Stamens and style of *Pisum maritimum,* Sea-side pea; 43. Calyx of the same; 44. Standard; 45. A wing; 46. One petal of the keel; 47. Pistil; 48. Stamens and pistil of *Hypericum elodes,* Marsh St. John's-wort; 49. Calyx magnified; 50. Back of the whole flower; 51. *Stuartia pentagyna;* 52. A petal separate, with part of the stamens, a. pistils; 53. *Melaleuca thymifolia;* 54. Bundles of stamens; 55. Calyx and pistil; 56. Separate petal) from a drawing by Arthur Stansbury for Sir James Edward Smith's *A Grammar of Botany, Illustrative of Artificial, as Well as Natural Classification,* 1822.

27. Wood engraving of Fig. 861.
Polygonum Pennsylvanicum. 862.
Enlarged flower laid open. 863. Section of
the ovary, showing the erect orthotropous
ovule. 864. Section of the seed, showing
the embryo, on one side of the albumen
for Asa Gray's *The Botanical Text-Book
For Colleges, Schools, and Private
Students,* 1842.

The farinaceous seeds of P. Fagopyrum (the Buckwheat)
are used for food. The roots of most species of *Rhubarb*

are purgative : but it is not yet known what particular
species of Tartary yield the genuine officinal article.

ORDER 112. PHYTOLACCACEÆ. Chiefly represented by the common Poke (Phytolacca decandra), and well
distinguished by a compound ovary of ten confluent (one-
seeded) carpels, the short styles or stigmas distinct; the
fruit a flattened berry. — The root is acrid and emetic: yet
the young shoots in the spring are used as a substitute for
Asparagus. The berries yield a copious deep-crimson
juice.

FIG. 861. Polygonum Pennsylvanicum. 862. Enlarged flower laid open. 863.
Section of the ovary, showing the erect orthotropous ovule. 864. Section of
the seed, showing the embryo, at one side of the albumen.

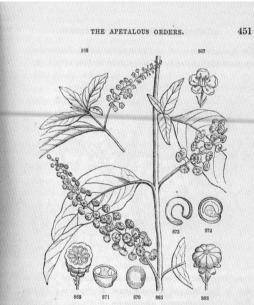

Group 3. *Flowers perfect, or sometimes polygamous, not disposed
in aments, furnished with a regular and often petaloid calyx.
Ovary one (rarely two) celled, with solitary ovules, or at least a
single seed in each cell. Embryo not coiled around albumen. —
Trees or shrubs, rarely herbs.*

ORDER 113. LAURACEÆ. Trees or shrubs, with al-
ternate leaves, their margins entire. Flowers sometimes
polygamo-diœcious. — Calyx of four to six somewhat united
sepals, which are imbricated in two series, free from the
ovary. Stamens definite, but usually more numerous than

FIG. 865, 866. Phytolacca decandra (Poke). 867. A flower. 868. Unripe fruit.
869. Cross section of the same, a little enlarged. 870. Magnified seed. 871. Section of the same across the embryo. 872. Vertical section, showing the embryo
coiled around the albumen into a ring. 873. Magnified detached embryo.

28. Wood engraving of Fig. 865, 866.
Phytolacca decandra (Poke). 867. A flower.
868. Unripe fruit. 869. Cross section of the
same, a little enlarged. 870. Magnified seed.
871. Section of the same across the embryo.
872. Vertical section, showing the embryo
coiled around the albumen into a ring. 873.
Magnified detached embryo for Asa Gray's
*The Botanical Text-Book For Colleges,
Schools, and Private Students,* 1842.

in 1858, *Introduction to Structural and Systematic Botany* in 1858, *School and Field Book of Botany* in 1868, and *Structural Botany* in 1879—the whole constituting a series of versions and editions of his instructional text that continued to the end of the century. Alphonso Wood, whose textbooks offended Gray's scientific standards but nevertheless stood as rivals to Gray's own, published his *First Lessons in Botany* in 1850, his *Class-Book of Botany* in 1861, *Leaves and Flowers* in 1863, and *How to Study Plants* in 1882, much of the same material reappearing in a variety of editions later revised by Oliver R. Willis. Textbook publication became a veritable industry in itself. Apart from the Phelps/Gray/Wood trio, a stream of texts of varying scholastic levels and merit were published from 1832 onward by John Comstock, William Ruschenberger, Harland Coultas, Frances Green and Joseph Congdon, Eliza Youmans, Charles Bessey, George Macloskie, George Goodale, and Liberty Bailey from 1832 to 1900. All were illustrated with what must collectively amount to thousands of text illustrations, modest in format and cost, the notable exception being Frances H. Green and Joseph W. Congdon's rather handsome *Analytical Class-Book of Botany* published in 1855 in a well-designed quarto with both plates and text illustrations of better than average quality. Gray's textbooks were particularly fully illustrated, especially those for which he had Sprague's assistance. The fifth edition of his *Botanical Textbook of Structural and Systematic Botany, and Vegetable Physiology,* published in 1858, boasted "over thirteen hundred woodcuts," many of truly "thumbnail" proportions. Probably the tiniest of all text illustrations were those provided in E. A. Apgar and A. C. Apgar's 1874 *Plant Analysis: Adapted to Gray's Botanies.* They provide an introductory "analytical arrangement of botanical terms," the type set in open line spacing with a little (ca. 1 cm) line-drawn figure set *between* each term and its definition.

Inexpensive instructional manuals were also a growing necessity outside the schoolroom. The burgeoning population required cheap books and periodicals on the elements and the practice of applied botany, i.e., horticulture,

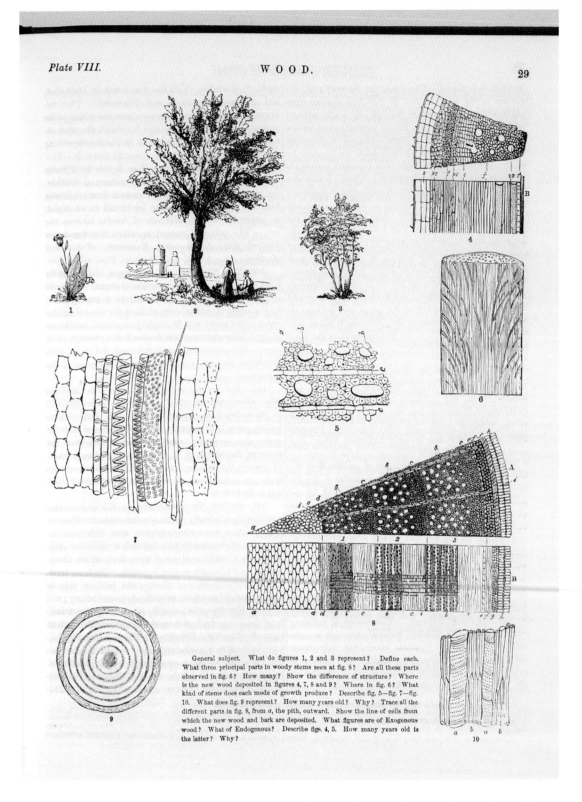

29. Wood engraving of Pl. VIII. Wood for Francis Harriett Green and Joseph W. Congdon's *Analytical Class-Book of Botany*, 1855.

agriculture, silviculture, pasture and field crops, vegetable and fruit varieties, the uses of the native tree flora, etc. These were ordinary people for whom the color-plate books mentioned previously were unaffordable luxuries. A rather handsome early example is William Coxe's 1817 *View of the Cultivation of Fruit Trees, … with Accurate Descriptions of the Most Estimable Varieties of Native and Foreign Apples, Pears, Peaches, Plums, and Cherries*, illustrated by sturdy cuts of 200 kinds of fruits of the natural size, a pioneer pomological Bible for Americans. In later years typically inexpensive manuals with modest text illustrations included Robert Manning's 1838 *Book of Fruits*, Andrew Downing's 1845 *Fruits and Fruit Trees of America*, John Thomas's 1847 *American Fruit Culturist*, Samuel Cole's 1849 *Book for Every Body: The American Fruit Book*, Andrew Fuller's 1867 *Small Fruit Culturist*, George Johnson's 1847 *Dictionary of Modern Gardening*, Richard Allen's 1856 *American Farm Book*, John Warder's 1858 *Hedges and Evergreens*, John Klippart's 1860 *The Wheat Plant*, and Peter Henderson's 1869 *Practical Floriculture* and 1875 *Gardening for Pleasure*, etc. The last pair of titles were products of the Orange Judd Company of New York, who, more than any other publisher, provided a wealth of cheap illustrated horticultural manuals in the later decades of the century.

A novel convention was introduced for the illustration of fruit varieties in the inexpensive manuals that relied on text illustrations rather than colored plates. Only the outline of the mature fruit, such as apples, peaches, plums, etc., was provided, and sometimes several overlapping outlines were grouped on the page. The idea was introduced by Downing in his 1845 book with the explanation, "Many of the more important varieties of fruit are shown in outline. I have chosen this method as likely to give the most correct idea of the form of a fruit, and because I believe that the mere outline of a fruit, like a profile of the human face, will often be found more characteristic than a highly finished portrait in color." The idea was much copied by other writers, but Downing's own principles were abandoned in his second edition of 1847 when he added color plates (Hedrick 1950).

Cerasus borealis,

THE NORTHERN CHERRY-TREE.

Synonymes.

Cerasus borealis,	MICHAUX, North American Sylva. DE CANDOLLE, Prodromus. LOUDON, Arboretum Britannicum.
Cerasus pennsylvanica,	TORREY AND GRAY, Flora of North America.
Cerisier du Canada,	FRANCE.
Canadischer Kirschbaum,	GERMANY.
American Bird Cherry-tree,	BRITAIN.
Small Cherry, Red Cherry-tree,	NEW ENGLAND.
Wild Red Cherry, Bird Cherry, Choke Cherry-tree,	OTHER PARTS OF ANGLO-AMERICA.

Engravings. Michaux, North American Sylva, pl. 90; Loudon, Arboretum Britannicum, ii., fig. 410; and the figures below.

Specific Characters. Leaves oval-oblong, acuminate, membranaceous, glabrous, denticulate, and almost in an eroded manner. Flowers on longish pedicels, and disposed nearly in a corymbose manner. Fruit nearly ovate, small; its flesh red.—*De Candolle, Prodromus.*

Description.

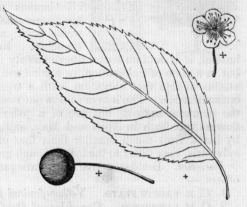

THE Cerasus borealis is a handsome small tree, growing to a height of twenty or thirty feet, with a trunk six or eight inches in diameter, and covered with a smooth brownish bark, which detaches itself laterally. Its leaves are from two to six inches long, and somewhat resemble those of the common almond. Its flowers put forth in May or June, and occur in small, white bunches, which give birth to a small, red, intensely-acid fruit, that arrives at maturity in July. It is described by Pursh to be agreeable to the taste, astringent in the mouth, and hence called *choke cherry;* but this name is ordinarily applied to another tree.

Geography, &c. The northern cherry is found in a common soil from Newfoundland to the northern parts of the Rocky Mountains, and as far south as Virginia. It was introduced into Britain in 1822, and is growing at present in Messrs. Loddiges' arboretum, and other European collections. This tree, like the paper birch, is remarkable for springing up spontaneously, in old cultivated fields, or in such parts of the forests as have been burnt over by accident or design. Of all trees of North America, no one is so nearly allied to the Cerasus vulgaris as the present species; and hence it has been recommended as a suitable stock to graft that cherry upon. The wood of this tree is exceedingly hard, fine-grained, and of a reddish hue; but the inferior size to which it usually grows, forbids its use in the mechanic arts.

34

17. Wood engraving of *Cerasus borealis,* The northern cherry-tree for Daniel Jay Browne's *The Trees of America, Native and Foreign, Pictorially and Botanically Delineated … Illustrated by Numerous Engravings,* 1846.

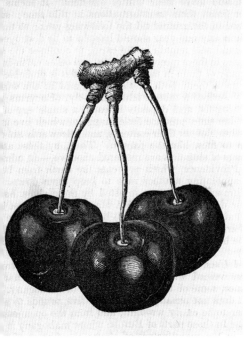

Manuals on native trees and grasses included Browne's 1832 *Sylva Americana* and 1843 *Trees of America*, both with singularly helpful text illustrations; Hoopes' handsome 1868 *Book of Evergreens*; Flint's 1857 *Grasses and Forage Plants*; Darlington's 1859 *American Weeds and Useful Plants*; Vasey's 1884 *Agricultural Grasses*; and Hackel's 1890 *The True Grasses*. All were valuable illustrated manuals that served the needs of special audiences at modest prices.

The usual method of illustrating tree species in earlier works was simply to provide a plate showing a leaf, a flowering branchlet and a mature fruit, much the same sort of material a botanist would put onto a herbarium sheet. Browne's works provided only small black text figures. In his *Sylva* he reduced illustration to a precise depiction of a silhouette leaf and an image of the fruit, but in his later *Trees* he provided tiny tree silhouettes and a flower, the results represented a style that we are more used to seeing in some modern pocket tree guides. Full tree shapes were not favored as illustrations in the 19th century. The sixth (posthumous) edition of Downing's *Treatise on the Theory and Practice of Landscape Gardening*, 1859, included a supplement by H. W. Sargent that provided 14 illustrations of newer deciduous and evergreen plants, presumably emphasizing their value in landscape *design*. At this point, we might draw attention to the work of Edward Vischer, a German immigrant to California. At the age of fifty, in the middle of a career in business, he took up drawing and photography. As he travelled about California, he made a collection of field sketches of landscapes and buildings, which he worked into finished drawings at home. Well-known for his views of old Spanish missions, he became fascinated by the giant sequoias. Recognizing that the immense changes taking place in the state were destroying much of the landscape, he sought to preserve a visual record of these immense trees and published *Vischer's Views of California* in 1862, *The Forest Trees of California* at about the same time, and in 1870 *Vischer's Pictorial of California*.

Above:

16. Wood engraving of *Cerasus vulgaris*, The common cherry-tree for Daniel Jay Browne's *The Trees of America, Native and Foreign, Pictorially and Botanically Delineated ... Illustrated by Numerous Engravings*, 1846.

38

Fig. 16.

NUTTALLIA ORNATA.

MISSOURI SWEET-POPPY.

72. Wood engraving of *Fig. 16. Nuttalia ornata*, Missouri sweet-poppy for Constantine Samuel Rafinesque-Schmaltz's *American Florist*, 1832.

Simple sketches for ramblers and young folk

There was also a wide audience of people leaving school who would retain a personal interest in the rudiments of schoolroom botany as aspiring amateur botanists and nature enthusiasts. Their needs were served by various handy books on field and wayside botany and "floras," manuals that catalogued, described, and to some extent cheaply illustrated the wild flora. The always unusual Constantine Rafinesque published in 1832 a little *American Florist … Figures of Beautiful or Curious American and Garden Flowers, Plants, Trees, Shrubs and Vines* in two parts with 72 bold, uncolored woodcuts. Each title page was headed "36 figures—36 cents" and bore the slogan, "Let us teach by pictures." Rafinesque's booklets, now exceedingly rare, were an early expression of a foreseen need for such cheap popular illustrations. There were various other popular "botanies" that fed both the minds of the public and the bank accounts of publishers throughout the century. Some good examples include S. G. Goodrich's 1838 *Peter Parley's Cyclopedia of Botany* (republished in 1849 as *Peter Parley's Illustrations of the Vegetable Kingdom*); Mary Lorimer's 1869 *Among the Trees: A Journal of Walks in the Woods and Flower-Hunting through Field and by Brook*; William Bryant's 1874 *Among the Trees*; Mrs. Dana's 1893 *How to Know the Wild Flowers*; and, on a more sophisticated plane, William Gibson's 1887 *Happy Hunting-Grounds: A Tribute to the Woods and Fields*, with some fine "text" illustrations by the author.

For the young, even the very young, there were illustrated books on plants and their lore such as the tiny (4 x 3 1/2 inches) Anonymous' 1840s *About Plants*, provided "with many engravings"; two anonymous American Sunday-School Union books; the 1844 *Flowers by the Way-Side*; the 1840s *Wonders of Vegetation*; Mary Mann's 1846 *The Flower People*; Theodore Thinker's 1847 *First Lessons in Botany; or, The Child's Book of Flowers*; Anonymous' 1857 *Pond Lily Stories*; Anonymous' 1865 *Thoughts among Flowers* (another tiny book at 4 x 2 1/2 inches); and Gertrude Hale's 1887 *Little Flower-People*.

MOUNTAIN-LAUREL.

intermeshed across the pathway in playful taunt, with "no thoroughfare" laughing in every strand and tendril; of morning gossamers and evening skies; of pink-domed piles of cloud rising to the zenith beyond the "sundown-tinted hill," with shadowed glen and purling brook beneath. There are massive banks of chestnut foliage fraying out in yellow tassels, and wild apples in crimson drift rows circling the sloping stone piles. There is a silent, ruined mill I well remember, and a long stretch across a breezy upland

26. Wood engraving of Mountain-laurel *[Kalmia]* for William Hamilton Gibson's *Happy Hunting-Grounds: A Tribute to the Woods and Fields*, 1887.

For the serious botanist, however, inexpensively systematically illustrated field "floras" were clearly not as favored in America as they were in Europe.[11] Rafinesque's 1832 slogan, "Let us teach by pictures," did not apparently meet with the approval of Asa Gray, America's greatest botanist. Gray's famous *Manual of the Botany of the Northern United States* reached its second edition in 1856 before illustrations were added, but they were not what one might have expected. His introduction says, "Another important feature of the present edition consists in the plates, fourteen in number, crowded with figures, illustrating the genera of the six Cryptogamous Orders (Mosses, Ferns, &c.) embraced in the work," and again in the 1862 fourth edition, "Eight plates have been added, crowded with figures, illustrating all the genera (66 in number) of Grasses." All are of needle-fine highly technical detail that could only be seen under a dissecting microscope.[12] Despite being written with English, rather than Latin descriptions, suggesting that it was addressed at a wide audience of varied botanical education, Gray provided no other illustrative aids to the identification of flowering plants in any edition of his *Manual* in the manner of his British counterpart, Bentham's *Handbook*.[13] Indeed, it was several decades before Nathaniel L. Britton and the Hon. Addison Brown provided the public with their *Illustrated Flora of the Northern United States* (New York, 1896–1898). Embellished with hundreds of small (2 x 2 1/2 inch) text illustrations, valuable aids to the reader in plant identification, it unfortunately ran to three large volumes, scarcely convenient use out of the house. And it was 1908 before Gray's successors, Benjamin L. Robinson and Merritt L. Fernald, "rearranged and extensively revised" *Gray's New Manual of Botany* to produce a "Seventh Edition—Illustrated." They used four artists to provide many text illustrations and distributed those "crowded" plate figures to the relevant passages of text.

The problem of providing profitable illustrations in color was one that had exercised the resourcefulness of publishers and printers for much of the century. W. P. C. Barton's *Vegetable Materia Medica* was published with "true imitations of the plants" in the form of hand-colored engravings, the first such American botanical illustrations, and the task required a team of six people. Hand-coloring was slow, expensive to do, and could be subject to variation in accuracy and quality even within different copies of the same edition. At its best it could rise to the level of high botanical art, at its worst it amounted to little more than ugly daubing that detracted from, rather than added to, any merit in the underlying printed image. As early as 1817 Bigelow's *American Medical Botany* had experimented with the idea of *printing* the colors, or at least some of them. Color printing, like hand-coloring, could vary enormously in quality and accuracy depending on factors such as printing expertise or the level of expense budgeted by the publisher, sometimes it achieved fine results in popular books as some of our exhibits reveal. "With colored plates" was a phrase beloved of the commercial publisher—and what publishers were not. There *was* a commercial market to be exploited in low quality flower illustrations, and plenty exist to prove the point.[14]

"Plain" or "colored"—from paintbrush to printing press

A broad miscellany of popular "colored" books straddled the middle years of the century. One of the more numerous groups are those on the language, symbolism and poetry of flowers. Most are small or modest format, many designed to appeal to ladies, many indeed written, compiled, and illustrated by ladies, generally embellished with a handful of colored bouquet plates or portraits of selected flowers. Some books of this genre sought to improve their fanciful content by adding a simple outline of botany. Out of a long list (Seaton 1995) a random selection includes, Mrs. Elizabeth Wirt's 1830 *Flora's Dictionary* with 6 plates; Anonymous' 1835 *Language of Flowers* with 6 plates; "A Lady's" 1836 *Book of Flowers, Flora and Thalia* with 24 plates; Frances Osgood's 1841 *Poetry of Flowers and the Flowers of Poetry* with 12 plates; Lucy Hooper's 1842 *Lady's Book of Flowers and Poetry* with 9 plates; Anonymous' 1843 *Language of Flowers* with 6 new plates; Mrs. Frances Osgood's 1845 *Flower Alphabet* with 20 plates;

Mrs. Anne Dinnies' 1847 *Floral Year* with 12 plates;
Frances Osgood's 1847 *Floral Offering* with 10 plates;
Sarah Josepha Buell Hale's 1848 *Flora's Interpreter, and
Fortuna Flora* with 2 plates; John Keese's 1850s *Floral
Keepsake and Language of Flowers* with 30 plates; Mrs.
C. M. Badger's 1867 *Floral Belles* with 16 plates; and Mrs.
Susie Skelding's 1883 *Flowers from Hill and Dale* with 4
plates, the first of about 15 such books by this lady, all
provided with lush color-printed plates. In a genre of their
own are the famous F. L. Grandville *Flowers Personified*
with 25 whimsical colored plates of "female figures
adorned with flower costume," translated from the French
and somewhat Americanized in an 1847–1849 New York
edition. In a similar vein, but quite different style, are
Anna Pratt's 1890 *Flower Folk* with Laura C. Hills' bright
illustrations.

31. Chromolithograph by F. F.
Oakley, Boston of [floral
bouquet] for Sarah Josepha
Buell Hale's *Flora's Interpreter,
and Fortuna Flora*, 1848.

PASSION-FLOWER.

FLEUR-DE-LA-PASSION, GRANADILLA, LA-GRENADILLA, FIORE-
DELLA-PASSIONE, PASSIFLORA.

CLASS, Monadelphia, from *mo-*   ORDER, Pentandria, from
nos one, and *adelphos*, brother.   *pente*, five, *aner*, stamen.
Because these flowers have their *Stamens* growing united by their filaments
into one body, and have *Five Stamens*, and consequently are of the
Sixteenth Class and *Fifth Order* of Linnæus.

Passiflora lutea,	Yellow Passion-flower.
'' *cærulea,*	Blue Passion-flower.
'' *alata,*	Winged Passion-flower.

According to some, there are thirty-seven species of the Passion-flower. The "Hortus Bri-
tannicus" makes sixty-three known species.

THE EMBLEM OF HOPE.

Yon mystic flower, with gold and azure bright,
Whose stem luxuriant speaks a vigorous root,
Unfolds her blossoms to the morn's salute,
That close and die in the embrace of night.
No luscious fruits the cheated taste invite—
Her short-lived blossoms, ere they lead to fruit,
Demand a genial clime, and suns that shoot
Their rays direct with undiminished light.
Thus Hope, the *Passion-flower* of human life,
Whose wild luxuriance mocks the pruner's knife,
Profuse in promise, makes a like display
Of evanescent blooms, that last a day !
To cheer the mortal eye, no more is given,
The fruit is only to be found in heaven.   *Cartwright.*

The Passion-flower affords us an example of a most perfect
plant, in all its various parts of stem, leaf, tendrils, involucre, cup,

14. Wood engraving of Passion-flower for Hermon Bourne's *Flores Poetici: The Florist's
Manual … with More Than Eighty Beautifully-Coloured Engravings of Poetic Flowers*, 1833.

In a different class were various popular color plate books, what one might call "parlor" botanies. An early, and rather handsome example, is Hermon Bourne's 1833 *Flores Poetici: The Florist's Manual,* "with more than eighty beautifully-colored engravings of poetic flowers," unusual in that they are actually hand-colored, wood-engraved text illustrations rather than separate plates. Others include Mrs. Embury's 1845 *American Wild Flowers in Their Native Haunts,* with 20 plates (with unconventional landscape backgrounds[15]); John Newman's 1847 *Boudoir Botany; or, The Parlor Book of Flowers,* with 65 plates; Henry Osborn's 1860 *Plants of the Holy Land* with 6 plates. The most unusual popular color plate "book" of flowers was the *Wild Flowers of America: Flowers of Every State in the American Union, by a Corps of Special Artists and Botanists.* This "botanical fine art weekly" appeared in New York in 18 issues between May and September 1894, the complete set including 288 color-printed flower portraits. The quality was not as poor as one might have expected for something that was, presumably, sold at newspaper and magazine stands around town.

45

12. Chromolithograph of Fig. 79. Night Flowering Catchfly, *Silene noctiflora,* July and Fig. 80. Tick Trefoil, *Meibornia (Desmodium) canadensis,* July for *Botanical Fine Art Weekly: Wildflowers of America,* 1894.

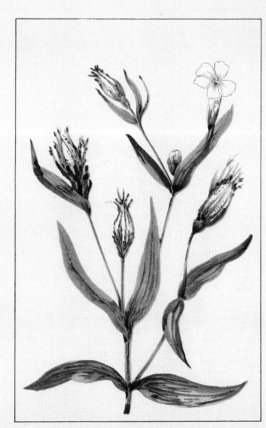

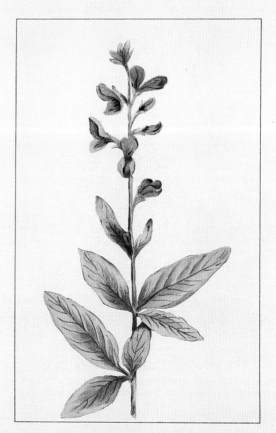

— 79 —

NIGHT FLOWERING CATCHFLY.

SILENE NOCTIFLORA.

JULY.

— 80 —

TICK TREFOIL.

MEIBOMIA (DESMODIUM) CANADENSIS.

JULY.

— 81 —
FRINGED GENTIAN.
GENTIANA AMERICANA (CRINITA).
JULY—AUGUST.

— 82 —
ELECAMPANE.
INULA HELENIUM.
AUGUST.

13. Chromolithograph of Fig. 81. Fringed Gentian, *Gentiana americana (Crinita)*, July–August, Fig. 82. Elecampane, *Inula helenium*, August for *Botanical Fine Art Weekly: Wildflowers of America*, 1894.

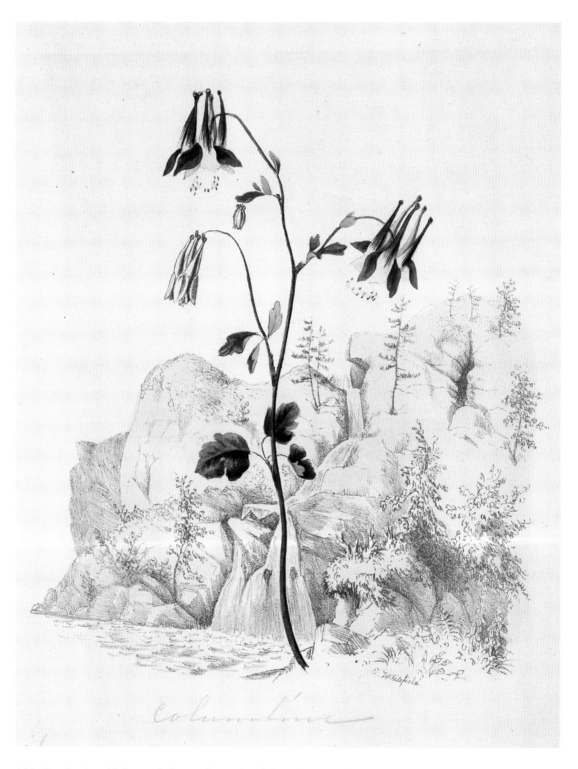

Columbine

104. Hand-colored lithograph from Edwin Whitefield's drawing of *Aquilegia canadensis*, Wild columbine for Emma C. Embury's *American Wild Flowers in Their Native Haunts*, 1845.

48

ADIANTUM CAPILLUS-VENERIS.

L. PRANG & COMPANY, BOSTON.

54. Chromolithograph from Alois Lunzer's painting of *Adiantum capillus-veneris*, True maiden-hair fern for Thomas Meehan's *The Native Flowers and Ferns of the United States*, 1878.

The chromolitho reaches maturity

The second half of the century saw the rise of a class of illustrated plant books that spoke of the arrival of a more affluent market for "nature" books, one willing to pay for books that in several cases were, for their day, equivalent to the modern "coffee table book." Richly color-printed (rather than the older hand-colored) illustrations, somewhat impractical large formats with fancy cloth gilt covers, clothed popular natural-history books that placed more emphasis on eye-catching illustration than on botanical text. The chromolithographic age had arrived. The procession of these "goodies" included George Goodale's 1876 *Wild Flowers of America* with 50 colored plates by Isaac Sprague; Daniel Eaton's 1878–1880 *Ferns of North America* with 80 colored plates by J. H. Emerton and C. E. Faxon; Thomas Meehan's 1878 *Native Flowers and Ferns of the United States* with 96 fine bouquets; Isaac Sprague's 1886 *Beautiful Wild Flowers of America* with 14 colored plates; Emma Thayer's 1885 *Wild Flowers of Colorado* with 24 "original water color sketches" (reissued in 1887 as *Wild Flowers of the Rocky Mountains*) and her sister 1887 work *Wild Flowers of the Pacific Coast* with 24 similar plates; Isaac Sprague's 1888 *Flowers of Field and Forest* with 10 "original water color drawings"; and Ferdinand S. Mathews' lavish 1890 *The Golden Flower Chrysanthemum* with 15 florid "studies from nature in water color by James & Sidney Callowhill, Alois Lunzer and F. S. M." To be absolutely fair to this genre of flower books, it should be remarked that several included serious botanical content and highly professional illustrations. It was just that the "pitch" was to the nature-loving public rather than the serious botanist.

87. Chromolithograph (artist's proof) of Isaac Sprague's painting of White bay, *Gordonia pubescens* L'Hér. for George L. Goodale, *The Wild Flowers of America*, 1886.

CULLINGFORDII

61. Chromolithograph from Sydney T. Callowhill's watercolor of *Cullingfordii* for Ferdinand Schuyler Mathews' *The Golden Flower Chrysanthemum*, 1890.

Do it yourself— "Drawing without a Master"

A lesser byway of American 19th-century botanical illustration is the small group of books of "how to do" flower painting and drawing. A considerable number of such books were being published in England and the Continent, so it was natural that American publishers should see a publishing opportunity for themselves. Titles included Thomas Richards' 1838 *The American Artist; or, Young Ladies' Instructor, in the Art of Flower Painting, in Water Colours, Illustrated by Twenty-Three Progressive Studies, Drawn and Coloured by the Author;* Mrs. Ann Hill's ca.1840 *Drawing-Book of Flowers,* which appeared in about three issues; Thomas Strong's ca.1840s *Drawing without a Master;* John Hopkins' ca.1846 *Burlington Drawing Book of Flowers*[16] (republished the following year as the *Vermont Drawing Book of Flowers*), and Anonymous' ca.1865 *Examples for Drawing and Coloring Flowers.* The usual formula was described in the subtitle of Richards' book, to provide examples of flower portraits in progressive stages of completion and of hand-coloring. Hopkins' plates were unusually gracefully drawn as shown by the proof impression in our exhibition. These books were addressed to amateurs and schools but probably had little value for serious botanical artists except perhaps at the elementary level.[17] As a further confirmation that interest in flower drawing was generating a market for publishers, books by three English authors were republished in American editions: François Francia's 1818 *Series of Progressive Lessons, Intended to Elucidate the Art of Flower Painting in Water Colours* (three times republished), James Andrews' 1852 *Studies in Flower Painting;* and Nathaniel Whittock's 1852 *Oxford Drawing Book, … to Which Is Added, Lessons in Flower Drawing, a Series of Plates by James Andrews.*

Although, as mentioned above, illustrations of whole tree forms were not much in evidence, there were three publications specifically devoted to tree drawing, chiefly for the assistance of landscape artists seeking fidelity in their depiction of landscape vegetation. Benjamin Coe's 1841

Drawing Book of Trees: Exhibiting the Whole Process of Sketching and Shading the Different Kinds of Foliage in the Most Familiar Manner, was republished in 1843, a mark of its success. Ten years later *Coe's New Drawing Lessons: Series 3, Landscapes with Instructions in Foliage* appeared with 48 plates, and in 1860 Benjamin Nutting published an *Introduction to Tree Drawing with Full Instructions.*

37. Lithograph of John Henry Hopkin's drawing of *[Papaver]* for his *Burlington Drawing Book of Flowers,* [ca.1846].

Hopkins fect.   Pl.6.

Pictures in periodicals— quantity over quality

We have already mentioned some of the colorful illustrated horticultural periodicals of the 1830s to 1850s. A succession of these continued through the century, and a number continued to provide regular color plates, as much for their selling appeal as for the botanical intelligence they conveyed. The changes in color plate methods, from the hand-colored engraving or lithograph to the rich tonal colors of the chromolithograph, were apparent in periodicals as much as in books. Later examples included *Meehan's Monthly: A Magazine of Horticulture, Botany, and Kindred Subjects*, illustrated with colored lithographs, that was published from 1891, and even the formal *Yearbook of the United States Department of Agriculture* began to include high quality color-printed plates at the end of the century.

Yearbook U. S. Dept. of Agriculture, 1908.   PLATE XLI.

D. G. Passmore

PATTEN APPLE.

67. Chromolithograph of Deborah Griscom Passmore's painting of Patten Apple *[Malus]* for the *Yearbook of the United States Department of Agriculture*, 1908.

KAWAKAMI

55

LONESTAR

Elsie E. Lower

PERSIMMONS.

53. Chromolithograph of Elsie E. Lower's painting of Persimmons *[Diospyros]* for the
Yearbook of the United States Department of Agriculture, 1908.

This will tend to repress undue luxuriance of growth, and promote the production of flowers.

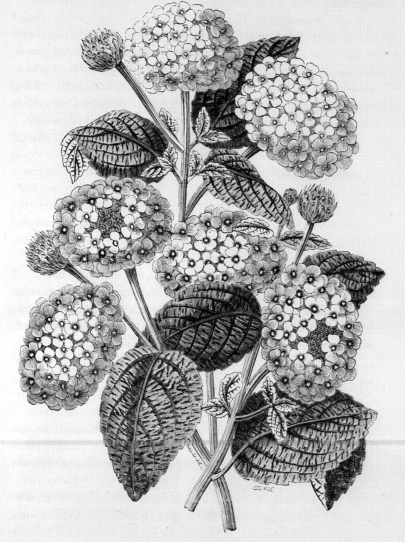

Let us follow a *lantana* through the year. The plant is purchased in

56

5. Wood engraving of *Lantana* for the *American Journal of Horticulture and Florist's Companion*, 1868.

But most periodicals in our field, particularly in the
1840s, 1850s and 1860s, were directed at a popular
audience that apparently wanted up-to-date news of
interesting discoveries, new plant varieties, new technical
improvements in horticulture and agriculture, gardening
tips, etc., and welcomed cheaply produced illustrations of
these. Cheap illustration meant black text illustrations or,
at best, the odd plate where budgets allowed. Periodical
publication meant that subscribers had to be provided
with their promised quantity of reading and pictorial
matter, no matter what. Illustrations had to be prepared
and printed quickly, sometimes apparently much too
quickly because blocks were borrowed from other publications or from business nurserymen, copied from other
publications, and so forth. Some examples are included in
our exhibition. The famous Concord Grape was boldly
illustrated, full-page, in 1854 in the *Magazine of Horticulture* An early depiction of the "Gigantic wellingtonia" with
a facing companion plate of the analytical botanical details
appeared in *The Horticulturist* in 1855, probably borrowed
or copied from some other publications. Rather better
quality engraved illustrations in the *American Journal of
Horticulture* for 1867 demonstrate an improvement in
standards. Even a newspaper type of periodical, namely,
the *American Agriculturist,* included some rather good text
illustrations of wheat varieties in the 1880s. Some other
illustrated periodicals that included a variety of interesting, sometimes amateurish, text engravings are the 17
volumes of *The Gardener's Monthly and Horticultural
Advertiser,* which ran from 1859 to1875, *Woodward's
Record of Horticulture for 1866 (–67),* and *L B Case's
Botanical Index; an Illustrated Quarterly Botanical Magazine,* which completed four volumes between 1877 and
1881.

GIGANTIC WELLINGTONIA

7. Lithograph of Gigantic *Wellingtonia [Sequoiadendron]* for Patrick Barry and J. Jay Smith's *The Horticulturist and Journal of Rural Art and Rural Taste*, January to December 1855.

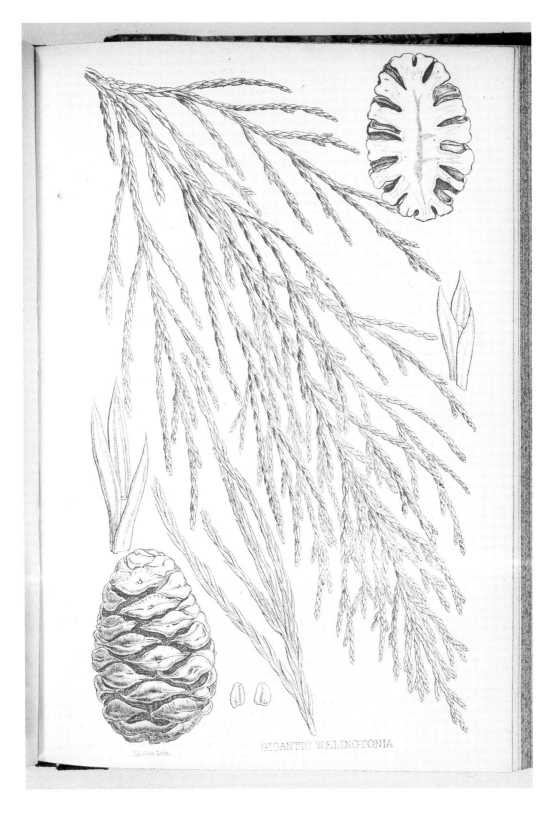

GIGANTIC WELINGTONIA

Shober Lith.

8. Lithograph of Gigantic *Wellingtonia* [detail] for Patrick Barry and J. Jay Smith's *The Horticulturist and Journal of Rural Art and Rural Taste*, January to December 1855.

THE NEW AMERICAN ROSE, MRS. W. C. WHITNEY. (See next page.)

6. Line-block reproduction from M. E. Fellows' drawing of The New American Rose, Mrs. W. C. Whitney for Liberty Hyde Bailey's *American Gardening*, February 1893.

The 1880s saw the launch of Charles Sargent's *Garden*
and Forest, apparently funded by him in some measure,
which set new standards for the American horticultural
periodical. It was able to provide some fine text illustrations reproducing botanical drawings by Charles Faxon
and others on large format pages with excellent quality
printing. *American Gardening*, a contemporary New York
publication edited by Liberty Bailey, provided similarly
fine, sometimes markedly arty, illustrations—the drawing
of "The New American Rose, Mrs. W. C. Whitney" by M. E.
Fellows being a good instance. Meantime, new color-
printing technology was given its own journal in the form
of *Meehans' Monthly*, a periodical that commenced in
1890, boasting that it was "illustrated with colored lithographs by L. Prang & Co. and numerous copper and wood
engravings." Louis Prang, the producer of its lush color
plates, was one of the leading color printers in the world at
that time.

Photography assists, but ultimately challenges

Mention of the intrusion of photographs into periodicals brings us to the final chapter of our 19th-century ramble. During the last quarter of the century, botanical, and indeed all other branches of book illustration, began to be influenced by the intrusion of photography. Linear text illustrations became larger, more detailed and more cleanly printed, lithographs became smoother and less like the stone drawn images of earlier decades; more sophisticated tonal effects were being developed in all processes; and with improvements in the surface finish of paper and more precise high-speed machine printing, the overall "look" of books and their illustrations improved. Botanical illustrators could expect to see much more faithful reproductions of their original artwork. America, more than any other country, was vigorously advancing the combination of photography and printed book and periodical illustrations.

To most readers the photographic element in the printmaking process that provided these improved images was a hidden factor except when actual photographs began to appear. Alpheus Hervey's 1893 *Sea Mosses*, a book on seaweeds, claimed that its colored illustrations were "from photographs of actual specimens," but they had none of the *look* of a photograph. Tonal illustrations in books and especially periodicals began appearing that were reproduced from original wash drawings. Different processes were in use such as heliotype, a photographically based engraving process, or collotype, a delicate lithographic-like process, but both of these had to be separately printed and inserted between the text pages. Most tonal illustrations were printed as text figures from photo-relief half-tones, but still did not look obviously "photographic."

However, modern books like Liberty Bailey's 1898 *Sketch of the Evolution of Our Native Fruits* and John Coulter's 1898–1899 *Plant Relations and Plant Structures* had a liberal mixture of line illustrations and photographs. A similar situation had become increasingly commonplace in periodicals, so that even the most casual reader couldn't help noticing that photography had arrived. Sargent's *Garden and Forest* provides another example, the November 1891

63

DUTCHMAN'S BREECHES, OR WHITE-HEARTS
(Bicuculla Cucullaria)

11. Photomechanical halftone from Henry Troth's photograph of Dutchman's breeches or White-hearts, *Bicuculla cucullaria [Dicentra cucullaria* (L.) Bernh.*]* for Neltje Blanchan's *Nature's Garden*, 1900.

CLAMMY LOCUST (*Robinia viscosa*)

76. Photomechanical 3-color halftone of A. Radclyffe Dugmore's photograph of Clammy Locust, *Robinia viscosa* for Julia Ellen Rogers' *The Tree Book*, 1907.

issue included a drawing of a flowering branch of *Viburnum tomentosum* faced by a photograph of the whole bush in flower on the opposite page. By 1900 George Atkinson's *Studies of American Fungi* boasted on the title page that it was illustrated "with 200 photographs by the author." Harriet Keeler's 1900 *Our Native Trees* had 178 photographs, and Neltje Blanchan's 1900 *Nature's Garden* had "illustrations photographed directly from nature by Henry Troth and A. R. Dugmore." A revolution was taking place, and professional nature/botanical photographers had arrived.[18] Color photography appeared boldly in book illustration in the mid 1900s; Julia Rogers' 1905 *Tree Book* had "sixteen plates in color and one hundred and sixty in black-and-white from photographs by A. Radclyffe Dugmore," an under-acknowledged pioneer nature photographer.

From our present point of view, the significance of the arrival of the photographically illustrated book is that the draughtsman now had unprecedented competition. It was now possible to produce illustrations from the live plant—from first exposure to printing block—by photographic and photo-mechanical means. For the entire century we have been describing, all printed illustrations required the hand of an artist to create the initial image that the printmaker, using mechanical and/or sometimes chemical methods, transformed into the printed picture.

66

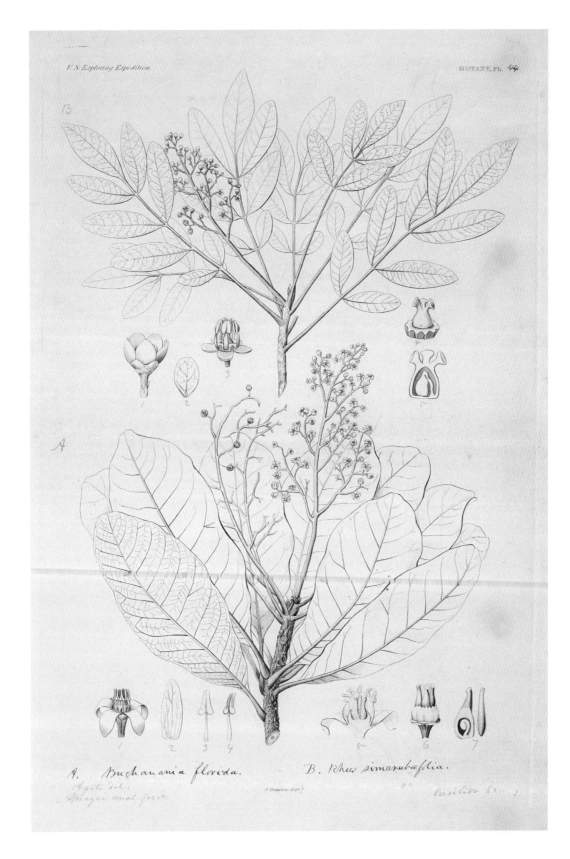

A. *Buchanania florida.*   B. *Rhus simarubæfolia.*

J. Drayton. del.

The printmaking methods exhibited

Intaglio plate prints

The details of the various branches of printmaking technology have been fully described in an earlier Hunt Institute catalogue (Bridson and Wendel 1986) and will not be reiterated here. We might just mention some of the methods that are exhibited. The century commences with conventional line-engraved, sometimes etched, plates, many with hand-coloring, being used as the only useful printmaking medium; wood engraving was in decline and little used. The quality of engraving varied considerably according to the skill of the early American trade engravers and the publisher's budgeted selling price. Excellence in botanical engraving was eventually reached in scientific works such as Gray's 1848 *Genera Florae Americae Boreali-Orientalis Illustrata*, with 186 fine plates, and Wilkes' 1855–1874 United States Exploring Expedition reports, with some 200 folio illustrations.

Some experimental forays were made into producing color-printed engravings, usually requiring some supplementary hand-coloring. Bigelow's 1817–1820 *American Medical Botany* was the most ambitious of these experiments with 60 prints that utilized aquatint for tonal effects.[19] The same principal was employed for the 105 line-engraved plates in William Barton's 1820–1823 *Flora of North America*, but with a greater reliance on hand-coloring.

Left:
3. Engraved proof plate from Alfred T. Agate's drawing of *Buchanania florida; Rhus simarubaefolia* for Asa Gray's "Atlas. Botany. Phanerogamia." in the *United States Exploring Expedition*, 1857.

PLATE IV.

68

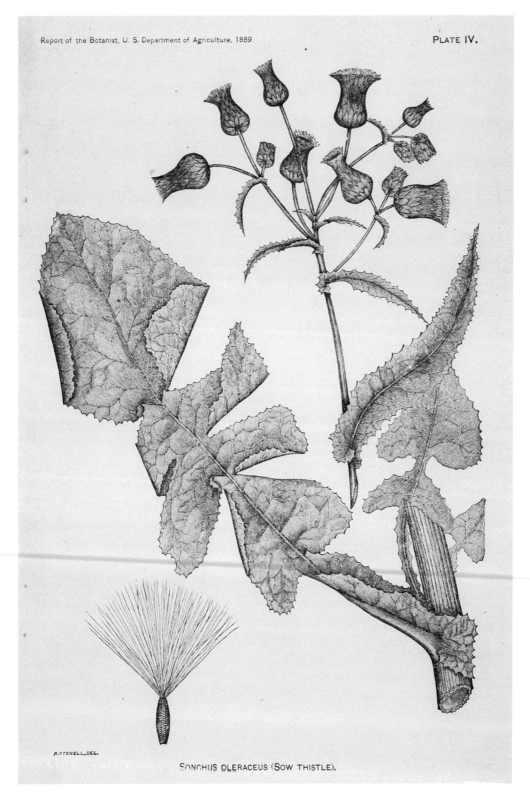

R.STOWELL.DEL.

SONCHUS OLERACEUS (SOW THISTLE).

91. Wood engraving from Louisa Maria Reed Stowell's drawing of *Sonchus oleraceus*, Sow thistle for the *Report of the Botanist, U.S. Department of Agriculture*, 1889.

Wood engravings

Following the early 19th-century English revival in wood-engraved book illustration, stimulated by the country genius of Thomas Bewick, it was natural that it should eventually be adopted in America. Its cheapness and convenience of printing[20] made it an attractive process for the emerging field of popular illustrated book publication, with textbooks being especially relevant here. That revolution really reached America in the 1830s, and styles were a little varied in the earlier years with immigrant engravers following different national traditions and skills while native engravers were still finding their feet in a newly developing field of craftsmanship. Henry's 1814 *American Medical Family Herbal* and Rafinesque's 1832 *American Florist* represent a sturdier style, more reminiscent of the woodcuts of earlier times, whereas Bourne's 1833 *Flores Poetici* and Browne's 1843 *Trees of America* display the more sophisticated, finely detailed style that was typical of mature 19th-century wood engraving.

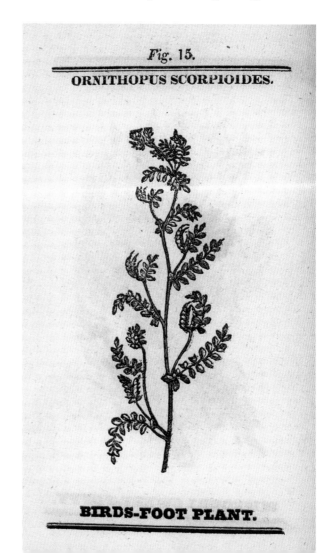

71. Wood engraving of
Fig. 15. Ornithopus scorpioides,
Birds-foot plant for
Constantine Samuel
Rafinesque-Schmaltz's
American Florist, 1832.

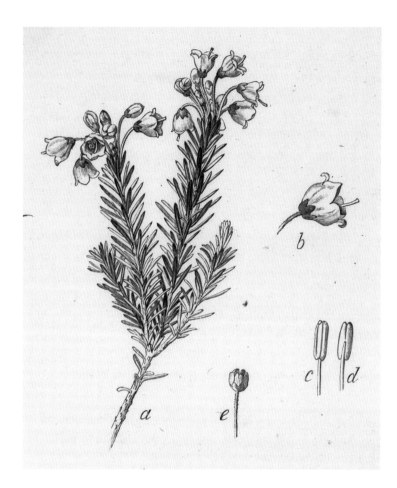

70

97. Wood engraving of *Erica* ? from a pen-and-ink drawing by Frederick Andrews Walpole.

98. Wood engraving of *Vaccinium ovalifolium* from a pen-and-ink drawing by Frederick Andrews Walpole.

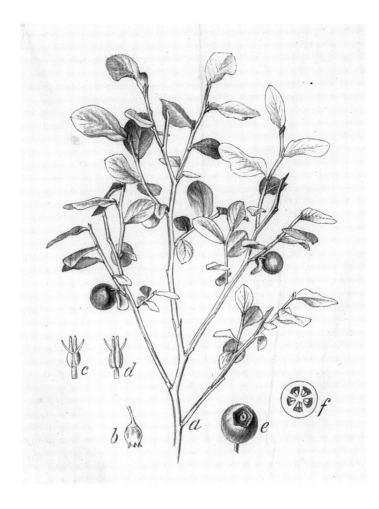

100. Wood engraving of *Vaccinium parvifolium*, Red huckleberry from a pen-and-ink drawing by Frederick Andrews Walpole.

99. Wood engraving of *Vaccinium membranaceum* from a pen-and-ink drawing by Frederick Andrews Walpole.

72

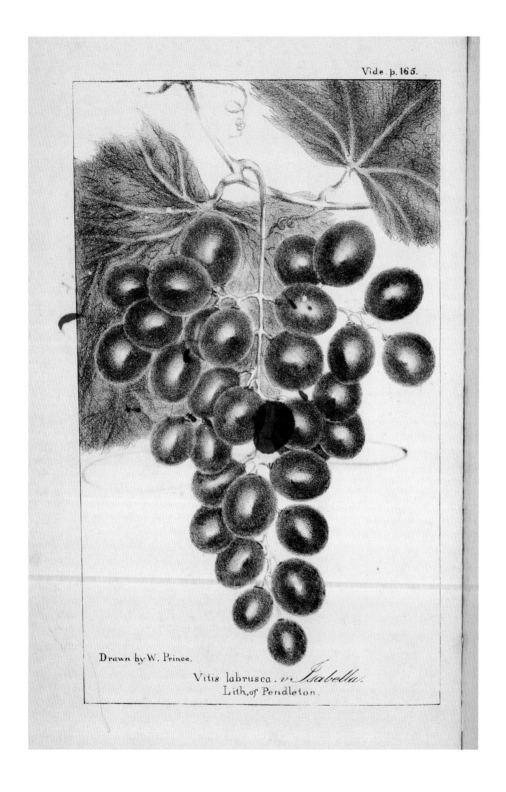

70. Lithograph of William Prince's drawing of *Vitis labrusca* v. Isabella for William Robert Prince's *Treatise on the Vine*, 1830.

Lithographs and chromolithographs

Lithography was a major event in printmaking processes for commercial use in America. First invented in Germany in 1798, it was first described to American readers in 1808 by the physician/naturalist, Dr. Samuel Mitchill. Experiments in lithography were reported in Philadelphia for several years, but Americans had to wait until 1819 to see the first lithograph published here.[21] The earliest use for botanical illustration is seen in the 1822 American edition of Smith's *Grammar of Botany* where it was used for Stansbury's linear copies of the 21 line-engraved plates from the English edition (the copper plates presumably being retained in London for later editions). It was a timid effort, perhaps, but it was, after all, only the second American book with lithographic illustrations. It was also the start of a revolution in printing; lithography completely ousted the older engraved metal processes for botanical illustration. Chalk-style lithography, most commonly seen in Europe, was also used in America—the frontispiece of Prince's 1830 *Treatise on the Vine* and Hopkins' ca.1846 *Burlington Drawing Book of Flowers* being good examples of its use for plant depiction, while Mrs. Embury's *American Wild Flowers in Their Native Haunts* nicely demonstrates chalk style in a different genre.

105. Hand-colored lithograph of Edwin Whitefield's drawing of *Uvularia perfoliata*, Bellwort for Emma C. Embury's *American Wild Flowers in Their Native Haunts*, 1845.

74

1. OPUNTIA Rafinesquii minor. 2. 3. OP. Raf. Grandiflora. 4. OP. Fuscoatra

75. Lithograph by Joseph Prestele from Paulus Roetter and Heinrich Balduin Möllhausen's drawing of *Opuntia rafinesquii minor* E., 2–3. *Op. rafinesquii grandiflora* E., 4. *Opuntia fusco-atra* E. [as published] for George Engelmann and J. M. Bigelow's "Description of the cactaceae" in the *Reports of Explorations and Surveys, to Ascertain the Most Practicable and Economical Route for a Railroad from the Mississippi River to the Pacific Ocean*, 1856.

ENANTIOPHYLLA HYDEANA, Coulter & Rose.

C. E. Faxon, del.

B. Meisel, Lith. Boston.

24. Lithograph of Charles Edward Faxon's drawing of *Enantiophylla hydeana* Coulter and Rose for John M. Coulter and J. N. Rose's "Notes on North American Umbelliferae." III. *Botanical Gazette*, 1893.

76

PELLAEA ORNITHOPUS.
L. PRANG & COMPANY, BOSTON.

55. Chromolithograph from Alois Lunzer's painting of *Pellaea ornithopus* for Thomas Meehan's *The Native Flowers and Ferns of the United States*, 1878.

However, American lithographers are noteworthy for their adoption and development of "engraved" stone work, a style that was not adopted for botanical work in England, for instance. The technique was introduced by some German workers such as the renowned Joseph Prestele and much favored by Asa Gray for his publications. Instead of the soft pencil-like lines so favored by English, French, and other lithographic artists, stone engraving produced lines of needle-sharp fineness. Roetter and Möllhausen's plates for Engelmann's 1856 *Description of the Cactaceae* demonstrate this technique at its very best. This sharp linear style prevailed in scientific plant illustration, becoming the style of choice down to the end of the century and beyond. In time lithographic stones were replaced by much lighter and more convenient grained zinc plates. Lithographic plates of this kind can be found in almost all the later 19th-century scientific periodicals. To the casual observer they look almost the same as metal-engraved prints, but the imprint *Lith.* reveals their nature.

On a quite different tack, lithographers began experiments with printing in colors. Our exhibition includes the first American book to contain true chromolithographs, Mattson's 1841 *American Vegetable Practice*, some plates being printed in up to five colors. This was but a small beginning in marked contrast to the highest point on chromolithographic excellence achieved 13 years later in Allen's justly famous *Victoria Regia* of 1854, with enormous chalk-style chromo-tinted illustrations. These six prints were both botanically accurate and stunningly beautiful. The most significant chromolithographic development in later years was the production of the whole image in colors, without any "key" drawing in black, as Allen's plates employed. The richly colored plates in Meehan's 1878–1880 *Native Flowers and Ferns of the United States* are good examples of this style, products of Louis Prang's famous chromolithographic printing firm.

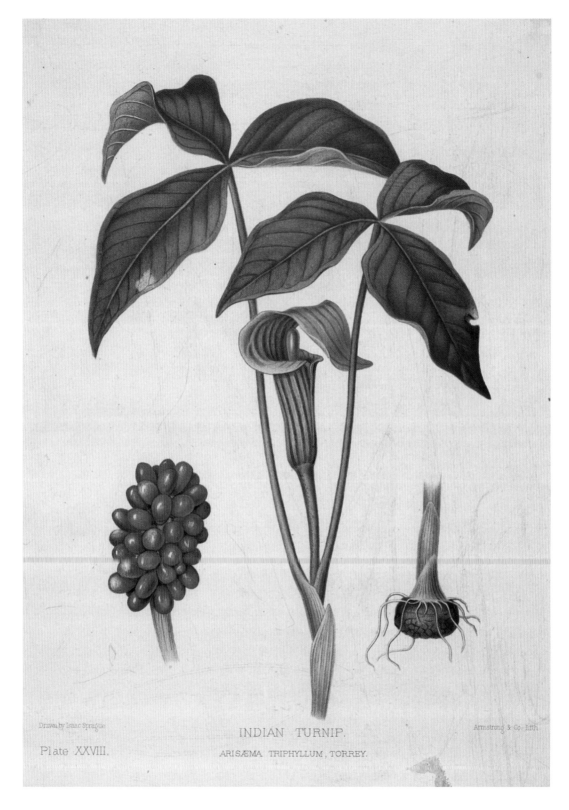

Drawn by Isaac Sprague

INDIAN TURNIP.

Armstrong & Co. Lith.

Plate XXVIII.

ARISÆMA TRIPHYLLUM, TORREY.

89. Chromolithograph from Isaac Sprague's painting of Indian turnip, *Arisaema triphyllum* Torrey for George L. Goodale's *The Wild Flowers of America*, 1886, or subsequent edition.

Origin by Isaac Sprague

Armstrong & Co. lith.

Plate XXVII. SYMPLOCARPUS FŒTIDUS, SALISBURY.

90. Chromolithograph from Isaac Sprague's painting of *Symplocarpus foetidus* Salisbury for George L. Goodale's *The Wild Flowers of America*, 1886, or subsequent edition.

80

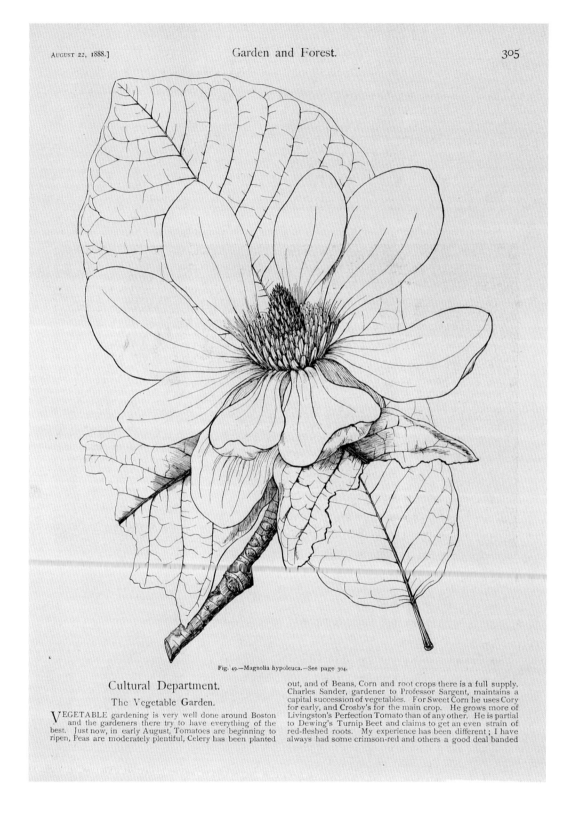

Fig. 49.—Magnolia hypoleuca.—See page 304.

Cultural Department.

The Vegetable Garden.

VEGETABLE gardening is very well done around Boston and the gardeners there try to have everything of the best. Just now, in early August, Tomatoes are beginning to ripen, Peas are moderately plentiful, Celery has been planted out, and of Beans, Corn and root crops there is a full supply. Charles Sander, gardener to Professor Sargent, maintains a capital succession of vegetables. For Sweet Corn he uses Cory for early, and Crosby's for the main crop. He grows more of Livingston's Perfection Tomato than of any other. He is partial to Dewing's Turnip Beet and claims to get an even strain of red-fleshed roots. My experience has been different; I have always had some crimson-red and others a good deal banded

78. Line block–relief of *Magnolia hypoleuca* for Charles Sprague Sargent's *Garden and Forest; A Journal of Horticulture, Landscape Art and Forestry*, 22 August 1888.

Photo-assisted reliefs

Meanwhile, behind the scenes, photography was gradually creeping into the printmaking workshop. From the 1870s onwards most of what appear to be wood-engraved text illustrations are in fact photo-relief line blocks, reproduced from pen-and-ink artwork frequently drawn in the conventional wood-engraving style. The revealing characteristic is that the lines generally have a uniformity of breadth and lack vigor, however closely placed by the artist. Gone is much of the "life" that the wood engraver gave to his lines by varying the sweep and strength of each line to create sophisticated, vigorous modelling and tonal effects. Of course, the printer strove to conceal the difference in favor of the reduction in time, labor, and cost that he gained by employing the new-style line blocks.[22] Processes varied with a succession of experimental advances—a somewhat complicated story—but the original principle, based on the work of the Frenchman, Charles Gillot, is preserved in the name of "Gillotype" generally given to earlier line blocks. Over the years photo-mechanical relief block production improved enormously, and the individuality of a pen-and-ink artist's style could be reproduced with fidelity. Two examples in our exhibition that show differing styles are the illustration of *Magnolia* in the 22 August 1888 issue of *Garden and Forest* and M. E. Fellow's drawing of the "Mrs. W. C. Whitney" rose from the 1893 volume of *American Gardening.*

Photo-lithographs

Photo assisted lithography developed over the same decades, but the printed results cannot usually be identified as photo-lithography—the artist's original drawing being simply transferred to the stone by photographic rather than autographic or conventional transfer methods. The plates for Greene's 1889–1890 *Illustrations of West American Oaks* were probably photo-lithographed. Collotype, another photographic process that shares the same planographic feature as lithography, provided finely detailed reproductions of original artwork. It was little-used in botanical work, but the exhibited example of a wash drawing of *Nymphaea polysepala* in the 1902 volume of *Report of the United States National Museum* demonstrates its quality.

82

102. Heliotype from Frederick Andrews Walpole's painting of *Nymphaea polysepala [Nuphar]* for Frederick V. Coville's "Wokas: A primitive food of the Klamath Indians" in the *Annual Report of the United States National Museum*, 1902.

*Halftones—
monochrome
and color*

Much effort was expended over the later years of the century in producing an artificial "grain" that could be used to reproduce "tones" in illustration. America was in the forefront of this development, competing fiercely with England, Germany, France and others. The technique took the form of breaking the image into a pattern of minute dots—a technique we see every day in today's newspapers. Once perfected it permitted the reproduction of tonal "wash" drawings and continuous tone photographs by relief blocks or lithography, especially the former. Artwork for book and periodical illustration could now be done in a mixture of gray and black washes and reproduced almost as readily as line-drawn work.

By the end of the century color-photographic methods were becoming commercially viable. "Tri-chromatic" half-tone color blocks were produced based on the use of three primary colors, red, yellow and blue, that could be printed individually or in combination to reproduce the whole range of the spectrum in three printings. In 1901 Willard Clute's *Our Ferns in Their Haunts* presented *all* its illustrations in line block, half-tone and three-color half-tone, and Ferdinand Mathews' 1902 *Field Book of American Wild Flowers* could boast on the title page, "with numerous reproductions of water colors and pen-and-ink studies from nature by the author." Three years later the comprehensive *Apples of New York*, by Spencer Beach and others, provided a photograph of every variety on 136 tri-chromatic and 77 halftone plates.

84

a

b

c

d

e

f

B. Meisel. lith. Boston.

R. Cowing, del.
Div. of Illustrations

ARENARIA COMPACTA.

20. Tinted lithograph of Roberta Cowing's drawing of *Arenaria compacta* for *Contributions from the United States National Herbarium*, 1893.

Camera *versus* pencil

Photography, considered in its early days to be the most "truthful" medium of depiction was found to have short-comings for the scientific illustration of plants where critical details of fine structure were not always clearly visible or where analytical floral detail was required. The many photographs in Blanchan's *Nature's Garden*, for example, are very clearly taken by skilled photographers, probably in studio lighting and with a backdrop that throws the object into as clear a contrast as possible. And yet many still fall short of the botanist's needs. The botanical artist also aims to be "truthful" in his or her depiction but unlike the camera is specially careful to clearly depict every critical detail that might be necessary in establishing the precise identity of the plant. Thus, in a sense, the artist is giving emphasis to the details in a way that the camera's uncritical eye cannot be trained to do. The scientific botanical drawing does not differ to any marked degree from the later 19th century to this day, by whatever means the image is put into print. At the end of the 19th century the United States Department of Agriculture (U.S.D.A.) included a Division of Illustration whose work can be found in plenty in the *Contributions from the United States National Herbarium*. The Division of Illustration was obviously alive to the advantages of the photomechanical revolution as well as being steeped in the traditions of the older processes. Amongst the Institute's collection of prints is a trio of U.S.D.A. turn-of-the-century reproductions of a Frederick Walpole scientific drawing—one made in halftone, one in collotype, and one in line block. We can only surmise that the Division of Illustration was trying out new processes to help in deciding which was best for its needs. Its publications reveal that line block was the preferred method. However, the 1901 volume of the *Contributions* demonstrates that all three processes were used, but selectively, for different kinds of illustrations; high quality collotype for clear vegetation and habitat views, halftones for smaller text photos and illustrations of whole plants and plant products, and line block for conventional linear scientific plant portraits.

86

RILEY.

SCIOTO.

PRINGLE.

DAMSON PLUMS.

34. Chromolithograph of Bertha Heiges' painting of Damson Plums *[Prunus]* for the *Yearbook of the United States Department of Agriculture,* 1905.

87

MONEYMAKER.

HOLLIS.

SUCCESS.

SCHLEY.

YOUNG.

PECAN VARIETIES.

E. I. Schutt.

JULIUS BIEN & CO. N.Y.

80. Chromolithograph of Ellen I. Schutt's painting of Pecan varieties for the *Yearbook of the United States Department of Agriculture*, 1905.

"Hanging" prints

There remains one aspect of 19th century printmaking that we have not considered, the separate, commercially published, print. Prints of exceptional flowers, novel introductions, or bouquets of flowers were plentifully published in Europe long before America's botanical printmaking era began. They were created as independent entities published for connoisseurs' portfolios or for framing, and formed part of a print world that included portraits, landscapes, town views, battle scenes, various historical events, etc. Separate prints of this type were published in America from the 17th century (see Museum of Graphic Art 1969), but, so far as we know, America produced no separately published flower prints of any kind before about 1830. In 1831 Moses Swett drew a fine chalk-style lithograph of a floral bouquet, shown in our exhibition. We know of no other similar print in any medium from this period.

Lith. & Published by Endicott & Swett, Graphic Hall Baltimore. 1831.

In about 1859 a stream of lithographic prints began to appear from the famous New York house of Currier & Ives. The firm was famous for its colored lithographic pictures of American life and views but little is heard of some of their lesser productions. Actually, between 1859 and 1875, they published in various formats over 130 plates of flowers (cultivated and wild), ferns, bouquets, vases of flowers, fruit (single and groups), and foliage (summer and autumn). These were essentially "hanging prints" for parlor decoration, and most undoubtedly perished where they hung in the course of years. Most were unsigned, only four have been noted as yet, two by "J. Schutz del.," and two by "F. F. Palmer del.," the former pair undated, the latter dated 1862 and 1863.[23] They can be classed in total as popular art, but closer study may reveal that some have real artistic or botanical merit. None are included in our exhibition.

Another group of "hanging prints" that merits special mention is the corpus of work from the previously mentioned chromolithographic firm of Louis Prang of Boston. Prang had a special fondness for flowers and floral decoration and commissioned a number of painters of his day such as Paul De Longpré, Mrs. E. T. Fisher, George Lambdin, Aloïs Lunzer, Annie C. Nowell, and Mrs. O. E. Whitney, to produce oil paintings and panel paintings of flowers and bouquets, some with a characteristic black ground. Between the 1860s and the 1890s, largely from this personal gallery of paintings, he produced large chromolithographic reproductions for individual sale as frameworthy pictures. Our exhibition includes an 1874 example by George Lambdin of a *Lilium*, printed in no fewer than 18 printings.[24] As Prang's biographer, Katherine McClinton, has observed,

> The flower chromos of L. Prang & Company are some of the most interesting prints available and it seems strange that they have never received the attention of collectors of flower illustrations. Their color compares favorably with that of the old prints of France and other European countries.... Not only are the flowers themselves—violets, fuchsias,

Left: 93. Hand-colored lithograph of Moses Swett's [Flowers] printed by Endicott and Swett, Graphic-Hall, Baltimore, 1831.

46. Chromolithograph from George C. Lambdin's painting of *[Lilium]*, 1875, printed by Louis Prang & Co.

and moss roses—the nineteenth century favorites, but the compositions of the flower bouquets are typically Victorian—pansies and azaleas; calla lily and geraniums, pinks and moss roses. ... Millions of these flower lithographs were sold throughout the country in the last quarter of the nineteenth century ... (McClinton 1973, pp. 91–102).

Other chromolithographic printer/publishers such as the two New York firms of Sarony, Major & Knapp and Fabronius, Gurney & Son are known to have produced similar floral prints, but information about them is very sparse. In the early 1870s *Vick's Magazine*, the brainchild of James Vick, seedsman and journalist, offered its readers an annual floral chromo "for the purpose of increasing the love of flowers." These bouquets were about 19 by 24 inches "on cloth and stretchers, just like an oil painting, ready for the frame;" by 1876 *Vick's* offered a set of eight, "framed in black walnut and gilt" if desired.

Finally there was a distinctive class of separately published prints that is strictly associated with the horticultural trade, especially the Rochester trade. The principal object of their creation was to provide colored pictures of varieties of flowers and fruit that travelling salesman could take on the road or that could be purchased by nurseries to make up sample books of their own annual offerings.[25] Since the object was to *sell* seeds or plants, the images were eye-catchingly colorful to the point of being garish, hand-colored or stencilled lithographs and chromolithographs being the usual medium. One of the leading Rochester firms that published these prints was Dellon Dewey. He produced sets or albums but also sold them as separate prints,[26] and various others are also known to have issued similar productions.[27] These were in effect a kind of horticultural "ephemera" for the selection changed from year to year. Fashions in garden and house plants changed, new introductions, varieties and hybrids were added, and some former favorites were dropped. As a result only scattered selections have survived, and even those are scarce. This curious byway of the American print trade is not represented in our exhibition.

Conclusion

Our "ramble" thus reaches the end of a century of American botanical printmaking. The story ends with the displacement of printmaking as an obligatory process for the multiplication of plant images. All the highly developed skills of engravers, etchers, copperplate printers, wood-engravers, lithographic draughtsmen, lithographic engravers and printers, and chromolithographers that had made possible the printed reproduction of botanical art were no longer essential for commercial book illustration. Specialized graphic-arts technicians, preparers of photo-mechanical printing surfaces, had replaced them all, and sophisticated power-driven machines put the images on paper.

But printmaking was not dead. In the 20th century it was free to become the sole province of artists who could use its various traditional, and some innovative, techniques to produce creatively conceived and executed images of plants in the form of what we now speak of as true "prints." These were usually published as separate entities, occasionally published as portfolio sets, or incorporated into specially designed and finely printed books. Twentieth-century artists' prints form the second portion of our exhibition.

— Gavin D. R. Bridson

Notes

1. See, for example, the illustrations in *American Printmaking: The First 150 Years* (Museum of Graphic Art 1969).

2. More information on works mentioned in this section may be found in both the catalogue entries and the provisional list of American botanical illustration to 1900 that is appended to this catalogue. Works mentioned that are outside the scope of that list are described in the following reference list.

3. See Wood (1973) for a brief outline of the general scientific content of this early period.

4. See Wood (1970) for a general survey of early-19th-century American scientific illustration.

5. The monochrome figures were actually bold and simple wood engraved figures placed with the text and reminiscent of Thomas Bewick's much admired illustrations to R. J. Thornton's *New Family Herbal* (London, 1810).

6. Under the series title "School of Flora," some of Rafinesque's woodcuts, accompanied by a full descriptive letterpress, were republished in *Atkinson's Casket; or, Gems of Literature, Wit and Sentiment* (Philadelphia, [Sam. C. Atkinson], vol. 1, 1831), a popular journal that, as the title suggests, catered to a broad audience.

7. The 70 well-known and very attractive plates in Andrew J. Downing's *The Fruits and Fruit Trees of America [etc.], Illustrated with Colored Engravings* (New York, J. Wiley, 1847) were actually lithographed, printed and colored in Paris, and are thus excluded from our consideration here.

8. P.-J. Redouté's great iconographies with their hundreds of color plates, James Bateman's monster *Orchidaceae of Mexico and Guatemala,* 1837–1843, with 40 life-sized images, and George Brookshaw's large folio *Pomona Britannica,* 1805–1812, with 90 magnificent plates, are three examples that spring to mind.

9. Sharp's illustrations were modelled on Walter H. Fitch and William J. Hooker's *Victoria Regia; or, Illustrations of the Royal Water Lily* (London, 1851), though Sharp succeeded in giving his own plates a distinctly individual character.

10. His remarkable career is minutely described and lavishly illustrated in Van Ravenswaay (1984).

11. There was not, for example, an American equivalent of George Bentham's *Handbook of the British Flora, ed. 2* (London, Lovell Reeve, 1865), with its hundreds of clear text illustrations. These were later published separately as Walter H. Fitch and Worthington G. Smith's *Illustrations of the British Flora: A Series of Wood Engravings of British Plants* (London, Lovell Reeve, [1879]), in what was virtually a pocket book with no less than 1,306 postage-stamp sized illustrations of great clarity, much valued by field naturalists.

12. An illustrated advertisement, showing a twin pocket lens, of a swivelling kind that is still manufactured today, mounted over a small dissecting stage, is included in some issues of Gray's *Lessons in Botany*, e.g., 1875: "Gray's Botanist's Microscope. This convenient instrument, devised and manufactured first for the use of the students at Harvard University, has given so great satisfaction there, and elsewhere, that we deem it a duty to make it better known, and offer it at a price within the reach of all students."

13. See Dupree (1959). One can't help feeling that, with Sprague's proven talent at his command, he might have usefully enlightened his *Manual* with the small text figures of the kind that he used so plentifully in his textbooks.

14. See McGrath (1966) for a detailed survey of this field.

15. "Haunts" are also depicted, to some extent, in such books as William Gibson's

1895 *Our Edible Toadstools and Mushrooms* and Willard N. Clute's 1901 *Our Ferns in Their Haunts.*

16. In fairness to Hopkins, formerly priest at the Calvary Episcopal Church in Pittsburgh and later first Bishop of Vermont, it should be said that he lithographed and printed his own plates, colored them with the help of his children, and sought to raise funds for the Episcopal Institute for Boys at Burlington by their publication. The book proved to be virtually unsaleable, an expensive commercial failure. Republication under a new title didn't help the situation.

17. An eccentric extension of plant drawing includes two books that describe how to make leaf pictures by "nature printing" methods, viz, Anonymous' 1864 *Phantom Flowers: A Treatise on the Art of Producing Skeleton Leaves* and Charles Himes' 1868 *Leaf Prints; or, Glimpses at Photography.*

18. A few years later Edwin Hale Lincoln published his *Wild Flowers of New England* (Pittsfield, 1904, 3 parts) with 75 plates. It was a forerunner of his great work, *Wild Flowers of New England Photographed from Nature and Published by E. H. Lincoln* (Pittsfield, 1911–1914, 16 parts in 8 vols.) with 400 fine platinum plates. Lincoln's work, probably the finest American photographic plant iconography, was issued in a small number of copies.

19. ... and perhaps more! An elaborate study of the history of this book, the experiments made in the preparation of the plates, and the possible methods finally used, can be found in Wolfe (1979).

20. Wood-engraved illustrations could be "dropped" into the text beside the relevant passage and printed with the letterpress as a single printing operation. Copper plate engravings or lithographs had to be separately printed and inserted between or at the end of the text pages, forcing the reader to go looking for the illustration that related to the passage being read.

21. The story is told in detail in Weimerskirch (1985).

22. It should be remarked that wood-engraved blocks were very durable and could print thousands of impressions. In addition, there was a process for making identical metal copies by electro-deposition, known as electrotypes. Printers could use electrotype copies of an old wood-engraved illustration that required no alteration for several decades—in school textbooks, for example. Thus, one tends to find a mixture of wood engravings and line blocks in the later editions of some works or in cheaper productions where the use of old blocks saved the expense of making new illustrations—as in the Orange Judd Co.'s publications.

23. See Conningham (1970) for a comprehensive list of their prints.

24. The Hunt Institute Art Department includes a complete set of the 18 color separations and progressive proofs for this production.

25. For information of this class of prints, see, for example, Van Ravenswaay (1977).

26. E.g., Dellon Marcus Dewey's *The Colored Fruit Book, for the Use of Nurserymen, Containing Accurate Specimens of Colored Fruits and Flowers, Carefully Drawn and Colored from Nature, and Designed to Represent a Medium and Fair Size of Each Particular Fruit* (Rochester, N.Y., D. M. Dewey, 1859), with a varied number of chromolithograph plates. Dewey "listed some 275 plates of fruits, berries, grapes, nuts, evergreen and ornamental trees, and flowers, including roses. These plates were priced at twenty-five cents each (if the whole collection was bought) and from thirty-seven to seventy-five cents each in lots of one to twenty" (Van Ravenswaay, 1977, p. 22). Also, Dellon Marcus

Dewey's *The Specimen Book of Fruits, Flowers, and Ornamental Trees, Carefully Drawn and Colored from Nature for the Use of Nurserymen* (Rochester, the Author, ca.1865–1866, 38+ chromolith. pls.) Copies exist with 38, 56, 65, 66, 92, 103, 117 plates.

27. Other sets that have been noted include, Amana Society, Iowa County, *Specimen Book of Fruits & Flowers Lithographed and Colored by G[ottlieb]. Prestele* (N.p., n.d.); D. W. Sargent, *The Specimen Book of Fruits, Flowers and Ornamental Trees, Carefully Drawn & Colored from Nature for the Use of Nurserymen.* (Rochester, ca.1860s?); E. O. Graham, Nursery, [Collection of 56 colored flower portraits (Rochester printed)] (New York, ca.1870s?); O. Andrews, Nursery, [Collection of 152 colored fruit portraits (Rochester printed)] (Great Barrington, ca.1881); Chas. W. Stuart & Co., Nursery, [A set of 76 (Rochester printed)] (New York, ca.1888). Dates are difficult to ascertain.

References

Audubon, J. J. 1827–1838. The Birds of America: From Original Drawings Made during a Residence of 25 years in the United States. 4 vols. London: Published by the author. 435 pls. (col.) in double-elephant folio.

Barnhill, G. B. 1987. The publication of illustrated natural histories in Philadelphia, 1800–1850. In: G. W. R. Ward, ed. 1987. The American Illustrated Book in the Nineteenth Century. Winterthur, Del.: Henry Francis du Pont Winterthur Museum; distributed by the University Press of Virginia, Charlottesville, Va. Pp. 53–88.

Bridson, G. D. R. and D. E. Wendel with the assistance of J. J. White. 1986. Printmaking in the Service of Botany. Pittsburgh, Pa.: Hunt Institute for Botanical Documentation. 166 pp.

Catesby, M. 1731–1743. The Natural History of Carolina, Florida and the Bahama Islands: Containing the Figures of Birds, Beasts, Fishes, Serpents, Insects and Plants, not Hitherto Described, or Very Incorrectly Figured by Authors, Together with Their Descriptions in English and French. To which, are added observations on the air, soil and waters; with remarks upon agriculture, grain, pulse, roots, etc. To the whole is prefixed a new and correct map of the countries treated of [etc.]. 2 vols. London: Printed at the expense of the author. 100+220 pls.

Catesby, M. 1737+. Hortus Britanno-Americanus; or, A Curious Collection of Trees and Shrubs, the Produce of the British Colonies in North America, Adapted to the Soil and Climate of England. 2 vols. London: Chris. Gray. 17 pls.

Conningham, F. A. [1970]. Currier & Ives Prints: An Illustrated Check List. Updated by Colin Simkin. New York: Crown Publishers. xx+300 pp.

Dunthorne, G. 1961. Eighteenth-century botanical prints in color. In: Hunt Botanical Library. 1958–1961. Catalogue of Botanical Books [etc.]. 2 vols. in 3. Pittsburgh, Pa.: Hunt Botanical Library. Vol. 2. Pp. xxi–xxxi.

Dupree, A. H. 1959. Asa Gray, 1810–1888. Cambridge, Mass.: Belknap Press of Harvard University. x+505 pp. & 9 pls.

Hedrick, U. P. 1950. A History of Horticulture in America to 1860. New York: Oxford University Press. xiii+551 pp.

McClinton, K. 1973. The Chromolithographs of Louis Prang. New York: Clarkson N. Potter, distributed by Crown Publishers, Inc. 246 pp. & [16] pp. of col. illus. [Includes details of flower paintings sold at auction by Prang in 1875, notes of various artists he employed, and reproductions of various of his productions, floral and otherwise.]

88. Chromolithograph
(artist's proof) of Isaac
Sprague's painting of
Canadian rock-rose,
Helianthemum canadense
Michx. for George L.
Goodale's, *The Wild
Flowers of America*, 1886.

McGrath, D. F. 1966. American Colorplate Books, 1800–1900. Ph.D. thesis. The University of Michigan. [iv]+ii–iv+231 pp. (Photocopy of his unpublished dissertation.)

Michaux, A. 1803. Flora Boreali-Americana: Sistens Characteres Plantarum quas in America Septentrionali Collegit et Detexit. 2 vols. Paris and Strasbourg. 51 pls.

Michaux, F. A. 1810–1813. Histoire des Arbres Forestiers de l'Amérique Septentrionale, Considérés Principalement sous les Rapports de leurs Usage dans les Arts et de leurs Introduction dans le Commerce. 3 vols. Paris. 140 pls.

Museum of Graphic Art, New York. 1969. American Printmaking: The First 150 Years. Text by Wendy J. Shadwell. New York: Published for The Museum ... by the Smithsonian Institution Press. 180 pp.

Pennsylvania Horticultural Society. 1976. From Seed to Flower: Philadelphia, 1681–1876. A horticultural point of view. Philadelphia, Pa.: Pennsylvania Horticultural Society. 120 pp.

Reveal, J. L. 1992. Gentle Conquest: The Botanical Discovery of North America. With illustrations from the Library of Congress. Washington, D.C.: Starwood Publishing. 160 pp., illus.

Rudolph, E. D. 1990. Isaac Sprague, "Delineator and Naturalist." Journal of the History of Biology 23: 91–126. [Appendix: Books and papers containing illustrations drawn by Isaac Sprague.]

Saint Pierre, B. de. 1797. Studies of Nature, transl. H. Hunter. 3 vols. Worcester: Printed for J. Nancrede. (First American edition.) [See vol. 2, pls. II–V.]

Seaton, B. 1995. The Language of Flowers: A History. Charlottesville, Va.: University Press of Virginia. xiii+234 pp. [See The language of flowers: An annotated bibliography, pp. 203–209; and Miscellaneous flower books: A bibliography, pp. 211–217.]

Van Ravenswaay, C. 1977. Fruit and flower plates. In: Van Ravenswaay, C. A Nineteenth-Century Garden. New York: Universe Books, a Main Street Press Book. Pp. 20–23. 73 pp., illus. (col.).

Van Ravenswaay, C. 1984. Drawn from Nature: The Botanical Art of Joseph Prestele and His Sons. Washington, D.C.: Smithsonian Institution Press. 357 pp., incl. 95 pl., & 43 illus.

Weimerskirch, P. J. 1985. Naturalists and the beginnings of lithography in America. In: A. C. Wheeler and J. H. Price, eds. 1985. From Linnaeus to Darwin: Papers from the Fifth Easter Meeting of the Society for the History of Natural History, 28–31 March, 1983. London: The Society for the History of Natural History. Pp. 167–177.

Wolfe, R. J. 1979. Jacob Bigelow's American Medical Botany, 1817–1821: An Examination of the Origin, Printing, Binding and Distribution of America's First Color Plate Book, with Special Emphasis on the Manner of Making and Printing Its Colored Plates. North Hills: Bird & Bull Press; Boston: Boston Medical Library. 121 pp. & 2 pls.

Wood, C. B., 3rd. 1970. Prints and scientific illustrations in America. In: J. D. Morse, ed. 1970. Prints in and of America to 1850. Charlottesville, Va.: University Press of Virginia for The Henry Francis du Pont Winterthur Museum. Winterthur conference report 1970. Pp. 161–191.

Wood, C. B., 3rd. 1973. American scientific illustration, 1675–1775. In: Colonial Society of Massachusetts. 1973. Boston Prints and Printmakers, 1670–1775: A Conference Held by the Colonial Society of Massachusetts, 1 and 2 April 1871. Boston. Pp. 221–239.

Wroth, L. C. 1938. The Colonial Printer, ed. 2. Portland, Maine: The Southworth-Anthoensen Press. xxiv+368+[1] pp. & pls. i–xxiv+A–F.

The 20th century: Printmaking for its own sake

Introductory notes

The second portion of our exhibition is devoted to prints with botanical or other plant themes made without the need to satisfy any particular scientific requirement. Some, indeed, are of such detail and accuracy as to elevate them to the status of scientific illustration, but that was not a primary consideration in making our selection. The prints are the product of a wide range of 20th-century American creative printmakers, and each print can be said to speak for itself in terms of subject, treatment, and technique. What we have tried to do in making our selection from the considerable Hunt Institute art resources is to find prints that were produced by the broad spectrum of relevant 20th-century printmaking processes. Most of these processes existed in the previous century, but here they often are handled in an idiosyncratic or innovative manner that adds to the personality of the individual printmaker's work.

As the 20th-century advanced American art came under the influence of a succession of powerful "modern" movements that we know as cubism, surrealism, social realism, abstract expressionism, minimalism, conceptualism, "pop" art, and so forth, movements that tended to push figurative printmaking themes to the margins of the art scene. Nevertheless, there has always been a group of printmakers who were inspired to continue portraying nature with fidelity born of keen observation of and familiarity with their subject coupled with a love of form and color who were yet able to infuse their prints with individuality. Their relatively small numbers are somewhat surprising when one considers that in the later decades of the 20th century there arose a greater awareness of and understanding of nature, coupled with the need to conserve its beauty and resources, than we had ever experienced before. To that sensibility may be attributed the tremendous upsurge in the practice and appreciation of botanical art that we have seen these last three decades. Curiously, it appears the allure of the plant has yet to inspire a corresponding growth in the printmaking activity.

Our exhibit shows selected examples of the work of some of these representational printmakers, including some who have adopted freer or experimental approaches to plant depiction, design, color and execution. As a botanical institute, the Hunt's acquisitions are principally images that are botanically recognizable below the level of plant family, others that are horticultural, and some that are purely decorative, but all representational. Thus our exhibit, taken from Institute collections, does not include images that fall within any of the abstract "isms" that are so significant in the wider world of modern art.

The 20th century opened with little original printmaking that could be called plant inspired. Etching was the most fashionable artistic printmaking process in vogue, a hang-over from the late 19th century. In his introduction to *American Prints in the Library of Congress* (1970), Alan M. Fern, of the Prints & Photographs Division, explains,

> Until the time of the Centennial Exposition in Philadelphia in 1876, printmaking was an occasional diversion for the serious artist in America. Bass Otis, Benjamin West (who in fact, did his lithographs in England), and the Peales made prints, as did painter-illustrators like Winslow Homer. In 1877, however, there arose a group of artists, devoted to the production of etchings, who were successful in reaching the art-buying public. Clubs of etchers and widely advertised editions of prints became common phenomena in the 1880's and 1890's. Meanwhile, [American] artists abroad were becoming increasingly interested in printmaking as a medium of direct expression; Whistler, Otto Bacher, Frank Duveneck, and Joseph Pennell were among the most prolific and inventive of American expatriates. These two groups of printmakers provided direction and tutelage for the next generation of American artists (Library of Congress 1970).

That etching revival started in France, spread to England and eventually reached America. Our researches suggest that the individual plant or animal was a rarely chosen subject during this period. The closest we find to prints with anything that might be called a "plant" theme was in the work of a group of etchers, New Englanders and others, who took landscape vegetation, especially tree-landscape, as their inspiration. For example, Albert Fitch Bellows, Edward Moran, Mary Nimmo Moran, Thomas Moran, Charles M. Prior, Alexander Schilling, James D. Smillie, Cadwallader Washburn, Donald Shaw MacLaughlan, Jules André Smith, Benjamin C. Brown and William Harry Warren Bicknell are some who produced work in the late 19th and early 20th centuries within this genre.

During years when modern movements in art were beginning to disturb traditional attitudes, the market for this kind of "outdoor" etching was much depressed. In 1934 an organization known as the Associated American Artists was formed, and its principal mission was to assist artists in reaching their audience by making art affordable. To that end some 50 department stores across the country undertook to display and offer for sale signed etchings and lithographs by AAA members. However, the vision of soft furnishings, wallpapers, and prints does not suggest a very discerning or inspiring audience for the printmaker.

In the 1930s the state of the nation and its economy helped to foster the fashion known as "social realism," what might be called "showing it like it is" in modern parlance. Indeed, in 1936 the American Artists' Congress exhibited a hundred prints under the title "America Today," and published an album of reproductions. The Introduction remarks that

> The exhibition, as a whole, may be characterized as "socially-conscious." It reflects a deep-going change that has been taking place among artists for the last few years—a change that has taken many of them not only to their studio window to look outside, but right through the door and into the street, into the mills, farms, mines and factories. More and more artists are finding the world outside their studios increasingly interesting and exciting, and filling their pictures with their reactions to humanity about them, rather than with *apples or flowers* [my emphasis] (American Artists' Congress 1936).

The only plant print in the album, "Calla Lily," is a drypoint by Kalman Kubinyi, who depicts the potted plant against a gloomy industrial backcloth of smoking mill chimneys, a railroad engine, a truck, two trudging workmen, and a daily newspaper with the visible headline "Yanks Win. Rebels Advan ....."

Fern's earlier quoted remarks continue, "The various federal art projects of the 1930's and the teaching of Stanley William Hayter in the 1940's are among other forces that have made printmaking a vital art in this country. Today, although the aesthetic and technical climate of printmaking has undergone a revolution, the graphic arts remain a primary means of expression for artists in the United States" (Library of Congress 1970). Although written 33 years ago, his final comment is certainly true today.

68. Drypoint etching, *Yucca*, by
Gerry Peirce, ca. late 1930–1940s.

Etching and drypoint, sometimes in combination, remain favorite processes for printmakers as a number of our exhibits show. It is possible to print intaglio prints on a relatively small and inexpensive rolling press in the artist's studio, and most engravers keep one, if only for proofing their work as it progresses. For large-scale work the artist must turn to one of the fully equipped studios. Stanley Hayter's New York "Atelier 17," transferred from Paris in 1940, was one of several intaglio workshops that fostered etching; Crown Point Press in Oakland, California, founded in 1962, was another. These tonal intaglio processes were employed relatively infrequently by 20th-century printmakers. A few can be found that use aquatint, soft-ground etching, or mezzotint in combination with etched line or drypoint work, but most intaglio work uses a linear syntax.

The long list of printmakers who have created a wide variety of botanical prints in the intaglio medium includes Katherine Ely Ingraham, Ruth Doris Swett, Gerry Peirce, Kalman Kubinyi, Gabor Peterdi, Richard Claude Ziemann, Jane Kogan, Virginia Louise Leak, Marvin Edward Spohn, Peter Takal, Richard Volpe, Steven Barbash, Leonard Baskin, Patricia Tobacco Forrester, Della Taylor Hoss, Howard Lessnick, Vaino Kola, Barry Moser, Marvin Hayes, Margaret Ann Moran, Lowell Nesbit, Arcadia Olenska-Petryshyn, Fernando Torm, Stephen Fisher, Donald A. Mackay and Arnold J. Bittleman.

96. Color etching, Wheat, by Richard Volpe, ca. late 1960s.

47. Zinc etching, *[Plectranthus],* by Virginia Louise Leak, ca.1960s.

Grasses   23/25   Richard Claude Ziemann 1956

107. Line engraving with etching, Grasses, by Richard Claude Ziemann, 1956.

50. Etching, Winter Poetry, by Howard Lessnick, 1971.

Winter Poetry   20/250   H. Lessnick 1971

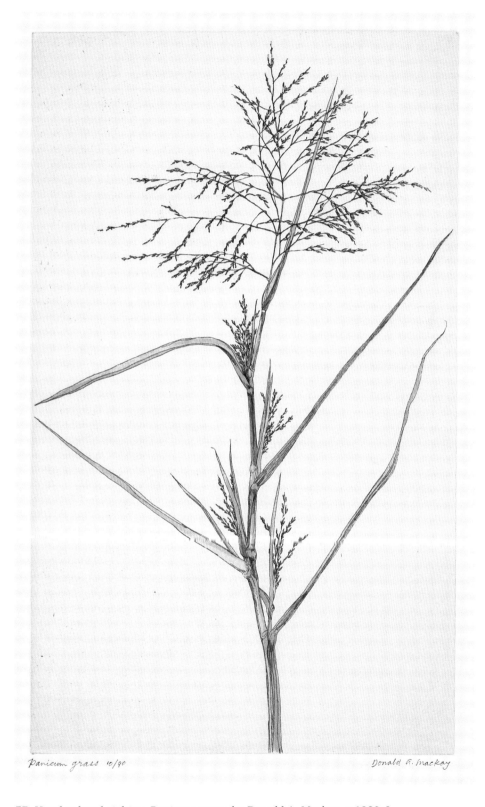

Panicum grass 10/90   Donald A. Mackay

57. Hand-colored etching, Panicum grass, by Donald A. Mackay, c.1980s?

25. Line etching/acquatint, Backwoods Norfolk, CT (Gothic Landscape 8), by Stephen Fisher, 1982–1985.

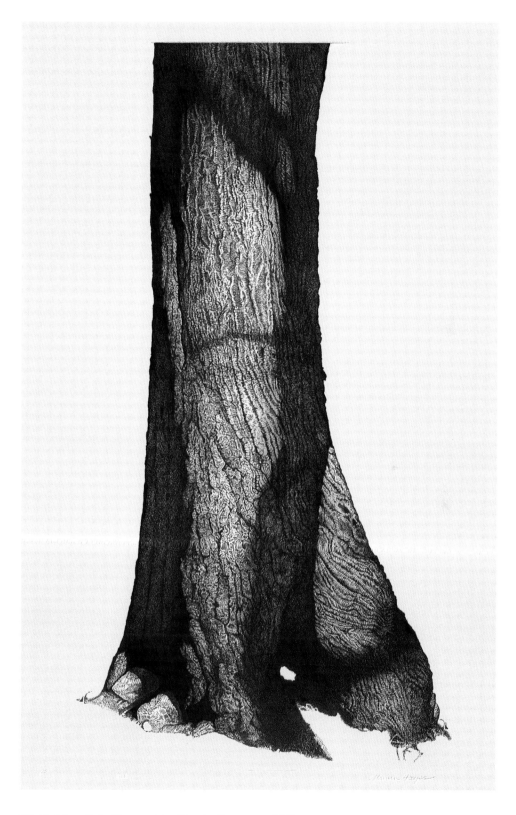

33. Etching, Oak *[Quercus]*, by Marvin Hayes, ca. 1970s.

In the 19th century the detailed precision of the needle and graver were used to depict the finest structural and floral details in hundreds of scientific and horticultural illustrations. They were made under the supervision of botanists and their style of presentation "standardized" as much as possible, leaving the printmaker no room for personal expression. Twentieth-century intaglio printmakers, relieved of this discipline have tended to focus on the larger aspects of form and color in their printmaking. Many have shown a marked interest in trees as a source of inspiration—entire trees of various characters and kinds, statuesque and quaint tree forms, tangles of branches, trunks and bark textures. This theme is demonstrated in the prints of artists such as George Elbert Burr, Roi Partridge, Donald Campbell Hardman, Helen A. Loggie, Harry Newman Wickey, Howard Norton Cook, Elizabeth White, Alfred Ray Burrell, Luigi Lucioni, Alfred Rudolph, Keith Shaw Williams, Claxton Byron Moulton, Mildred Brooks, Gabor Peterdi, Rudy Otto Pozzatti, Richard Claude Ziemann, Robert Bero, Peter Takal, and Vaino Kola.

Left: 106. Etching, Two Brothers *[Quercus]*, by Keith Shaw Williams, ca.1940s.

Above: 52. Etching, The Wraith *[Pinus]*, by Helen Loggie, 1930.

Above: 43. Etching, Everett's Tree *[Fagus]*, by Vaino Kola, 1974.

Right: 95. Color etching, Plants *[Aloe, Areca, Philodendron, Sansevieria]*, by Donella Reese Vogel, 1970.

Color intaglio

Many intaglio prints in the previous century were hand-colored to add to the information they convey but also to enhance their attractiveness. Most were used as book illustrations and were reliant upon mass-production methods for their multiplication. In the 20th century color intaglio prints have been freed of such limitations. Color now forms part of the creative process of printmakers, is entirely their conception and frequently printed by their own hand or, at least, under their close supervision. There is great variety in the finished artwork in this category created by artists such as Ruth Cyril, Lowell B. Nesbit, Walter Cleveland, Sally Moran Kugelmeyer, Donella Reese Vogel, Marsha Kristen Heinbaugh Howe and Elaine Simel.

43/100 PASQUE FLOWER   M. Howe '72

39. Color etching. Pasque flower *[Anemone]*, by Marsha Kristen Heinbaugh Howe, 1972.

I 15/20 Dandelion Mr Howe '74

41. Color etching, Dandelion *[Taraxacum]*, by Marsha Kristen Heinbaugh Howe, 1974.

40. Color etching, Teasel *[Dipsacus]*, by Marsha Kristen Heinbaugh Howe, 1974.

II 5/20 Teasel Mr Howe '74

Above: 4. Wood engraving, Tomato plant with hornworm larva *[Lycopersicon]*, by Grace Albee, 1940.

Right: 56. Wood engraving, Cabbages *[Brassica]*, by Warren Mack, ca.1939.

Relief prints

Relief printmaking processes underwent some striking developments in the 20th century. Following the work of William Morris and his Kelmscott Press in England, wood-engraved or woodcut illustrations featured prominently in the self-consciously refined productions of the "private press" movement where the craftsmanship and artistry of the finished product overrode almost any economic consideration. This became a fertile field for wood-engraver artists, several of whom found inspiration in plants or plant themes for their work. As a medium, wood engraving frequently encourages small-scale work, intimate and mannered in its approach. End-grain engraving of the 19th-century Bewick school, both white and black line, was generally used for small text illustration, no more than about two inches square, a limitation imposed by the smallness of the trunk of the Box tree. (That limitation was overcome for newspaper and magazine illustration by bolting a number of blocks together to create a larger engraving surface).

Cabbages   2/50   Warren Mack

116

Iris stylosa and christmas Roses 1935 — 65   clare leighton

49. Wood engraving, *Iris stylosa* and Christmas roses, by Clare Veronica Hope Leighton for her
Four Hedges: A Gardener's Chronicle, 1935.

48. Wood engraving, Weeds, by Clare Veronica Hope Leighton for her *Four Hedges: A Gardener's Chronicle*, 1935.

Cupressus sempervirens L.   E. Abbe

1. Wood engraving, *Cupressus sempervirens* L., by Elfriede Abbe for her *Plants of Virgil's Georgics*, 1962.

Medicago arborea L.

E. Abbe

2. Wood engraving, *Medicago arborea* L., by Elfriede Abbe for her *Plants of Virgil's Georgics*, 1962.

"Calendula"   Asa Cheffetz

19. Wood engraving, *Calendula*, by Asa Cheffetz, ca. 1930s.

Woodcut, which uses the *long* grain, is usually cut on fruit tree wood, such as cherry. Larger surfaces are possible this way, but relatively small-scale images still seem to be favored. Twentieth-century artists rejected the minutely detailed, crabbed and crowded syntax of 19th-century engravers in favor of much bolder linear or block work providing pronounced black/white contrasts and admitting much individuality in treatment. Woodcut and wood engraving have been more closely associated with artistic book illustration than other 20th-century printmaking processes, and several artists have published book illustrations as well as separate artist prints.

36. Woodcut, *Gladiolus*, by Jacques Hnizdovsky, 1964.

65. Woodcut, Deadly nightshade *[Datura]*, by Arthur Barry Moser, 1976.

45. Hand-colored woodcut, *[Viola]*, by Fritz Kredel, 1963.

44. Hand-colored woodcut, *[Taraxacum]*, by Fritz Kredel, 1963.

A third, much favored, relief process is linocut. Linoleum was introduced as a relief printing medium in the second decade of the century but became really widely known following the Great War. Its cheapness, consistence, ease of working, and availability in large dimensions soon found favor, and a broad range of relief printmakers have used it with wonderful effect. There has been a steady stream of 20th-century printmakers who created botanical prints on wood or linoleum, including Edna Boies Hopkins, Asa Cheffetz, Clare Veronica Hope Leighton, Paul Landacre, Warren Bryan Mack, Grace Albee, Leo John Meissner, Jacques Hnizdovsky, Valenti Angelo, William Steeple Davis, Elfriede Abbe, Fritz Kredel, Robert Bero, Maureen S. Kruckeberg, Charles Bruce Carter, Joe Ardourel, Emilio Sanchez, Arthur Barry Moser, Richard Wagener and Jim Dine.

18. Woodcut, Ben's cornfield, by Charles Bruce Carter, 1966.

Color relief

Both wood and lino have been used for color prints, either from the single-block on which the artist "painted" his colored inks and printed the block at one impression, or by the use of a separate block for each color, printed in a series. At the beginning of the century, in both America and Europe, a great interest developed in the extraordinary wealth and diversity of Japanese color prints. This was accompanied by a greater awareness and appreciation of the qualities and virtue of Japanese papers for printmaking. The artistic and technical approach to American color relief printmaking benefited from this Japanese influence.

Gooseberries   5/30   Alice Pauline Schafer, Imp.

79. Color linocut, Gooseberries *[Ribes]*, by Alice P. Schafer, ca. late 1940–1950s.

Aesculus Hippocastanum   4/15   Virginia Ward, *Imp.*

103. Color linocut, *Aesculus hippocastanum,* by Virginia Ward, ca.1970s.

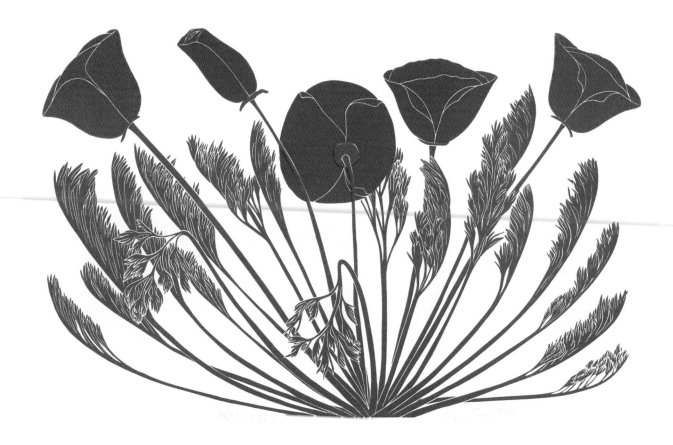

22. Color linocut, Poppy *[Eschscholzia],* by Henry Evans, 1974.

A modest-sized hand-press can be set up in an engraver's studio relatively easily and cheaply. Although special printing skills were required to succeed in color ink mixing—overprinting to achieve combination colors, and accurate color registration—wood engravers have often acquired them and successfully printed their own work. Color-printed relief botanical prints from wood or linoleum have been created by artists such as Gustav Baumann, Frances Hammel Gearhart, Blanche Lazzell, Margaret Jordan Patterson, William Seltzer Rice, Cora M. Boone, Cornelis Botke, Stanton Macdonald-Wright, Henry Herman Evans, Boyd Everett Hanna, James Dexter Havens, Mervin Jules, Margaret Jordan Patterson, Alice Pauline Schafer, Virginia Ward, Ed Baynard, and Luigi Rist. Of all these Evans was by far the most prolific.

23. Color linocut, Iris, by Henry Evans, 1973.

Scarlet Runner Beans 84/60 *James D. Havens, A.N.A. Del. Sc. Imp. 1957.*

32. Color woodcut, Scarlet runner beans *[Phaseolus]*, by James Dexter Havens, 1957.

42. Color woodcut, Poppies, by Mervin Jules, ca.1960s.

15. Hand-colored lithograph, Sere and yellow *[Quercus]*, by John Brandon, ca.1930–ca.1940s.

By the end of the 19th century American lithography had acquired the reputation of being an almost entirely commercial printing-trade medium. The most notable exception to this situation being the masterly lithographic work of James M. Whistler. Following Whistler's death, Joseph Pennell and a few others in 1908 created the Senefelder Club to try to re-establish artistic credibility for the medium. In the hands of Pennell and a few others, some commendable prints were created, but their brave efforts could not re-establish lithography's reputation, and the field dwindled to a few dedicated artists. Artists who drew on stone, on zinc, or on special paper for transfer to stone, rarely printed their own work, depending on the technical expertise of experienced hand-printing specialists. There were few printers outside the trade who could print artists' work; George C. Miller, Bolton Brown, and Lynton R. Kistler of Los Angeles were some who stimulated artists to take a renewed interest in the medium. In the postwar years, Kistler's new Los Angeles studio, Robert Blackburn's Printmaking Workshop in New York, Tamarind Lithography Workshop in Los Angeles, the Pratt Contemporaries Graphic Art Centre in New York, Gemini GEL (Graphic Editions Limited) at Los Angeles, Tyler Graphics at Bedford Village, New York, Universal Limited Art Editions of West Islip, New York, and others have brought about a renaissance in the medium. As printmakers enlarged their "canvas," so to speak, some large, power-driven machines with sophisticated ancillary facilities were required, hence the growth of these specialized lithographic printing studio businesses.

Lithography can be achieved in a variety of ways, but the conventional method was to draw on stone with pen and ink, or with a special chalk, or dab or rub the stone with powdered lithographic chalk. Some artists who made prints using such methods include Bolton Coit Brown, Henri Gilbert De Kruif, Charles Sheeler, Ralph Griswold, Emil Ganso, John Brandon, Vera Andrus, Stow Wegenroth, Lilian May Miller, Alice L. Gerschel, Wilfred Readio, James Patrick, Adolf Arthur Dehn, Elizabeth Saltonstall, Jan Stussy, Henry E. Winzenried, Jack

Above: 30. Lithograph, British Queen *[Laeliocattleya],* by Ralph Griswold, ca.1931.

Right: 73. Lithograph, Tangle 4 *[Galanthus, Hosta],* by Wilfred Readio, ca.1930–ca.1940s.

Perlmutter, Charles Ephraim Burchfield, Peter Takal, Victoria Hutson Huntley, Ellsworth Kelly, Stanley Maltzman, Robert Kipniss, Michael Knigin, Roy Drasites, David Hockney, and Roger Medearis. In the later decades lithographers often modified traditional lithographic style to the point where the appearance of the finished print looked vastly different from lithography as known to Victorian printmakers, and sometimes the identity of the process can scarcely be determined from the printed results at all.

63. Lithograph, Native Oak *[Quercus]*, by Roger Medearis, 1981.

59. Lithograph, Thistle *[Cirsium?]*, by Stanley Maltzman, 1972.

Color lithographs

Commercial color-printed lithography, universally known as chromolithography, was a highly successful and widespread 19th-century commercial printing process. It was much maligned by modern printmakers whose creative chromatic work was to be distinguished by the term "color lithography." Much influence was derived from French lithographic artists of the later 19th century who worked in a style markedly different from chromolithography. Color lithography multiplies printing difficulties, and a fastidious artist can spend weeks or even months with a master printer in proofing, altering, reproofing, modifying ink recipes, and so forth, until the artist's conception is finally achieved. A number of 20th-century printmakers have produced botanical prints in a wide variety of styles of color lithography among whom are Russell T. Limbach, Margaret Lowengrund, Lowell B. Nesbit, Deborah Kogan, Lois Long, Gary Alan Bukovnik, Laura Grosch, Alex Katz, Kenjilo Nanao, Carl E. Schwartz, Alan Magee, Mary Ann Cabot (formerly Booth-Owen), Joseph Raffael, and Fritz Scholder.

58. Color lithograph, Ceremony of Innocence *[Cucurbita]*, by Alan Magee, 1984.

Silk-screen prints

Silk screen, or serigraphy as it was christened by Carl Zigrosser in about 1940, is a 20th-century invention, developed to practical successfulness in the 1930s. It is the most simple of the printmaking processes, the most characteristically American, has always been a color process, and is, more than any other, readily printed by the artist himself. Initially, the process was exploited for poster and other commercial color work and professional studios have long been in existence. In the 1960s and later decades some studios were founded that catered strictly to printmaking artists such as the Ives-Silman workshop in New Haven, the Chiron Press and the Styria Studio in the New York area, and Cirrus Editions in Los Angeles. Many technical developments in the process have facilitated its operation and enlarged its appeal as an art medium. Much earlier work in this medium was influenced by the social realism and subsequent art movements, eventually becoming familiar to a vast public audience in the 1960s through the work of Andy Warhol. The plant world provides thousands of species in an infinite variety of forms and a full palette of colors, and several artists in recent years have reveled in portraying their vision of botanical prints of large format featuring broad expanses of riotous solid colors. Some earlier artists who have made botanical prints in this medium include the pioneers Anthony Velonis and Guy MacCoy, and Ben Shahn (who printed some of his work in black outline finished with hand-coloring). During and after the great 1960s' revival, various artists have made striking botanical prints, among them Henry Mockel, Alex Katz, Andy Warhol, Charles Burton Harper, Alma Gene Bauer, John Gordon, Lowell Nesbi, Tjelda vander Meijden (formerly Michas), Joe Price, and Michael E. Arth. Techniques have varied from the starkly simple work of Alex Katz or Andy Warhol, to the 74-screen finesse of Joe Price's "Red Ripe" shown here.

RED RIPE   65/100

69. Seventy-four screen serigraph, Red Ripe, by Joe Price, 1984.

Above: 64. Serigraph, Developing inflorescence, Mojave yucca, *Yucca schidigera*, by Henry Mockel, ca.1960s.

Right: 94. Serigraph, Oriental poppy *[Papaver]*, by Tjelda vander Meijden (formerly Michas), 1980.

Nature printing

Making prints direct from the plant or its shadow without the intervening hand of a draughtsman has fascinated printmakers from time to time over several centuries. Long ago Leonardo da Vinci made some trial nature prints in his notebooks. In the 1730s Benjamin Franklin used nature printing as a means of defeating counterfeiters. Meanwhile in Europe some magnificent and extensively illustrated books were produced by nature-printing methods. Again in mid-19th-century England and Austria nature printing went through a renaissance before vanishing from use for many decades. In the 1950s two American enthusiasts began to exhibit nature prints. Arthur Wisner Rushmore made his black impressions from carefully inked specimens and Robert W. Little, starting from the same basic method, went on to produce creatively treated color-printed images and in 1976 published a book on the process.

Two printmakers who extended the "nature" image into an entirely novel field were a pair of radiographers, Harold Frank Sherwood and Albert G. Richards. Both made some striking X-ray images of plants, both published articles on their work, and in 1990 Richards published a book on his work.

51. Nature print, New York Fern, *Adiantum pedatum*, by Robert W. Little, ca. early 1970s.

ADIANTUM *pedatum*
June 1974
ROBERT W. LAINE

Digital prints

In the first section of this exhibition we noted that the final decade of the 19th century was marked by vigorous experimentation that contributed to what we now recognize as the photo-mechanical revolution. By the end of that century it became possible to create printed images from camera to page without the intervention of what had previously been essential manual printmaking crafts. The final decade of the 20th century has seen a similar period of experimentation. From early simple computer imaging programs, such as MacDraw and MacPaint, adventurous experimenters and artists were encouraged to create whatever they possibly could. Before long various illustration programs were introduced, advanced computer programs were designed that enabled the manipulation of images and the creation of sophisticated visual effects, and improved methods of ink-jet and laser printing enabled computer graphics to be printed in "book" quality. Photography was brought into the picture, and the whole basis of its process was revolutionized by switching from film to electronic digitization. As if mirroring the events of the late 19th century, the 1990s saw the field of computer graphics undergo such enormous changes that by the turn of the century the "digital revolution" could be proclaimed, and we now find ourselves living in a new graphics world.

Michael Maskarinec, a local digital printmaker, has provided us with a digital print to round off our sample of 20th-century printmaking, perhaps a pointer to significant printmaking developments in the new century. Maskarinec's digital print was made in 2000 using the Adobe Illustrator program. A "state-of-the-art" description of digital methods in use at the time can be found in various publications of which two typical works are *Adobe Illustrator 8.0* (1998) and *The Painter 6 Wow! Book* (2000).

— Gavin D. R. Bridson

60. Six color inkjet print from 1200 dpi digital file, Succulent Garden (Aloe, Snake plant, *Sansevieria*, *Sedum*, Golden Barrel cactus *Echinocactus grusonii*), by Michael Maskarinec, 2000.

Sources of information

Acton, D. 1990. A Spectrum of Innovation: Color in American Printmaking, 1890–1960. New York: W. W. Norton & Co., Worcester Art Museum. 304 pp.

Adams, C. 1983. American Lithographers, 1900–1960: The Artists and Their Printers. Albuquerque: University of New Mexico Press. x+230 pp.

Adobe Creative Team. 1998. Adobe Illustrator 8.0: Classroom in a Book. Berkeley, Calif.: Peachpit Press for Adobe Press. 417 pp.

Allan, L. 1997. Contemporary Printmaking in the Northwest. Sydney, NSW: Craftsman House. G+B Arts International. 231 pp.

American Artists' Congress. 1936. America Today: A Book of 100 prints. New York: Equinox Cooperative Press. 14 pp. & 100 pls.

Armstrong, E. and S. McGuire. 1989. First Impressions: Early Prints by Forty-Six Contemporary Artists. New York: Hudson Hills Press, in association with Walker Art Center, Minneapolis. 149 pp.

Breuer, K., R. E. Fine and S. A. Nash. 1997. Thirty-Five Years at Crown Point Press: Making Prints, Doing Art. Berkeley, Calif.: University of California Press. xii+204 pp.

Brooklyn Museum. 1977. Thirty Years of American Printmaking, Including the 20th National Print Exhibition. By Gene Baro. New York.

Brown, K. 1996. Painters and Sculptors at Crown Point Press: Ink, Paper, Metal, Wood. San Francisco: Chronicle Press. 287 pp.

Castleman, R. 1973. Contemporary Prints. New York: The Viking Press, A Studio Book. 172 pp.

Corcoran Gallery of Art, Washington. 1997. Proof Positive: Forty Years of Contemporary American Printmaking at ULAE [Universal Limited Art Editions]. Washington, D.C.: Distributed by Harry N. Abrams, Inc. 272 pp.

Devon, M., ed. 2000. Tamarind 40 Years. Albuquerque: University of New Mexico Press. xi+206 pp.

Feldman, F. and J. Schellmann. 1997. Andy Warhol Prints. A Catalogue Raisonné, 1962–1987, ed. 3. Revised and expanded by Frayda Feldman and Claudia Defendi. New York: Distributed Art Publishers in association with Ronald Feldman Fine Arts, Inc./ Edition Schellmann, The Andy Warhol Foundation for the Visual Arts, Inc. 304 pp.

Fine, R. E. and M. L. Corlett. 1991. Graphicstudio: Contemporary Art from the Collaborative Workshop at the University of South Florida. Washington: National Gallery of Art. 351 pp.

Hunt Botanical Institute. 1966. An Exhibition of Botanical Linocuts by Henry [Herman] Evans. 6 November 1966 to 25 March 1967. Pittsburgh, Pa. 24 pp. & 96 prints.

Hunt Institute for Botanical Documentation. 1979. A Northeast Folio. J. V. Brindle and J. J. White. Produced to accompany an exhibition of works by contemporary botanical printmakers ... 14 May to 14 September 1979. Pittsburgh, Pa. 18 ff.

Hunt Institute for Botanical Documentation. 1985–1998. Catalogue of the Botanical Art Collection at the Hunt Institute. Compiled by

James J. White with the assistance of Elizabeth R. Smith. Pittsburgh. 9 parts. 1777 pp. [Pts. 1–6: Plant portraits, Artists A–Z and Unknown; Pt. 7: Decorative, horticultural and non-botanical subjects, Supplement to Parts 1–6, Plant portraits; Pt. 8: Index by higher taxa to Parts 1–6 and Supplement, Plant portraits; Pt. 9: Index by genera to Parts 1–6 and Supplement, Plant portraits.]

Johnson, U. E. 1980. American Prints and Printmakers: A Chronicle of Over 400 Artists and Their Prints from 1900 to the Present. Garden City, N.Y.: Doubleday & Co. xxii+266 pp. & 29 pls. (col.).

Library of Congress. 1970. American Prints in the Library of Congress: A Catalog of the Collection. Baltimore, Md.: The Johns Hopkins Press, for the Library of Congress. xxi, 568 pp.

Little, R. W. 1976. Nature Printing. Pittsburgh, Pa.: Privately published. 96 pp. & 10 pl. (col.).

O'Gorman, J. E. 1988. Aspects of American Printmaking, 1800–1950. Syracuse, N.Y.: Syracuse University Press. x, 245 pp.

Print Council of America. 1959. American Prints Today, 1959. New York. [70] pp.

Richards, A. G. 1990. The Secret Garden: 100 Floral Radiographs. Ann Arbor, Mich.: Almar Co. 13 pp. & 100 pl.

Rosenthal, M. 1993. Artists at Gemini G.E.L.; Celebrating the 25th Year. New York: Harry N. Abrams, Inc., in association with Gemini G.E.L. 208 pp.

Smithsonian Institution Traveling Exhibition Service. 1975. American Prints from Wood: An Exhibition of Woodcuts and Wood Engravings. Organized by Jane M. Farmer. Washington, D.C. 64 pp.

Sparks, E. 1989. Universal Limited Art Editions. A History and Catalogue: The First Twenty-Five Years. New York: Harry N. Abrams, for The Art Institute of Chicago. 552 pp.

Tallman, S. 1996. The Contemporary Print. London: Thames & Hudson. 304 pp.

Threinen-Pendarvis, C. 2000. The Painter 6 Wow! Book. Berkeley, Calif.: Peachpit Press. [viii]+360 pp.

Walker Art Center, Minneapolis. 1987. Tyler Graphics: Catalogue Raisonné, 1974–1985. New York: Abbeville Press. 430 pp.

Watrous, J. 1984. Printmaking: A Century of American Printmaking, 1880–1980. Madison, Wis.: University of Wisconsin Press. x, 334 pp.

Abbe, Elfriede (1919–)

1. (page 118) *Cupressus sempervirens* L., 1962
Wood engraving
Image: 15 x 7 cm   Paper: 32 x 23 cm   Edition: 4/50
Publication: Elfriede Abbe, *Plants of Virgil's Georgics.* Ithaca, Cornell University Press, 1962.

2. (page 119) *Medicago arborea* L., 1962
Wood engraving
Image: 15 x 7 cm   Paper: 32 x 23 cm   Edition: 4/50
Publication: Elfriede Abbe, *Plants of Virgil's Georgics.* Ithaca, Cornell University Press, 1962.

Catalogue
of the
exhibition
(including biographical data and index)

Abbe was born in Washington, D.C., and educated at the Art Institute of Chicago (1937) and Cornell University, College of Architecture (B.F.A., 1940). She later worked as a scientific illustrator in the Division of Biological Sciences (1942–1974) at Cornell. As a graphic artist, sculptor, typographer and book designer, she has participated in numerous one-person and group exhibitions and received many awards. Her work is represented in several collections including the Museum of Fine Arts, Boston; Dumbarton Oaks; Library, Royal Botanic Gardens, Kew; Harvard University; the National Gallery; and the Library of Congress. Since 1949 she has continued to design books through her private press in Manchester Center, Vermont. The Hunt Institute included her wood engravings in its first four International Exhibitions of Botanical Art & Illustration (1964, 1968, 1972, 1977) and her botanical sculptures in its *Spring Exhibition* (1969). The wood blocks for these prints were cut by Abbe in Italy from living plants, 50 of those mentioned by the Roman poet Virgil in the Georgics. The research and travel for this production were aided by a grant from the Hunt Botanical Library (now the Hunt Institute).

Agate, Alfred T. (1812–1846) and Sprague, Isaac (1811–1895)

3. (page 66) *Buchanania florida; Rhus simarubaefolia*
Engraved proof plate
Image: 42.5 x 28.5 cm   Paper: 55 x 37 cm
Printmaker: Casilear [on proof but not published plate]
Publication: Asa Gray, Atlas. Botany. Phanerogamia. In: C. Wilkes etal. 1845–1876. *United States Exploring Expedition.* Vol. 14. New York, G. I. Putman, 1857. Pl. 44.

Probably born in Sparta, New York, Agate studied under his brother (Frederick S.) and T. S. Cummings. He exhibited at the National Academy (1831) and worked in New York City (1831–1838). He was the artist for the 1838–1842 exploring expedition of Charles Wilkes, and he returned to Washington (1842) to prepare the sketches and paintings for publication. Agate was an associate (1832) and later an honorary member, professional (1840) of the National Academy. His work is reproduced in the *United States Exploring Expedition* (1845–1876).

Albee, Grace (1890–1985)
4. (page 114) Tomato plant with hornworm larva *[Lycopersicon]*, 1940
Wood engraving
Image: 15 x 12.5 cm   Paper: 28 x 20 cm   Edition: 3/100

Born in Scituate, Rhode Island, Albee studied at the Rhode Island School of Design (1910–1912). She and her husband, mural painter Percy F. Albee, moved with their five children to Paris in 1928. There she studied with Paul Bornet and had her first one-person exhibit (1932). She and her family returned to New York City (1933) and later moved to Bucks County, Pennsylvania (1937), where the landscape became an inspiration for her wood engravings. Her work was included in numerous one-person and group exhibitions, including the Pennsylvania Academy of Fine Arts, Philadelphia; National Academy of Design; Metropolitan Museum of Art; and the American Institute of Graphic Arts, New York. A retrospective of her prints was exhibited at the Brooklyn Museum (1976), and her work is in the permanent collection of the Library of Congress and the National Museum of Women in the Arts, Washington, D.C. Her engravings also were included in two exhibitions at the Hunt Institute, *A Northeast Folio* (1979) and the *5th International Exhibition of Botanical Art & Illustration* (1983). She received awards from the English Royal Society of Painters and Sculptors and was a member of the National Academy of Design.

Allen, John Fisk [see also Sharp, William]
Allen was a horticulturist, amateur botanist and author of *The Culture of the Grape* (Boston, 1847) and *Victoria Regia* (Boston, 1854).

American Journal of Horticulture and Florist's Companion. Boston, Tilton & Co., 1868. Vol. 3, p. 329.
5. (page 56) *Lantana*
Wood engraving
22 x 14.5 cm

Annin & Smith [see Swett, Moses]

Charles Armstrong and Co. [see Sprague, Isaac]
Charles Armstrong & Co., chromolithographers of Boston, became one of the giants of the American printing industry until the mid-1880s. Among their many productions were a number of important flower books such as G. B. Emerson's 1875 *Report on the Trees and Shrubs Growing Naturally in the Forests of Massachusetts*, G. L. Goodale's 1876–1882 *Wild Flowers of America*, D. C. Eaton's 1878 *The Ferns of North America*, and W. W. Johnson's 1884 *Forest Leaves*. Some of Sprague's plates for Goodale's book are shown [see figures 86 and 87].

Bailey, Liberty Hyde (1858–1954)

American Gardening. New York, A. T. De La Mare Ptg. and Pub. Co., Ltd., February 1893. Vol. 14, no. 2, p. 79.

6. (page 60) The New American Rose, Mrs. W. C. Whitney
Line-block reproduction from a drawing by M. E. Fellows
24 x 17.5 cm

Bailey (1858–1954) was born in South Haven, Michigan. He received a B.S. (1882) and M.S. (1885) from Michigan State Agricultural College, assisted Asa Gray at Harvard University (1883–1884), and returned to Michigan State to become professor of horticulture and landscape gardening (1884–1888). He was professor of horticulture at Cornell University (1888–1903), became dean of the Agricultural College and director of the Agricultural Experiment Station until his retirement (1913), and donated his herbarium and library to the university (1935). Along with editing *American Gardening*, Bailey published several papers on the genus *Carex* (1883–1900), was editor of the *Cyclopedia of American Horticulture* (1907–1909, 4 vols.) and the *Standard Cyclopedia of Horticulture* (1914–1917, 6 vols.), and established the journal *Gentes Herbarum* (1920–1984). He died in Ithaca, New York.

Barnet and Doolittle [see Doolittle, Isaac and Smith, Sir James Edward]

Barry, Patrick (1816–1890), author of the *Fruit Garden* from January to June, and **J. Jay Smith**, editor of the *N. Silva* from July to December.
The Horticulturist and Journal of Rural Art and Rural Taste. Philadelphia, Robert Pearsall Smith, January to December 1855. Vol. 5, facing pages between 296 and [297].

7. (page 58) Gigantic *Wellingtonia [Sequoiadendron]*
Lithograph
22.5 x 16.5 cm

8. (page 59) Gigantic *Wellingtonia* [detail]
Lithograph
22.5 x 16.5 cm

Barry, a pioneer pomological author of national stature, was born near Belfast and died in Rochester, New York. He succeeded to the editorship of *The Horticulturist* following the untimely death of A. J. Downing and moved the journal to Rochester. Under his tenure the periodical was noted for its hand-colored plates of fruits and flowers, improved typography, and the authority of its text. In 1851 he published *The Fruit Garden*, an illustrated work of long-lasting popularity, and he compiled a great catalogue of fruits for the American Pomological Society. Barry was president of the Western New York Horticultural Society for over 30 years and did much to make Rochester into a national center of the fruit-growing industry in his day.

Barton, William P. C. (1786–1856)

9. (page 13) *Rudbeckia laciniata.* Jagged-leaved Rudbeckia

Engraving, hand-colored

27 x 22 cm

Printmaker: F. Kearny

Publication: Barton, *A Flora of North America.* Vol. 1. Philadelphia, M. Carey & Sons, 1821. Pl. 16.

Barton, born in Philadelphia, became professor of botany at the University of Pennsylvania (1815). He illustrated *Vegetable Materia Medica of the United States* (1817–1818) and *A Flora of North America* (1820–1923). He made a strenuous effort to achieve high standards with his illustrations, employing several leading Philadelphia engravers, and remarking that, "It is confidently believed by the author, that they [the plates] will be found the most successful attempts at imitation, by SOUND engraving, of the French style, yet made in this country." He started Barton's Therapeutic Institute (May 1831) in his private residence at No. 208 Chestnut Street, Philadelphia, where he began an independent lectureship of materia medica, botany and toxicology, three times a week for "two lunar months." He was the first chief of the U.S. Navy Bureau of Medicine (1842).

Bigelow, Jacob (1787–1879)

American Medical Botany ...with Coloured Engravings. Boston, Cummings and Hilliard, 1817–1820. Pl. XIII, p. opp. [133].

10. (page 17) *Kalmia latifolia*

Color line engraving

26 x 17.5 cm

Bigelow was born in Sudbury, Massachusetts, was educated at Harvard (1806) and the University of Pennsylvania (M.D., 1810), and began his practice in medicine in Boston (1810). He was professor of materia medica at Harvard Medical School and physician at the Massachusetts General Hospital (1815–1855). Bigelow drew many of the plates included in this publication and developed the process for printing *American Medical Botany*, which is one of the first color-plate books published in America. A collection of some of Bigelow's botanical illustrations for this publication and some of his herbarium specimens from a European tour (ca.1839) are in the archives of the Harvard University Herbaria. Bigelow was one of the founders of the Massachusetts Horticultural Society (1829), co-authored the first U.S. Pharmacopoeia (1820), and was president of the American Academy of Arts and Sciences (1847–1863).

Bigelow, J. M. [see Roetter, Paulus and Möllhausen, Heinrich Balduin]

Blanchan, Neltje (1865–1918)
Nature's Garden ...with Colored Plates and Many Other Illustrations Photographed from Nature by Henry Troth and A. R. Dugmore. New York, Doubleday, Page & Co., 1900. P. [opp. 179].
11. (page 63) Dutchman's breeches or White-hearts, *Bicuculla cucullaria [Dicentra cucullaria* (L.) Bernh.*]*
Photomechanical halftone
Photograph from nature by Henry Troth
25.5 x 18.5 cm

Blanchan (1865–1918) was the pen name for Nellie Blanchan (DeGraf) Doubleday, wife of Frank Nelson Doubleday, founder of Doubleday & Company Publishers. She was an ecologist and authored many books on nature and birds including *Wildflowers: An Aid to Knowledge of Nature's Garden* (New York, Doubleday, Page & Company, 1909) *The American Flower Garden* (1909), *Birds Worth Knowing* (1917), and *Bird Neighbors* (1922).

Botanical Fine Art Weekly: Wildflowers of America. New York, G. H. Buek and Co., 1894.
12. (page 45) Fig. 79. Night Flowering Catchfly, *Silene noctiflora*, July
Fig. 80. Tick Trefoil, *Meibornia (Desmodium) canadensis*, July
Chromolithograph
20.5 x 29.5 cm
13. (page 46) Fig. 81. Fringed Gentian, *Gentiana americana (Crinita)*
July–August
Fig. 82. Elecampane, *Inula helenium*, August
Chromolithograph
20.5 x 29.5 cm

Previously known for the 47 famous color plates to Harry A. Ogden's 1889 *Uniform of the Army of the United States Illustrated from 1774 to 1884*, G. H. Buek printed and published these 288 chromolithographs for popular consumption in 18 weekly parts in 1894, a most unusual production. It featured flowers of every state in America with text about the flower and its habitat. Nothing else seems to be recorded from Buek's press.

Bourne, Hermon (1800–)
Flores Poetici: The Florist's Manual ... with More Than Eighty Beautifully-Coloured Engravings of Poetic Flowers. Boston, Munroe & Francis; New York, Charles S. Francis, 1833. P. 28.
14. (page 44) Passion-flower
Wood engraving
23 x 13.5 cm

Bourne's illustrations are slightly unusual in that they were hand-colored

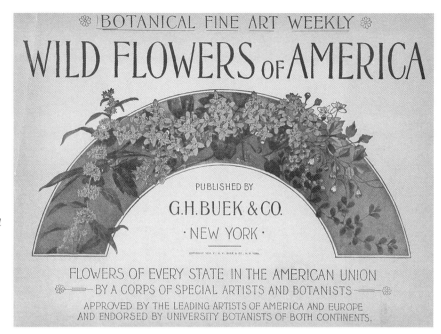

Title page of *Botanical Fine Art Weekly*: Wild Flowers of America, 1894.

wood engravings. Illustrations in that medium were usually left uncolored because the hand-coloring tended to muddy the strength of the black-line work.

Bouvé, Ephraim W. [see Sharp, William]

Brandon, John (1870–1958)
15. (page 132) Sere and yellow *[Quercus]*, ca.1930–ca.1940s
Lithograph, hand-colored
Image: 25.5 x 22 cm   Paper: 36.5 x 30 cm

Brandon was born in Franklin, Tennessee, and lived in Sacramento, California. He studied with Clifton Carbee in Boston and exhibited at the Kingsley Art Center (1931–1947). His work is in the collection of the California State Library.

Browne, Daniel Jay (1804–ca.1867)
The Trees of America, Native and Foreign, Pictorially and Botanically Delineated ... Illustrated by Numerous Engravings. New York, Harper, 1846. Pp. 264–265.
16. (page 37) *Cerasus vulgaris*, The common cherry-tree
Wood engraving
24 x 16.5 cm
17. (page 36) *Cerasus borealis*, The northern cherry-tree
Wood engraving
24 x 16.5 cm

Browne also authored *The Sylva Americana; or, A Description of the Forest Trees* (Boston, 1832), *Letters from the Canary Islands* (Boston, 1834), and

The American Poultry Yard (New York, 1850), *The American Bird Fancier* (New York, ca.1850), and *The Field Book of Manures* (New York, 1856). Browne had a rather undistinguished career as head of the agricultural division of the U.S. Patent Office (1853–1859).

G. H. Buek and Co. [see Botanical Fine Art Weekly]

Butler, J. J. [see Gray, Asa]

Callowhill, Sydney T. [see Mathews, Ferdinand Schuyler]

Carter, Charles Bruce (1930–)
18. (page 125) Ben's cornfield, 1966
Woodcut
Image: 37.5 x 62 cm   Paper: 54.5 x 70.5 cm   Artist's proof
Carter was born in North Adams, Massachusetts, and currently lives in Glenfield, New York. He studied at Albright Art School, Buffalo, New York (diploma, Fine Arts, 1951), State University of New York, Buffalo, (B.S., 1952), and Pennsylvania State University (M.Ed., 1955, D.Ed., 1958). He was a professor at Carnegie Mellon University (1964–1993) and also lectured at numerous universities and museums. He received several awards and fellowships, including the National Endowment for the Arts fellowship, and the Dr. Janusz Korczak International Memorial Medal, Warsaw, Poland. He is a member of the International Society of Wood-cutters and Wood Engravers, Winterthur, Switzerland; Boston Printmakers; and the Los Angeles Print Society. His work has been included in many solo, national, and international printmaking exhibitions. His work is in the collection of several universities and museums, including Carnegie Mellon University; Nova Scotia School of Art and Design, Halifax; Pennsylvania State University; Kunst Foreningen Museum, Oslo; Museum of Xylography, Capri, Italy; National Archives, Department of Military History, Washington, D.C.; National Museum of Art, Hanoi, Vietnam; Philadelphia Museum of Art; and the Westmoreland Museum of Art, Greensburg, Pennsylvania. His work was included in *Fields of Grass: The Varied Uses of Grass* (1986–1987), a collaborative exhibition with the Hunt Institute and the Smithsonian Institution. Twenty woodcuts from *The Vietnam Series*, with a commentary by the artist, were reproduced in the journal *Witness* (2(1): Spring 1988).

Casilear [see Agate, Alfred T.]

Cheffetz, Asa (1896–1965)
19. (page 120) *Calendula*, ca.1930s
Wood engraving
32 x 22.6 cm

Cheffetz was born in Buffalo, New York, and studied at the Boston Art Museum and the National Academy of Design, New York. His work was exhibited in numerous printmaking exhibitions and is in the collection of several museums in the United States and abroad, including the Library of Congress, Art Institute of Chicago, Boston Museum of Art, Cleveland Museum of Art, Metropolitan Museum of Art, Pennsylvania Academy of Fine Arts, and the state of Israel collection. In 1944, he designed and engraved the official bookplate for the Library of Congress. This print was featured in the Hunt Institute's *5th International Exhibition of Botanical Art & Illustration* (1983).

Coulter, John M. [see Faxon, Charles Edward]

Coville, Frederick V. [see Muller, Frank and Walpole, Frederick Andrews]

Cowing, Roberta (active 1887–1920)
20. (page 84) *Arenaria compacta*
Tinted lithograph
24.5 x 15 cm
Publication: *Contributions from the United States National Herbarium.*
1893. Vol. 4, pl. 5 [opp. p. 328].
Indefinite loan from Smithsonian Institution

Cowing was born in Indiana and was an illustrator for the United States Department of Agriculture, Division of Botany. Her work is included in the *Yearbook of the United States Department of Agriculture* and the *Contributions from the United States National Herbarium.* Some of her illustrations of fungi are housed in the Mycology Laboratory, National Fungus Collection, Beltsville, Maryland.

Doolittle, Isaac [see also Smith, Sir James Edward]p
Isaac Doolittle was one of America's first lithographers. He was instructed in the art of lithography in Paris. In ca.1821 he entered into partnership with William Barnet, who, like him, had learned lithography in Paris. They established a lithographic printing shop in New York, the first one in America. The partnership was short-lived; Barnet returned to Paris in 1822, and Doolittle moved to Bennington, Vermont, to work in an iron foundry. During that brief period they printed 21 plates for the 1822 edition of Sir James Smith's *Grammar of Botany*, only the second American book to have lithographic illustrations. The illustrations, put onto stone by Arthur J. Stansbury, were simple line-drawn copies of the original English engraved plates.

Downing, Andrew Jackson (1815–1852)
The Horticulturist and Journal of Rural Art and Rural Taste. Albany, N.Y., Luthur Tucker, July 1846–June 1847. Vol. 1, no. 12, pg. opp. [537].
21. (page 20) The Cedar of Lebanon. Full grown tree at Foxley, planted by Sir Uvedale Price. [Scale 1 in. to 12 feet]
Wood engraving
23 x 16.5 cm

Downing (1815–1852) was born in Newburgh, New York. In 1834 he and his brother Charles went into partnership in the nursery begun by their father in 1801. Andrew Downing became the owner (1839), offering numerous varieties of fruit trees, as well as other perennials. He was considered "the father of landscape architecture in America," and he is best known for his garden designs inspired by the natural English garden style. Downing believed that the architecture of the rural home and the surrounding landscape should compliment one another and also advocated the importance of naturalistic parks in urban spaces. Along with editing *The Horticulturist* (published 1846/47–1875), he was the author of *A Treatise on the Theory and Practice of Landscape Gardening* (1841), *Cottage Residences* (1842), *The Fruits and Fruit Trees of America* (1845) with his brother Charles, and *Architecture for Country Houses* (1850). He was commissioned to design the grounds of the Capital, Smithsonian and White House, but died in a tragic steamboat accident before they were completed.

Dugmore, A. Radclyffe (1870–1955) [see Rogers, Julia Ellen and Blanchan, Neltje]
Dugmore was an pioneering English nature and wildlife artist and photographer, who became especially well known in America, where much of his work was published. In the 1890s he became assistant and photographer to W. E. D. Scott, a well-known ornithologist, and some of his first photographs were published in Scott's *Bird Studies* (1898). Dugmore wrote and illustrated *Bird Homes … with Hints on the … Photographing of Young Birds* with 66 photographs (15 col.) (1900), and two years later *Nature and the Camera: How to Photograph Live Birds and Their Nests … Flowers, Trees and Fungi* …with 40 plates, a very early "how-to-do-it" manual for the subject. He wrote and illustrated several more famous books on wildlife photography down to the mid-1920s.

Emma C. Embury [see Whitefield, Edwin]

Endicott [see Swett, Moses]

Engelmann, George [see Roetter, Paulus and Möllhausen, Heinrich Balduin]

Evans, Henry (1918–1990)
22. (page 128) Poppy *[Eschscholzia]*, 1974
Linocut, color
33 x 50.5 cm
Edition: 13/350
23. (page 129) Iris, 1973
Linocut, color
31.5 x 50.5 cm
Edition 10/78

Evans was born in Superior, Wisconsin, educated at the University of California, Berkeley, and the University of Arizona, Tucson, and was a self-taught botanical artist. He founded Peregrine Press, which operated from 1949 to 1958, and was a botanical printmaker from 1958 until his death. His work was exhibited in numerous one-person and group exhibits at the Smithsonian Institution; Royal Horticultural Society, London; California Academy of Sciences, San Francisco; Field Museum, Chicago; Los Angeles County Museum; and the National Arboretum, Washington, D.C. His work is in the permanent collection of the Library of Congress, Washington, D.C. The Hunt Institute included his work in its *2nd, 3rd,* and *4th International Exhibition of Botanical Art & Illustration* (1964, 1972/73, 1977/78), *5 Westcoast Printmakers* (1976), and in five of its travel exhibitions.

Faxon, Charles Edward (1846–1918)

24. (page 75) *Enantiophylla hydeana* Coulter and Rose
Lithograph
30.5 x 25.5 cm
Printmaker: Meisel, B., Boston
Publication: John M. Coulter and J. N. Rose, Notes on North American Umbelliferae. III. *Botanical Gazette.* Crawfordsville, 1893. Vol. 18, no. 1, pp. 54–56, pl. 5.

Faxon was born in Roxbury, Massachusetts (now Jamaica Plains), and his brother Edwin guided and taught Charles and his brothers about nature. Charles taught himself to draw, and he received his B.S. in civil engineering from the Lawrence Scientific School, Cambridge (1867). In the 1870s Faxon made some of the color illustrations for D. C. Eaton's *Ferns of North America.* He was instructor of botany at the Bussey Institution of Harvard College (1879–1884) and a member of the Academy of Arts and Sciences. Faxon became assistant director of the Arnold Arboretum (1882), where he headed the herbarium and library and illustrated Charles Sprague Sargent's *Silva of North America* (1891–1902, 14 vols.) over a period of 21 years, providing 744 illustrations. He provided 34 illustrations for John Donnell Smith's descriptions of Guatemalan plants for the *Botanical Gazette* (1888–1894), 285 drawings for *Garden and Forest* (1888–1898), and 642 for C. S. Sargent's *Manual of the Trees of North America* (1905).

Fellows, M. E. [see Bailey, Liberty Hyde]

Fisher, Stephen (1954–)

25. (page 106) Backwoods-Norfolk, CT (Gothic landscape 8), 1982–1985
Line etching/aquatint
Image: 38.2 x 63 cm   Paper: 53 x 73.8 cm   Edition: 43/100
Stephen Fisher received his M.F.A. (1981) from Yale University. Formerly a visiting assistant professor of art at colleges in Virginia, Massachusetts,

Connecticut and Oklahoma, and printmaking technician at Rhode Island School of Design, he is currently chair of the Art Department at Rhode Island College. His prints have been included in several one-person and group exhibitions in the United States and abroad, and he has received numerous honors and awards for his work, most recently at the *15th National Biennial Exhibition Los Angeles Printmaking Society*, 1999. His prints are in the collections of the Brooklyn Museum, the Newport Art Museum and several corporations and universities. The print in this exhibition was also included in the Hunt Institute's *6th International Exhibition of Botanical Art & Illustration* (1988) and *Gifts of Winter* (2000/2001). Fisher's etchings and aquatints are built up over a period of several months. He draws and etches the foreground, the background, and then the middle ground, building up a complex variation in tonality with several etching times at each stage. He often makes a small edition at this point and then reworks the plate by dropping a dark value over most of it. Fisher scrapes and burnishes so as to push the richness and complexity of the tonal variation as far as he can.

Gibson, William Hamilton (1850–1896)
Happy Hunting-Grounds: A Tribute to the Woods and Fields. New York, Harper & Brothers, 1887. P. 151.
26. (page 40) Mountain-laurel *[Kalmia]*
Wood engraving
30 x 22.5 cm

Gibson was born in Sandy Hook, Connecticut, and briefly studied at the Brooklyn Polytechnic Institute until the death of his father. He temporarily made a living in insurance, and during this time his interest in natural history illustration developed, along with his work in the medium of wood engraving. His illustrations were popular in the *American Agriculturist, Hearth and Home*, and *Harpers Monthly*. Gibson lectured on natural history subjects and also illustrated many of his own publications including *The Complete American Trapper* (1876), *Pastoral Days: Memories of a New England Year* (1880), *Highways and Byways* (1882), *Strolls by Starlight and Sunshine* (1890), *Sharp Eyes: A Rambler's Calendar* (1891), *Our Edible Toadstools and Mushrooms* (1895), and *Eye Spy: Afield with Nature among Flowers and Animate Things* (1897). Gibson died in Washington, Connecticut.

Goodale, George L. [see Sprague, Isaac]

Gray, Asa (1810–1888) [see also Sprague, Isaac and Agate, Alfred T.]
The Botanical Text-Book For Colleges, Schools, and Private Students. New York, Wiley and Putman, 1842. Pp 450–451.
27. (page 32) Fig. 861. *Polygonum Pennsylvanicum*. 862. Enlarged flower laid open. 863. Section of the ovary, showing the erect orthotropous

ovule. 864. Section of the seed, showing the embryo, on one side of the albumen.

Wood engraving

19.5 x 12 cm

28. (page 32) Fig. 865, 866. *Phytolacca decandra* (Poke). 867. A flower. 868. Unripe fruit. 869. Cross section of the same, a little enlarged. 870. Magnified seed. 871. Section of the same across the embryo. 872. Vertical section, showing the embryo coiled around the albumen into a ring. 873. Magnified detached embryo.

Wood engraving

19.5 x 12 cm

Gray was born in Sanquoit, New York, and is considered one of America's greatest systematic botanists. He received his doctor of medicine (1831) from the College of Physicians and Surgeons, Fairfield, New York. He became curator and librarian of the Lyceum of Natural History, New York City (1835), and during this time he wrote his first textbook *Elements of Botany* (1836). Gray became professor of botany, in the newly formed University of Michigan, Ann Arbor (1838), spending a year in Europe collecting books for the university's library, meeting the leading botanists, and comparing herbarium collections sent there from America. The university did not accept students until 1841, and Gray, who was on an unpaid leave, remained in New York to co-author two volumes of the *Flora of North America* (1838 and 1843) with his friend and mentor John Torrey. The flora of this country was one of his major interests through his entire career. The university was unable to finance his professorship, so Gray offered his resignation and accepted the Fisher Professorship of Natural History at Harvard University (1842–1873), where he lectured and directed the newly formed botanic garden. The specimens Gray collected and exchanged with botanists in the United States and abroad, and the botany books he collected for himself in Europe on his earlier trip became the core of the collection of the Gray Herbarium and botanical library, which he formed at Harvard University. Gray had some difficulty in obtaining suitable artists for his earlier publications. For this 1842 textbook, "The illustrations ... were drawn on wood by Miss Agnes Mitchell, and engraved by Mr. J. J. Butler." Three years later he met and employed the gifted Isaac Sprague, who worked for Gray for the rest of his career. Gray contributed regularly on the subject of American botany to the *American Journal of Science and Arts*, and authored *Manual of the Botany of the Northern United States* (1847), and several other botany textbooks, including *Field, Forest and Garden Botany* (1868) and *First Lessons in Botany and Vegetable Physiology* (1857). After his retirement from Harvard, he continued his work on the flora of North America, publishing two volumes of the *Synoptical Flora of North America* (1878 and 1884). After he met Charles Darwin at Kew (1855), they were in regular correspondence, and Gray was a proponent in America for Darwin's theories on evolution. Gray's collected writings on the subject were published in *Darwiniana* (1876). He died in Cambridge, Massachusetts.

Green, Frances Harriett (1805–ca.1878) and **Joseph W. Congdon**.
Analytical Class-Book of Botany. New York, D. Appleton & Co., 1855. P. 29.
29. (page 34) Pl. VIII. Wood.
Wood engraving
24.5 x 19.5 cm

Green was born in Smithfield, Rhode Island, and died in California. This publication is a fine example of the competent use of wood engraving for inexpensive educational illustration. Green stated in her preface, that

> Having been for several years a teacher of botany, I have had considerable opportunity of experimenting on the happiest means of imparting this delightful science. The importance of Pictorial Illustrations, systematically combined for regular exercises, early suggested itself. A new system of teaching was thence wrought out, consisting of a set of Diagrams made to Illustrate Oral Lessons ... Those Lessons and Diagrams are reproduced in the present work ... The Illustrations are presented to the eye in large groups, and are either immediately, or very nearly, associated with the corresponding portions of the Text.

Griswold, Ralph (1894–1981)
30. (page 134) British Queen *[Laeliocattleya]*, ca.1931
Lithograph
Image: 19.5 x 15.5 cm   Paper: 28.5 x 25 cm

Griswold was born in Warren, Ohio, and received a B.S. (1910) and M.S. (1919) in landscape art from Cornell University after serving in the American Expeditionary Forces in World War I. He was Fellow of Landscape Architecture (1920–1923) at the American Academy of Rome, and he traveled through Europe documenting Renaissance Gardens. On his return to the United States, he joined the landscape design firm of A. D. Taylor in Cleveland. He relocated to Pittsburgh, Pennsylvania (1927), started a private business for residential design, and collaborated on the design of the private row-houses of Chatham Village. He was Superintendent of the Bureau of Parks (1934–1945), revitalizing the park system in Pittsburgh, and he was commissioned to restore the garden and grounds of the Old Economy settlement outside of Pittsburgh (1930). He designed Point State Park, where the Allegheny and Monongahela Rivers meet to become the Ohio River, as part of the Pittsburgh "Renaissance." In the early 1950s he worked on the landscape architecture of an Archeological Park at Agora, Greece, using native plants mentioned in ancient Greek texts. In the mid-1950s and 60s Griswold was a research fellow and later a consultant and member of the Garden Advisory Committee for Dumbarton Oaks. In the 1970s he wrote about the history and plans for reconstruction of the gardens of Colonial Williamsburg. Griswold took up lithography and watercolor painting during the early years of his professional career in Pittsburgh, having recognized the importance of the medium from his experience in commissioning work from artists for design proposals. He studied with Wilfred Readio [see this artist's work in the exhibition], head of the Art Department at Carnegie Institute of Technology. [See Shah, Behula. 1999. Ralph Esty Griswold, landscape architect. *Bulletin of the Hunt Institute for Botanical Documentation.* 11(2): 4, 9.]

163

Hale, Sarah Josepha Buell (1788–1879)

Flora's Interpreter, and Fortuna Flora. Boston, Bazin & Ellsworth, 1848. Frontispiece.

31. (page 43) [floral bouquet]

Chromolithograph

19 x 11.5 cm

Lithographer: F. F. Oakley, Boston

Hale was born in New Hampshire and taught at home by her mother and brother. Early in her marriage, she and her husband started a literary club, and she began writing poetry. After his death from pneumonia in 1822, Hale was left with their five children to support. She and her sister started a millinery business, but Hale quit after her books *The Genius of Oblivion and Other Poems* and *Northwood* were successful. In 1828 The Reverend John Lauris Black asked her to be the editor of the *Ladies Magazine and Literary Gazette* (later *American Ladies Magazine*). The magazine was purchased in 1830 by Louis Godey and renamed *Godey's Lady's Book.* Hale was given the job of editor, where she remained until 1877. Through her editorials in the magazine, she became an advocate for the education and economic independence of women. She founded the first society to better the working conditions for women and children, urged the renaming of Vassar College from Vassar Female College, and was responsible for women becoming part of the teaching staff there. Hale also was a proponent for the nationalization of the Thanksgiving holiday.

Hall & Mooney [see Sprague, Isaac]

Havens, James Dexter (1900–1960)

32. (page 130) Scarlet runner beans *[Phaseolus]*, 1957

Woodcut, color

Image: 34 x 26.5 cm   Paper: 34 x 26.5 cm   Edition: 36/80

Havens was born in Rochester, New York, and educated at the University of Rochester, Rochester Institute of Technology, and the Charles H. Woodbury Summer School. Havens was director of the Print Club of Rochester for many years. He exhibited in numerous printmaking exhibits, and his work is in the collection of many museums including the Brooklyn Museum, Library of Congress, Metropolitan Museum of Art, and the Norton Simon Museum. This wood engraving was part of the Hunt Institute's *5th International Exhibition of Botanical Art & Illustration* (1983). In 2001 the Memorial Art Gallery of the University of Rochester, New York, exhibited *Woodblock Prints by James Havens: A Centennial Celebration,* featuring 40 woodblock prints from their collection.

Hayes, Marvin (1939–)
33. (page 107) Oak *[Quercus]*, ca.1970s
Etching
Image: 60 x 37.5 cm   Paper: 76.5 x 45.5 cm   Artist's proof
Born in Canton, Mississippi, Hayes has a B.F.A. from Lamar University, Beaumont, Texas. He also studied at the Art Student's League and received an M.F.A. from Columbia University (1966). He worked as a commercial artist illustrating books and magazines and is currently a freelance artist in Wilton, Connecticut, where he works mainly in egg tempera and etching. His work is included in the collections of the Westmoreland Museum of Art, Greensburg, Pennsylvania; Museum of Modern Art, New York; the National Portrait Gallery, London; the Vatican; and the Musée d'Art Moderne, Bibliothèque Nationale, and Lourvre, Paris. The Hunt Institute included his work in *A Northeast Folio* (1979) and the *4th International Exhibition of Botanical Art & Illustration* (1977/78).

Heiges, Bertha (active 1896–1907)
34. (page 86) Damson Plums *[Prunus]*
Chromolithograph
22.5 x 14.5 cm
Publication: *Yearbook of the United States Department of Agriculture.* 1905. Pl. LXIII
Heiges was born in Pennsylvania and was an artist for the United States Department of Agriculture, Division of Pomology, providing illustrations for some of their publications.

Henry, Samuel
A New and Complete American Medical Family Herbal. New York, S. Henry, 1814. P. 198.
35. (page 16) Mullen [Mullein], *Verbascum*
Wood engraving
23 x 13.5 cm

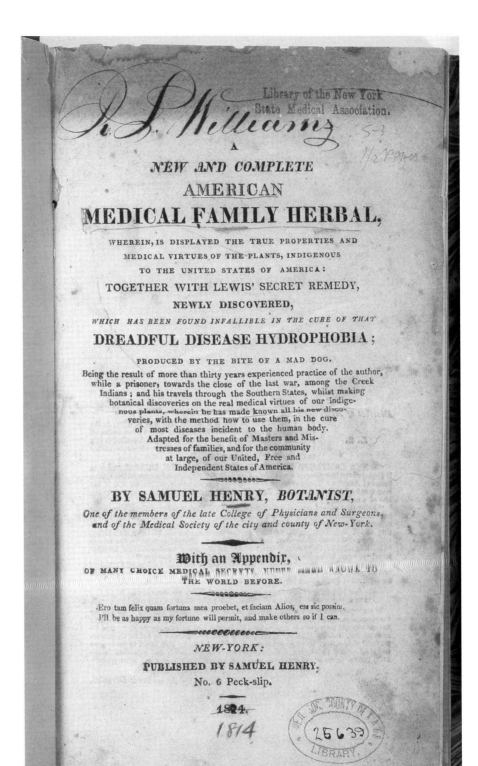

A

NEW AND COMPLETE

AMERICAN

MEDICAL FAMILY HERBAL,

WHEREIN, IS DISPLAYED THE TRUE PROPERTIES AND
MEDICAL VIRTUES OF THE PLANTS, INDIGENOUS
TO THE UNITED STATES OF AMERICA:

TOGETHER WITH LEWIS' SECRET REMEDY,

NEWLY DISCOVERED,

WHICH HAS BEEN FOUND INFALLIBLE IN THE CURE OF THAT

DREADFUL DISEASE HYDROPHOBIA;

PRODUCED BY THE BITE OF A MAD DOG.

Being the result of more than thirty years experienced practice of the author,
while a prisoner, towards the close of the last war, among the Creek
Indians ; and his travels through the Southern States, whilst making
botanical discoveries on the real medical virtues of our indigenous plants, wherein he has made known all his new discoveries, with the method how to use them, in the cure
of most diseases incident to the human body.
Adapted for the benefit of Masters and Mis-
tresses of families, and for the community
at large, of our United, Free and
Independent States of America.

BY SAMUEL HENRY, *BOTANIST,*

*One of the members of the late College of Physicians and Surgeons,
and of the Medical Society of the city and county of New-York.*

With an Appendix,

OF MANY CHOICE MEDICAL SECRETS, NEVER BEFORE KNOWN TO
THE WORLD BEFORE.

Ero tam felix quam fortuna mea proebet, et faciam Alios, ess sic possim.
I'll be as happy as my fortune will permit, and make others so if I can.

NEW-YORK :

PUBLISHED BY SAMUEL HENRY,
No. 6 Peck-slip.

1824.
1814

The engraver of these bold wood engravings is not recorded, but they are very much in the tradition of Thomas Bewick, the master English artist who brought about the revival of wood engraving in England, Europe and America. The titlepage notes that the botanist Samuel Henry was one of the members of the late College of Physicians and Surgeons and of the Medical Society of the City and County of New-York.

Hnizdovsky, Jacques (1915–1985)
36. (page 121) *Gladiolus*, 1964
Woodcut
Image: 81.5 x 13.5 cm   Paper: 92.5 x 26 cm   Edition 71/100

Hnizdovsky was born in Pylypcze, Ukraine, studied at the Academies of Art in Warsaw and Zagreb and exhibited in Germany before coming to New York City (1949). There he worked as a freelance artist making prints, and illustrating books such as the *Poems of John Keats* (S. Kunitz, ed., New York, 1964), *The Poems of Samuel Taylor Coleridge* (1967), *Tree Trails of Central Park* (1971), *Flora Exotica* (1972), and the *Poems of Thomas Hardy* (1979). This prolific artist, whose work was influenced by Japanese prints and folk art, also worked in the printmaking mediums of linocut and etching. A monograph of his work was published, *Jacques Hnizdovsy, Woodcuts and Engravings* (Abe M. Tahir, Gretna, 1976). His work was exhibited in the *American Graphics Exhibition in the U.S.S.R.*, the *Triennale Internazionale della Xilografia*, Italy, and in two exhibits at the Hunt Institute, *A Northeast Folio* (1979) and the *4th International Exhibition of Botanical Art & Illustration* (1977/78). A major exhibition of his work was at the Ukrainian Museum of New York (1995), and his work is included in their permanent collection as well as in several galleries, museums and private collections, including the Museum of Fine Arts, Boston; Cleveland Museum of Art; and the Library of Congress.

Hopkins, John Henry (1792–1868)
37. (page 53) *[Papaver]*
Lithograph
48 x 30.5 cm
Publication: Hopkins, John Henry. *The Burlington Drawing Book of Flowers*. R. Craighead, [ca.1846]. Pl. 6.

Hopkins was born in Dublin and moved to America with his parents (1800), settling in Philadelphia. In the early 1820s he worked as an ironmaster in western Pennsylvania, studied and practiced law in Pittsburgh, and also taught drawing at a private academy. Hopkins became the rector of the Episcopal Church of Pittsburgh (1823) and first Protestant Episcopal Bishop of Vermont in Burlington (1831). Hopkin's interest in the arts continued, and he published *Essay on Gothic Architecture* (1836) and a series of *Vermont Drawing Books* (1838–1843), illustrated with plates of flowers, figures and landscapes drawn by Hopkins, litho-graphed by his son John Henry Hopkins, Jr., and hand-colored by other members of the family. Hopkins became Presiding Bishop of the Protestant Episcopal Church (1865). [See G. Groce and D. Wallace, *The New-York Historical Society's Dictionary of Artists in America, 1564–1860*, New Haven, Yale University Press, 1957. P. 326].

Hopkins, Jr., John Henry [see Hopkins, John Henry]

Hovey, Charles Mason (1810–1887)
The Magazine of Horticulture, Botany and All Useful Discoveries and Improvements in Rural Affairs. Boston, Hovey and Co., 1854. Vol. 20, no. 2, p. opp. [47].

38. (page 21) The Concord Grape (Fig. 2.)
Wood engraving
22 x 14 cm

Hovey was born in Cambridge, Massachusetts, and there he owned a nursery with a large variety of fruit trees. He founded the *American Gardener's Magazine* in 1834 (which became the *Magazine of Horticulture*), and was editor until 1868. Modeled after Loudon's English "Gardener's magazine," it enjoyed the longest period of prosperity of any American horticultural journal and provides a record of the growth to maturity of New World horticulture. He also published *The Fruits of America* (Boston, 1847–1856), described by Hedrick in *A History of Horticulture in America to 1860* (New York, 1950) as "the book of books in horticulture so far as size, color plates, and fine printing go." In 1836 he introduced the Hovey strawberry, generally seen as the starting-point of commercial strawberry-growing in America. Hovey was a member of the Cincinnati and Cleveland Horticulture Society.

Howe, Marsha Kristen Heinbaugh (1943)
39. (page 112) Pasque flower *[Anemone]*, 1972
Etching, color
Image: 11.5 x 10   Paper: 19 x 15 cm   Edition: 43/100
40. (page 113) Teasel *[Dipsacus]*, 1974
Etching, color
Image: 9 x 5.5 cm   Paper: 18.5 x 10 cm   Edition: 5/20
41. (page 113) Dandelion *[Taraxacum]*, 1974
Etching, color
Image: 7 x 5.5 cm   Paper: 19 x 11 cm   Edition: 15/20

Howe was born in Chardon, Ohio, and she received a B.F.A. in printmaking and painting (1968) from Syracuse University's School of Art. She was an illustrator for Gibson Greeting Cards, Denver, and senior illustrator for Current Inc., Colorado Springs. Howe's work has been included in several one-person and group exhibitions, and her etchings were included in the Hunt Institute's *4th International Exhibition of Botanical Art & Illustration* (1977/78). She continues to pursue printmaking and painting in Manitou Springs, Colorado.

Hullmandel, C. J. [see Sharp, William]

Jules, Mervin (1912–1994)
42. (page 131) Poppies, ca.1960s
Color woodcut
Image: 50.5 x 41 cm   Paper: 61.5 x 49 cm   Edition: 16/60

Jules was born in Baltimore, Maryland, and educated at Baltimore City College (1930), Maryland Institute of Fine and Applied Art (1933), and the Art Student's League (1934), where he studied with Thomas Hart Benton. He was part of the Fine Art Project, (silkscreen unit) with the New York Works Progress Administration (WPA). Jules was a visiting artist at several universities in the Northeast and Midwest, a professor at Smith College (1945–1969), and chairman of the Art Department at City College of New York (1969). His work was included in numerous one-person and group exhibitions in galleries and museums, including the Hunt Institute's *2nd, 3rd* and *4th International Exhibition of Botanical Art & Illustration* (1968, 1972, 1977/78) and several of its travel exhibitions. Jules also received numerous awards and was made fellow of the Royal Society of Art, United Kingdom. His woodcuts are in the collections of several museums, including the Art Institute of Chicago; Metropolitan Museum of Modern Art, New York; Museum of Fine Arts, Boston; Library of Congress, Washington, D.C.; Philadelphia Museum of Art; Brooklyn Museum; Fogg Art Museum, Harvard University; Whitney Museum of American Art; and the Tel Aviv Museum.

Kola, Vaino (1937–)
17. (page 110) Everett's tree *[Fagus]*, 1974
Etching
Image: 42.5 x 45 cm   Paper: 50 x 51.5 cm   Edition: 12

Kola was born in Finland and received a B.F.A. from the Massachusetts College of Art (1959) and an M.F.A. with honors from Yale University (1962). He has given many public lectures and taught at Yale University (1960–1961); Chatham College, Pittsburgh (1962–1965); Lasell Junior College, Newton, Massachusetts (1968–1969); Impression Workshop, Boston (1966–1968); Lake Placid Workshop (summer 1971–1973); Boston University, School of Fine and Applied Arts (1972); and Wheaton College, Norton, Massachusetts (1969–1994). Kola was co-director of the Pittsburgh Graphic Workshop (1963) and an intaglio printmaker at Atelier Nord, Oslo (1975–1976). His work has been included in numerous one-person and group print exhibitions in galleries and museums. Kola was awarded a Ford Foundation Grant for experimental work in color intaglio technique (1969–1970), the Mellon Fellowship (1982–1983), Wheaton College Faculty Research Grants (1975, 1970, 1985, 1988), and the Massachusetts Artist Foundation Fellowship (1989). The Hunt Institute exhibited a selection of his work in *A Northeast Folio* (1979). His work is in the collection of many corporations and universities and numerous museums in the United States and Finland, including the Worcester Art Museum, Minneapolis Institute of Art, and Brooklyn Museum of Art. In 1994 he moved to Deer Isle, Maine, and set up a studio to concentrate solely on his artwork. His artworks are included in *The Art of Maine Winter* (Carl Little, Camden, Maine, 2002).

Kearny, F. [see Barton, William P. C.]

Kredel, Fritz (1900–1973)
44. (page 124) *[Taraxacum]*, 1963
Woodcut, hand-colored
31 x 24 cm
45. (page 123) *[Viola]*, 1963
Woodcut, hand-colored
31 x 23.5 cm

Kredel was born in Michelstadt, Germany, and was a graduate of Real-Gymnasium in Darmstadt. He studied under Rudolph Koch and Victor Hammer. He exhibited in the United States and abroad and was awarded the Gold Medal for book illustration at the Paris World Exposition (1937). Kredel lived in New York and illustrated for private presses, as well as the trade, children's books and works of prose and poetry. A retrospective of his work was exhibited at the Grolier Club, New York City (2000), of which he was a member, and at the Odenwald Museum in Michelstadt, Germany. An archive of Kredel's work is part of the Sterling Library's Arts of the Book Collection at Yale University. Kredel was represented in the Hunt Institute's first International, *Contemporary Botanical Art & Illustration* (1964).

Lambdin, George C. (1830–1896)
46. (page 90) *[Lilium]*, 1875
Chromolithograph (18 color separations)
Image: 51 x 33 cm   Paper: 53.5 x 35 cm

Lambdin was born in Pittsburgh, Pennsylvania, and initially received training in art from his father, the portraitist James Reid Lambdin. He moved with his family to Philadelphia (1838) where he lived most of his life, although he studied in Munich and Paris (1855) and Rome (1870). He began exhibiting paintings with religious and literary themes at the Philadelphia Academy of Fine Arts (1848). In the 1860s he turned to genre painting, often including images of children and, later, scenes from the Civil War. In the 1870s, with the popularity and new varieties of plants for home gardens, he was painting floral still lifes (often using the subject of roses in their natural uncut form, and often with dark backgrounds), and this popular work was reproduced as affordable chromolithographs by Louis Prang (1824–1909), Boston. In the 1880s he began writing and lecturing on art history and theory and was active in many art societies, including the Philadelphia Society of Artists. He was elected to the National Academy of Design (1868), and he was on the faculty of the School of Design for Women (1885–1887). [See R. Weidner, *The Lambdins of Philadelphia: Newly Discovered Work.* Philadelphia, Swartz Gallery, 2002.]

Leak, Virginia Louise (1940–ca.1978)
47. (page 103) *[Plectranthus],* ca.1960s
Etching (zinc)
Image: 22 x 18 cm   Paper: 41.5 x 34.5 cm
Leak was born in Iowa City and received her B.A. from Lindenwood College (1962) and an M.A. from the University of California (1965). Her zinc etching was exhibited in the Hunt Institute's first international, *Contemporary Botanical Art & Illustration* (1964).

Leighton, Clare Veronica Hope (1901–1988)
48. (page 117) Weeds
Wood engraving
Image: 17.5 x 12.5 cm   Paper: 25 x 16.5 cm
Publication: C. Leighton, *Four Hedges: A Gardener's Chronicle.* London, Victor Gollancz, 1935.
49. (page 116) *Iris stylosa* and Christmas roses
Wood engraving
Image: 14.5 x 12 cm   Paper: 17.5 x 14.5   Edition: 19/30
Publication: C. Leighton, *Four Hedges: A Gardener's Chronicle.* London, Victor Gollancz. P. 140.

Leighton was born in London and studied at the Slade School of Fine Arts (1921–1923) and the Central School of Arts and Crafts, University of London. She moved to the United States (1939), became a citizen (1945), and lived and maintained a studio in Connecticut after 1950. She has authored and illustrated 14 of her own books and illustrated numerous other books for gardeners and botanists. Leighton also designed for stained glass and mosaic including 33 windows for St. Paul's Cathedral in Worcester, Massachusetts. The Wedgwood Company commissioned her for a series of wood engravings of New England industries printed on a set of plates. Her work was represented in the Hunt Institute's *1st* and *2nd International Exhibition of Botanical Art and Illustration* (1964, 1968/69). A retrospective of her work was on display at the Boston Public Library (1977). Her work is in the collections of many libraries and museums including the Metropolitan Museum of Art, Library of Congress, New York Public Library, Boston Public Library, Fogg Art Museum at Harvard University, British Museum, and the Victoria and Albert Museum. She was made a member of the National Institute of Arts and Letters, the National Academy of Design, and the Royal Society of Painters, Etchers, and Engravers, London. *Clare Leighton: Wood Engravings and Drawings* (Stevens, A. and D. Leighton, Woodstock, New York, 1992) looks at her 40-year career as a wood engraver.

Lessnick, Howard (1939–)
50. (page 104) Winter Poetry, 1971
Etching
Image size: 14.5 x 28   Paper: 28 x 37.5 cm   Edition: 20/250

Lessnick was born in Brooklyn, New York, and received a B.S. (1962) and an M.S. (1967) from State University of New York at Cortland. As a freelance painter and printmaker, he has exhibited in numerous one-person and juried exhibitions. His work is in the permanent collection of the University of New York, Cortland, University of Scranton, and the Roberson Center for the Arts and Sciences.

Lewis & Brown [see Whitefield, Edwin]
The senior partner, George W. Lewis, founded a lithographic business in 1841 and continued with various partners for several years. The chalk-style lithographs by Lewis & Brown of Whitefield's illustrations (for Embury's *American Wildflowers in Their Native Haunts,* 1845) are fine examples of his firm's work. Most are hand-colored, but some show touches of color printing.

Little, Robert W. (1912–1991)
51. (page 145) New York Fern, *Adiantum pedatum,* ca. early 1970s
Nature print
44.5 x 30 cm

Born in Patton, Pennsylvania, Little received a B.S. (1941) and an M.S. (1945) from the University of Pittsburgh. He studied art at the university as well as the Carnegie Institute of Technology. He was a professor of biology and plant taxonomy at California State College in Pennsylvania (now California University) for five years in the early 1970s. While there he also taught an individual class on nature printing. Little later taught nature printing at Touchstone for two or three years and lectured at Powdermill Nature Reserve of Carnegie Museum, Pioneer Crafts Council at Mill Run, and the Pennsylvania Western Pennsylvania Conservancy. He exhibited at universities and galleries in the southwestern Pennsylvania area and was included in the Hunt Institute's *3rd International Exhibition of Botanical Art & Illustration* (1972/73). His nature prints also were part of international exhibits in Tokyo and at the Santa Barbara Museum of Natural History. He was one of two American artists included in a book of Gyotaku (nature prints) published in Tokyo, and he was a member of the Gyotaku-no-kai (association of nature printers in Japan). Little authored two books on this subject—*Nature Printing* (Pittsburgh, 1976), a history of the art and a guide to technique, and *Creative Concepts in Nature Printing* (Pittsburgh, 1985), less a how-to and more a description of difficult and experimental techniques. He lived on a 25-acre farm in Acme, Pennsylvania, where he maintained a nature printing studio and had a special interest in bonsai.

Loggie, Helen (1895–1976)
52. (page 109) The wraith *[Pinus]*, 1930
Etching
Image: 25 x 18.5 cm   Paper: 39 x 26 cm

Born in Bellingham, Washington, Loggie studied at Smith College, the Art Student's League, and with artists of the Ash Can School. Her work has been included in numerous group exhibits and is in the collection of numerous museums and universities including the Library of Congress, Museum of Fine Arts of Houston, Metropolitan Museum of Art, Philadelphia Museum of Art, Pennsylvania State University, Glasgow University, Scotland, and the British Museum, England. *The Flowering Earth: The Drawings and Etchings of Helen Loggie* was exhibited at the Frye Art Museum, Seattle, Washington (2000). The *Helen Loggie Archives* is part of the print and drawing collection at the Western Gallery, Western Washington University, Bellingham.

Lower, Elsie E. (active 1900–1909)
53. (page 55) Persimmons *[Diospyros]*
Chromolithograph
22.5 x 14.5 cm
Publication: *Yearbook of the United States Department of Agriculture.* 1908. Pl. XLVIII

Lower was born in Pennsylvania and was an artist for the United States Department of Agriculture, Division of Pomology, providing illustrations for some of their publications. Some of her illustrations of fungi are housed in the Mycology Laboratory, National Fungus Collection, Beltsville, Maryland. The U.S.D.A. was apparently reluctant to give up chromolithography as an illustration medium for some of its *Yearbook* illustrations at this late date. Most other publications of this type had already changed over to the modern tri-chromatic half-tone medium [see Rogers, no. 76 below, for example]. However, this is a fine example of the virtue of chromolithography for this type of work, and its demise was probably caused by economic considerations since photo-mechanical work was quicker and cheaper to print.

Lunzer, Alois (1840–?)

54. (page 48) *Adiantum capillus-veneris*, True maiden-hair fern

Chromolithograph

26 x 17.5 cm

Publication: Thomas Meehan, *The Native Flowers and Ferns of the United States.* Ser. 2, vol. 2, pt. 40. Boston, L. Prang and Co., 1878. Pl. 16.

55. (page 76) *Pellaea ornithopus*

Chromolithograph

25.5 x 18.5 cm

Publication: Thomas Meehan, *The Native Flowers and Ferns of the United States.* Ser. 2, vol. 2, pt. 40. Boston, L. Prang and Co., 1878.

Born in Austria, Lunzer came to the United States and was one of the flower painters who worked for the chromolithographers Louis Prang & Co. As an employee of Prang, he also worked under the supervision of botanist Thomas Meehan (Professor of Botany, Pennsylvania State Board of Agriculture) to produce the illustrations for the publications for which these chromolithographs were a part. These finely printed chromolithographs are typical of the quality of work for which Louis Prang became justly famous in America and beyond. Lunzer also provided several illustrations for issues of *Meehan's Monthly* (1891–1902), and he is one of the artists whose watercolor paintings were reproduced in *The Golden Flower Chrysanthemum* (1890) [see Mathews, Frederick Schuyler].

Mack, Warren (1869–1952)

56. (page 115) Cabbages *[Brassica]*, ca.1939

Wood engraving

Image: 17.5 x 23 cm   Paper: 26.5 x 36 cm   Edition: 2/50

Mack was born in Flicksville, Pennsylvania, and received a Ph.D., Lafayette College (1915); B.Sc., Pennsylvania State College (1921); M.Sc., Massachusetts Agriculture College (1923); Ph.D., plant physiology, Johns Hopkins University (1929); and D.Sc.(Hon.) Lafayette College (1946). He was an instructor (1923–1929), professor (1930–1937), and chairman (1937–1952) of horticulture at Pennsylvania State University. As a horticulturist and plant physiologist, Mack co-authored, with Dr. Walter Thomas, over 49 papers on plant nutrition. As a self-taught graphic artist, his work was exhibited from 1931 in numerous printmaking exhibitions. His work is in the collection of many libraries and museums including the New York Public Library, the Library of Congress (Pennell Collection), Glasgow University, Fogg Art Museum at Harvard University, and Pennsylvania State University (Mack Collection). He was made a fellow of the National Academy of Design (1944). His work was included in the Hunt Institute's first international, *Contemporary Botanical Art & Illustration* (1964), and *Gifts of Winter* (2000/01).

Mackay, Donald A. (1914–)

57. (page 105) Panicum Grass, ca.1980s?

Etching, hand-colored

Paper: 30 x 18 cm Edition: 4/25

Born in Halifax, Nova Scotia, Mackay was educated at the Massachusetts School of Art, Boston; Pratt Institute Center for Printmaking, New York; the University of Morelia, Mexico; and studied graphics with Alfredo Zalce. He makes his career as a freelance artist and has exhibited in numerous one-person and group exhibitions including the American Watercolor Society, Society of American Graphic Artists, Boston Print Club, Philadelphia Print Club, and the Smithsonian Institution traveling exhibit *50 American Drawings*. His work is in the collection of the Minnesota Museum of American Art and Vanderbilt University. His work has been reproduced in numerous magazines and children's books. A selection of his etchings and lithographs was exhibited in the Hunt Institute's *4th International Exhibition of Botanical Art and Illustration* (1977/78).

Magee, Alan (1947–)

58. (page 139) Ceremony of Innocence *[Cucurbita]*, 1984

Lithograph, 9 color

Image size: 46.5 x 64.5 cm   Paper: 57 x 75.5 cm   Edition: 63/100

Magee was educated at the Tyler School of Art and the Philadelphia College of Art. In 1969 he began working in New York as an editorial and book illustrator. His award-winning illustrations have appeared in magazines such as *Time, Playboy, Atlantic Monthly* and *New York* magazine and in books published by Avon, Ballantine, Bantam, and Pocket Books. In the late 1970s he began to concentrate on his personal paintings and lithographs and had his first solo exhibit at Staempfli Gallery, New York. Annually he has had one-person exhibitions in the United States and Europe, and a retrospective of his work, *Alan Magee, 1981–1991*, traveled to several U.S. museums. His paintings have been published in *Stones and Other Works* (New York, 1986) and *Alan Magee 1981–1991* (Rockland, Maine, 1991). He has received awards from the American Academy and Institute of Arts and Letters and the National Academy of Design. His work is included in several museum, corporate and private collections, and he is currently represented by Hollis Taggart Galleries, New York, and Hackett-Freedman Gallery, San Francisco.

Maltzman, Stanley (1921–)

59. (page 137) Thistle *[Cirsium?]*, 1972

Lithograph

Paper: 47.5 x 36 cm   Edition: 33/100

Printmaker: George C. Miller & Son, New York City

Stanley Maltzman studied commercial art at the Phoenix School of

Design and was formerly an Art Director at Vick Chemical Company. His artwork has been included in several one-person and group exhibitions and has received several awards, and his work is included in university, corporate and museum collections. Maltzman has held workshops on drawing the landscape, and his *Drawing Nature* (Cincinnati, Ohio, 1995) was received so well that it was reprinted in paperback. He recently published *Drawing Trees Step by Step* (Cincinnati, Ohio, 2000). His lithographs were included in the Hunt Institute's *4th International Exhibition of Botanical Art & Illustration* (1977/78), *Gifts of Winter* (2000/01), and one of the Institute's travel exhibitions on the theme of poisonous plants.

Maskarinec, Michael (1954–)

60. (page 147) Succulent Garden (Aloe, Snake plant, *Sansevieria, Sedum,* Golden Barrel cactus *Echinocactus grusonii*), 2000
6 color inkjet print from 1200 dpi digital file
Image: 65.5 x 50.5 cm Paper: 78 x 60.5 cm
Printer: Page Imaging, Pittsburgh, Pa.

Maskarinec was born in Youngstown, Ohio, studied classical guitar and painting at Youngstown State University (1973–1974), and attended the Art Institute of Pittsburgh (1978). He worked for a design firm and as a freelance designer for five years and has been the creative director at WQED, Pittsburgh, since 1984. Maskarinec is a member of, and has exhibited with, Group A and the Associated Artists of Pittsburgh. His work has been published in several garden magazines, on product packaging, and for a poster calendar for the Pittsburgh Parks Conservancy. This image was first sketched in pencil, then scanned in the drawing software Adobe Illustrator (for Macintosh), using an electronic drawing stylus on a pad, along with a mouse and keyboard. This program creates vectors, which describe graphics according to their geometric characteristics (a shape with a certain radius, at a specific location on the page, and filled with a specific color or designed gradation). One can move, resize, or change the structure without losing its detail or clarity. It is printed on High Country digital artist watercolor paper with archival inks with a fade resistant life-span of 40 years under normal conditions.

Mathews, Ferdinand Schuyler (1845–1938) [see Lunzer, Alois]
The Golden Flower Chrysanthemum. Verses by [various authors]. Illustrated with Reproductions of Studies from Nature in Watercolor by James and Sydney Callowhill, Alois Lunzer and F. S. M. [F. Schuyler Mathews]. Boston, L. Prang and Co., 1890. Pl. [6].

61. (page 51) *Cullingfordii*
Chromolithograph from the original watercolor by Sydney T. Callowhill
29.5 x 24.5 cm

Mathews was born in New Brighton, Staten Island, New York. Along with

176 Title page of Ferdinand Schuyler Mathew's *The Golden Flower Chrysanthemum*, 1890.

editing *The Golden Flower Chrysanthemum*, this prolific botanist and artist also was the author and illustrator of *Familiar Flowers of Field and Garden* (1895), *Familiar Trees and Their Leaves* (1896), *Familiar Features of the Roadside; The Flowers, Shrubs, Birds, and Insects* (1897), *Wayside Trees* (1899), *Field Book of American Wild Flowers* (1902), and *Field Book of American Trees and Shrubs* (1915). Louis Prang's love of floral subjects for his chromolithograph productions is extravagantly demonstrated in the enthusiastic illustrations for this 1890 "coffee-table book."

Mattson, Morris

The American Vegetable Practice; or, A New and Improved Guide to Health Designed for the Use of Families in Six Parts. Vol. 1. Boston, Daniel. L. Hale, 1841. P. opp. 203.

62. (page 18) Wild red raspberry, *Rubus strigosus*
Chromolithograph
22.5 x 13.5 cm
Printer: Sharp, Michelin & Co.

The first American book to contain true chromolithographs with some colors overprinted, this was the pioneer work of an English immigrant lithographer, William Sharp. The titlepage notes that Morris Mattson was a physician to the Reformed Boston Dispensary and lecturer on physiology and the practice of medicine.

Medearis, Roger (1920–2001)
63. (page 136) Native Oak *[Quercus]*, 1981
Lithograph
49.5 x 68.3 cm

Medearis was born in Missouri and studied at the Kansas City Art Institute with Thomas Hart Benton and John S. deMartelly. During World War II he drew battle charts for the U.S. fleet and training charts for the Field Artillery. After the war he set up a studio in Connecticut (1946) and had a successful exhibit at the Kende Gallery in New York. With the shift away from realism to abstract expressionism in the art world, Medearis was unable to sell his work, and decided to return to the Midwest. There he worked at the Container Corporation of America for over ten years. In the 1960s, he moved to California where his interest in painting returned and his personal style developed, first to the figurative, and then to the landscape of the west, where he worked in egg tempera, acrylic, oil and lithography. His work has been exhibited in many one-person and group exhibitions and is in many private and museum collections, including the Butler Institute of American Art, the National Museum of American Art, and the San Jose Museum of Art. The Hunt Institute included his work in the *6th International Exhibition of Botanical Art & Illustration* (1988).

Meehan, Thomas [see Lunzer, Alois]

Meisel, B. [see Faxon, Charles Edward and Muller, Frank]

Michelin, Francis [see Sharp, William]

George C. Miller & Son [see Moltman, Stanley]

Mitchell, Agnes [see Gray, Asa]

Mockel, Henry (1905–1981)
64. (page 142) Developing inflorescence, Mojave yucca, *Yucca schidigera*, ca.1960s
Serigraph
44.5 x 29 cm   Edition: 16/100

Mockel was the son of a Berlin publisher, studied at the Gymnasium, Berlin (1911–1923), and had a journeyman's certificate in bookbinding by the age of 18. He moved to the United States (1923), studied engineering at City College of New York (1927–1930), and attended the Grand Central School of Art (1931–1935). Mockel worked for the telephone company for 15 years, was a private art teacher at the Bronx School of Art for three years, and an artist and farmer in Maine and Cooperstown, New York (1946–1957). He and his wife moved to California (1958) where they opened the Pioneer Art Gallery in Twentynine Palms (1961). Originally his printmaking medias were etching and woodblock, but after a fire destroyed his entire studio, he turned to serigraphy. His artwork has appeared in numerous one-person and group exhibitions in the United States and is in private, corporate and arboretum collections. Mockel's work was in the Hunt Institute's *4th International Exhibition of Botanical Art & Illustration* (1977/78). He and his wife Beverly co-authored *Desert Flower Notebook* and *Hot Air from the Desert*. Two years before his wife's death, his studio was sold (1988) and continues under the name of the Desert Studio of Henry R. Mockel.

Moody, William [see Strong, Asa B.]
William Moody shared the task of printing Asa Strong's plates with Francis Michelin (one time partner of the celebrated William Sharp); both operated printing offices at separate addresses in Nassau Street, New York. Some of the plates are signed "drawn on stone by D. W. Moody." We can find no biographical information about either of these Moodys nor Michelin, but it is perhaps worth mentioning that there were several lithographic printers by the name of Moody in London and Birmingham, England.

Morgan, H. J. [see Rothrock, Joseph Trimble]

Moser, Arthur Barry (1940–)
65. (page 122) Deadly nightshade *[Datura]*, 1976
Woodcut
Image size: 20 x 15   Paper: 38 x 28 cm   Artist's proof
Moser was born in Chattanooga, Tennessee, studied industrial design at Auburn University, and received a B.S. from the University of Chattanooga (1962). He also has studied with George Cress, Leonard Baskin, Jack Coughlin, and Harold McGrath. He lives in East Hampton, Massachusetts, and teaches graphic art and art history at Williston-Northampton School. Moser operates Pennyroyal Press and is president of Hampshire Typothetae. Plants are prominent in his drawings, etchings and wood engravings, and illustrations were published in *The Flora of Massachusetts* (University of Massachusetts Press) and *Thistles and Thorns* (University of Nebraska, Abattoir Editions). His work has been included in numerous one-person and group exhibitions in the United States and abroad and is in several private and public collections of university and botanical gardens, including Harvard University, Princeton University, New York Botanical Garden, Missouri Botanical Garden, and Morton Arboretum. Moser's work was included in the Hunt Institute exhibitions *Northeast Folio* (1979) and the *4th International Exhibition of Botanical Art & Illustration* (1977/78).

Muller, Frank (active 1891–1897)

66. (page 28) *Frasera tubulosa* Coville

Lithograph

30.5 x 26.5 cm

Publication: Frederick V. Coville, Botany of the Death Valley Expedition. *Contributions from the United States National Herbarium.* 1893. Vol. 4, p. 344, pl. 13 (opp. p. 344).

Printer: B. Meisel, Boston

Muller was an illustrator for the United States Department of Agriculture.

Oakley, Francis F. [see Hale, Sarah Josepha Buell]

Francis F. Oakley, who printed the chromolithographs for Sarah Hale's work *Flora's Interpreter, and Fortuna Flora* (Boston, 1848), was one of the commercial pioneers of this medium in America. He disappears after the Civil War.

Page Imaging [see Maskarinec, Michael]

Passmore, Deborah Griscom (1840–1911)

67. (page 54) Patten Apple *[Malus]*

Chromolithograph

22.5 x 14.5 cm

Publication: *Yearbook of the United States Department of Agriculture.* 1908. Pl. XLI.

Passmore was born in Delaware County, Pennsylvania, and studied art at the Philadelphia School of Design and the Academy of Fine Arts. She traveled in Europe visiting galleries, and she was inspired by the work of Marianne North at the Royal Botanic Gardens, Kew. Passmore began painting the wildflowers of North America (these unpublished works as well as a folio of "flowers in watercolor" are in the collection of the National Agricultural Library). She was encouraged by W. W. Corcoran, founder of the Corcoran Gallery of Art, to open a studio in Washington, D.C. to give individual art instruction. Passmore provided paintings for the exhibits at the 1876 Centennial Exposition, Philadelphia, and for the Department of Agriculture Building at the 1893 World's Columbian Exposition, Chicago. She was an illustrator for the U.S. Department of Agriculture (1892–1909) and painted thousands of fruits for the Division of Pomology (these illustrations are in the collection of the National Agricultural Library) some of which were reproduced in several U.S.D.A. publications. She, soon after, also supervised the other staff artists.

Peirce, Gerry (1900–1969)

68. (page 101) Yucca, ca. late 1930–1940s

Etching, drypoint

Image: 22.5 x 30.5 cm   Paper: 30 x 41.5 cm   Edition: 16/50

Born in Jamestown, New York, Peirce studied at the Cleveland Institute of Art and the Art Students League in New York. He was a member of and exhibited regularly with several print groups including the Society of American Graphic Artists (1935–1945) and the Chicago Society of Etchers. He also was a member of the American Watercolor Society. In 1948 he developed, and taught at, the Gerry Peirce School of Watercolor Art in Tucson, Arizona. His work is included in several permanent collections including the Museum of Fine Arts, Boston, Cleveland Museum of Art, Museum of Modern Art, Tucson Museum of Art, Library of Congress, and the Denver Art Museum. Peirce illustrated *Plants of Sun and Sand: The Desert Growth of Arizona* (Stanford Stevens, Tucson, 1939) and was the author of *How Percival Caught the Tiger* (1936), *How Percival Caught the Python* (1937), and *Painting the Southwest Landscape in Watercolor* (New York, 1961).

Pendleton, William S. [see Prince, William Robert]

Pendleton's was one of America's earliest lithographic businesses beginning in Boston (1825) and later with offices in New York and Philadelphia. William S. Pendleton is most famous for his uncolored Rembrandt Peale portrait of George Washington, described by Harry Peters (*America on Stone*, 1931) as "Perhaps ... the greatest American lithograph."

L. Prang & Co. [see Lambdin, George; Lunzer, Alois; and Mathews, Ferdinand Schuyler]

Prestele, Joseph (1796–1867) [see Sprague, Isaac]

Prestele was born in Germany and studied botany, drawing and painting. He became proficient in lithography while in Munich, and from 1816 to 1828 he was the staff artist (working in watercolor) at the Royal Botanic Garden in Munich, drawing many of the plants for *Flora Monacensis* (1811–1818). He drew specimens for the garden director Carl F. P. von Martius' *Nova Genera et Species Plantarum quas in Iitinere per Brasiliam Annis,* for Carl Friedrich von Ledebour's *Icones Plantarum...Floram Rossicam* (1829–1834), and for Philipp Franz von Siebold's *Flora Japonica* (1823–1830). Prestele joined the Community of True Inspiration (ca.1835) and moved to their leased estates in Hessen-Darmmstadt. There he produced botanical drawings of German poisonous plants, engraved them on stone, and hand-tinted the plates. Due to religious persecution Prestele immigrated to America with other members of the Inspirationist sect to live in their communal society established in western New York (1843). As an artist lithographer Prestele interpreted the drawings of Isaac Sprague onto stone for publications by Asa Gray and John Torrey, the Smithsonian Institution, and expedition reports for the U.S. government. He produced plates for the periodical *The Horticulturist and Journal of Rural Art and Rural Taste,* and with the assistance of his son Gottlieb, he also illustrated and produced colored fruit and flower plates used by nurserymen to promote the sale of plants. Prestele relocated with his sect (now renamed the Amana Society) to eastern Iowa (1858) and because of the unavailability of scientific commissions returned to the making of nurserymen plates. Within the sect individual expression now was more limited, and the plates produced at this time by Prestele and his son only bear the name of the Amana Society. [See Charles Van Ravenswaay, *Drawn from Nature: The Botanical Art of Joseph Prestele and His Sons*, Washington, D.C., Smithsonian Institution Press, 1984.]

Price, Joe (1935–)
69. (page 141) Red ripe, 1984
Serigraph (74 screens)

Image: 30.5 x 45.5 cm   Paper: 40.5 x 55.5 cm   Edition: 65/100

Price was born in Louisiana and grew up in Alabama. He received a bachelor in theater arts from Northwestern University and worked in theater, film and television in New York City and Los Angeles. He worked in commercial art to supplement his income, and he received an M.A. in graphic design from Stanford University (1970) and became a professor of studio art at the College of San Mateo until his retirement (1994). Seventy-four separate screens of transparent color and gradations were used to produce this serigraph, which was also displayed in the Hunt Institute's *6th International Exhibition of Botanical Art & Illustration* (1988). Price has received many awards for his serigraphs, which have been included in numerous printmaking exhibitions in the United States and abroad, and his work is part of many private and corporate collections. His serigraphs are included in numerous museum collections including the San Francisco Museum of Modern Art, Philadelphia Museum of Art, and the Library of Congress.

Prince, William Robert (1795–1869) [see also Pendleton, William S.]
Aided by William Prince.
Treatise on the Vine. New York, T. & J. Swords [etc.]; Philadelphia [etc.], 1830. Frontispiece.
70. (page 72) *Vitis labrusca* v. Isabella
Lithographed by William S. Pendleton

William Robert Prince was born in Flushing, New York, and was the fourth-generation nurseryman in his family, which had established the Linnaean Botanic Garden and Nursery, Flushing, Long Island (1737). He accompanied John Torrey (1796–1873) and Thomas Nuttall (1786–1859) on their travels in the eastern United States and collected plants for the family's nursery. He experimented with European grapevines to improve the native varieties and sold them through the nursery. *Treatise on the Vine* was considered one of the better works written on viticulture in America. His father, William Prince had introduced *Vitis labrusca* v.

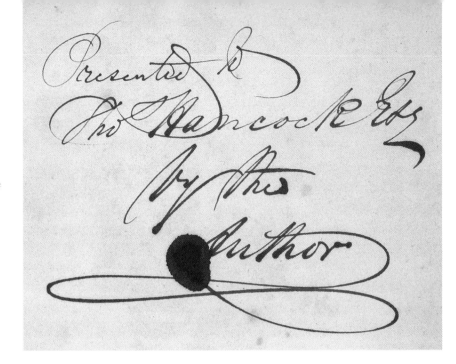

The author William Robert Prince's dedication of his book *A Treatise on the Vine*, 1830. (see stain on frontispiece illustration *Vitis labrusca* v. Isabella, page 72).

182

Isabella in the nursery and provided the drawing used for the frontispiece. This is a personally dedicated copy that William Robert Prince inscribed to a friend with a great calligraphic flourish on the reverse of this plate, hence the visible stain where the ink soaked through. His father also provided assistance on this publication as well as the *Pomological Manual* (1831) and *Manual of Roses* (1846).

William Prince (1766–1842) [see Prince, William Robert]

Rafinesque-Schmaltz, Constantine Samuel (1783–1840)
American Florist. Philadelphia, 1832. 18 pls. (36 figures). Fig. 15 and 16.
71. (page 69) Fig. 15. *Ornithopus scorpioides*, Birds-foot plant
Wood engraving
18 x 11 cm
72. (page 38) Fig. 16. *Nuttalia ornata*, Missouri sweet-poppy
Wood engraving
18 x 11 cm

The naturalist and author Rafinesque-Schmaltz was born in Constantinople and lived in France, Italy and Sicily (spending 10 years there as secretary to the U.S. Consul and collecting specimens and publishing scientific treatises). He settled permanently in the United States (1815) and became a citizen (1832). He made several collecting trips in the eastern United States and held the position of professor of botany and natural science at Transylvania University, Lexington, Kentucky (1819–1826), publishing many papers on the scientific names of thousands of plants and animals. After returning to Philadelphia (1826), he lectured and continued to publish on various natural history subjects under the patronage of Charles Wetherill, among them *Flora Telluriana* (1836), *A Life of Travels and Researches in North America and South Europe* (1836), and *The Good Book, and Amenities of Nature; or,*

Annuals of Historical and Natural Sciences (1840). Rafinesque made his own drawings, usually in a simple outline style, but nevertheless very characteristic. There is no text besides the legend to each illustration in *American Florist*. The engraver of these vigorous cuts is not acknowledged, and there is not even a printer's imprint. However, a broadside "American florist—Second series" is known, with "eighteen figures of handsome American garden flowers [numbered from 19 to 36]," published at Philadelphia in the same year and with the imprint of William Sharpless, printer, No. 2, Decatur street, Philadelphia. It was, we assume, an earlier issue of the latter part of the version we show, produced from the same press.

Title page of Constantine Samuel Rafinesque-Schmaltz's *American Florist*, 1832.

36 FIGURES—36 CENTS.

AMERICAN FLORIST,

CONTAINING:

36

FIGURES OF BEAUTIFUL OR CURIOUS

AMERICAN AND GARDEN FLOWERS, PLANTS,

TREES, SHRUBS AND VINES;

NATIVES OF NORTH AMERICA, OR CULTIVATED
IN GARDENS.

BY C. S. RAFINESQUE,

Professor of Historical and Natural Sciences.

Let us teach by Pictures.

PHILADELPHIA.
1832.

Readio, Wilfred (1895–1961)

73. (page 135) Tangle 4 *[Galanthus, Hosta]*, ca.1930–ca.1940s
Lithograph
Image: 30 x 37   Paper: 38 x 46 cm   Edition: 6/12

Readio was born in Northampton, Massachusetts, and received a B.A. in 1918 at Carnegie Institute of Technology (now Carnegie Mellon University). He was an instructor (1919–1922), assistant professor (1922–1926), associate professor (1928–1939), and professor and chairman (1939–1955) of the Department in Fine Arts, Carnegie Institute of Technology. His work was part of many group exhibits and is included in many institutions and private collections. Readio was a member of the Associated Artists of Pittsburgh, and his work was exhibited in the Hunt Institute's first international, *Contemporary Botanical Art & Illustration* (1964).

Roetter, Paulus (1806–1894) and **Möllhausen, Heinrich Balduin** (1825–1905) [see Prestele, Joseph]

74. (page 26) *Opuntia tessellata* E. [as published]
Lithograph
Image: 24.5 x 18.5 cm   Paper: 30.5 x 24.5 cm   Artist's proof
Publication: Engelmann, George and J. M. Bigelow. Description of the cactaceae. In: *Reports of Explorations and Surveys, to Ascertain the Most Practicable and Economical Route for a Railroad from the Mississippi River to the Pacific Ocean.* Vol. 4, no. 3. Washington, D.C., A. O. P. Nicholson, 1856. Pl. 21.
Printmaker: Joseph Prestele

75. (page 74) *Opuntia rafinesquii minor* E., 2–3. *Op. rafinesquii grandiflora* E., 4. *Opuntia fusco-atra* E. [as published]
Lithograph
Image: 24.5 x 18.5 cm   Paper. 24.5 x 18.5 cm   Artist's proof
Publication: Engelmann, George and J. M. Bigelow. Description of the cactaceae. In: *Reports of Explorations and Surveys, to Ascertain the Most Practicable and Economical Route for a Railroad from the Mississippi River to the Pacific Ocean.* Vol. 4, no. 3. Washington, D.C., A. O. P. Nicholson, 1856. Pl. 11.
Printmaker: Joseph Prestele

Roetter was born in Nuremburg, Germany, and studied art in Nuremberg, Düsseldorf, Munich and Paris. He moved to Switzerland (1825) where he painted miniature landscapes for the tourist trade and taught at Thun and Interlaken for the next 20 years. He immigrated to the United States (1845) to form a communistic settlement, but after it failed he moved to St. Louis and became an Evangelical pastor and school teacher. He was first instructor in drawing at Washington University (1853–1861). Roetter had a close association with George Engelmann and provided 61 drawings for the latter's "Cactaceae of the Boundary" in the *Report on the United States and Mexican Boundary Survey* (1859). He also continued with his landscape painting. After the Civil War, during which Roetter served with the Home Guard, he became an associate of Louis Agassiz (the systematist and paleontologist at Harvard), providing drawings of biological specimens. He returned to St. Louis (1884) ten years before his death. [See G. Groce and D. Wallace, *The New-York Historical Society's Dictionary of Artists in America, 1564–1860*, New Haven, Yale University Press, 1957. P. 543]

Möllhausen was born and educated near Bonn, Germany. After his years in the military, he traveled to the United States and settled in Belleville, Illinois (1849). He later became a member of two federal exploring parties to the American West. He was part of the Rocky Mountain expedition of Prince Paul of Württemberg (1851), but it only reached Fort Laramie before he was chosen to turn back. He returned to Germany to continue his artistic study and there met geographer Alexander von Humboldt, who recommended his appointment as topographer and draftsman for Lt. A.W. Whipple's surveying expedition along the 35th parallel from Arkansas to California (1853–1854). He was "artist and collector in natural history" for Lt. Joseph C. Ives' exploration of the Colorado River from its mouth to the Gulf of California (1857–1858). He returned to Germany (1858) and completed watercolors for Ives' report. Some of his sketches were lithographed for the official reports of these expeditions and some appeared as illustrations in his *Diary of a Journey from the Mississippi to the Coasts of the Pacific* (London, 1858). His travels were an inspiration for his more than 45 novels and short stories, and Möllhausen was considered the German Fenimore Cooper. [See G. Groce and D. Wallace, *The New-York Historical Society's Dictionary of Artists in America, 1564–1860*, New Haven, Yale University Press, 1957. P. 448 and *The Handbook of Texas Online*, www.tsha.utexas.edu/handbook/online/articles/view/MM/fmobt.html].

Rogers, Julia Ellen (1866–?)
The Tree Book ... with Sixteen Plates in Colour and One Hundred and Sixty in Black-and-White from Photographs by A. Radclyffe Dugmore. New York, Doubleday, Page & Co., 1907. P. opp. 346.
76. (page 64) Clammy Locust, *Robinia viscosa*
Photomechanical 3-color halftone
25 x 18.5 cm

Rogers studied at Iowa State University and Cornell University (M.S., 1902). She was a high school teacher in Iowa (1881–1900) and in 1903 began to lecture on natural history subjects. She also authored *The Book of Useful Plants* (1913). She later lived in New Jersey and Long Beach, California.

Rose, J. N. [see Faxon, Charles Edward]

Rothrock, Joseph Trimble (1839–1922) [see also T. Sinclair and Son]
Report upon United States Geographical Surveys West of the One Hundredth Meridian.... Vol. 6, Botany. Washington, Government Printing Office, 1878. Frontispiece

77. (page 29) A cactus grove, Arizona (species–*Cereus giganteus*) [*Carnegiea gigantea* (Engelm.) Britt. et Rose], 1871
Chromolithograph
Illustrator: H. J. Morgan
Printmaker: T. Sinclair and Son lith., Philadelphia.
29.5 x 23 cm

Rothrock was born in McVeytown, Pennsylvania, and educated at the Lawrence Scientific School, Harvard (B.Sc., 1864) [interrupted by his service in the Civil War, 1863–1864], and the University of Pennsylvania (Dr. Med., 1867). He was part of Robert Kennicott's Alaskan expedition (1865–1866), professor of botany at the State Agricultural College of Pennsylvania [now Pennsylvania State University] (1867–1869), a physician and surgeon in Wilkes-Barre, and one of the founders of the Wilkes-Barre Hospital. He was surgeon and botanist to G. N. Wheeler's exploring expeditions west of the 100th meridian (1873–1875), and professor of botany, University of Pennsylvania (1877–1891). Rothrock was the first forestry commissioner of the state of Pennsylvania (1895–1904). The roadside marker by the Pennsylvania Historical and Museum Commission in McVeytown states that he was a "conservationist and father of the State Forest idea in Pennsylvania," and "pioneer in the development of forest fire control, reforestation and scientific forestry." He lived in West Chester, Pennsylvania, the last 30 years of his life.

Sargent, Charles Sprague (1841–1927)
Garden and Forest; A Journal of Horticulture, Landscape Art and Forestry. 1888+. Vol. 1, 22 August 1888, p. 305.

78. (page 80) Fig. 49. *Magnolia hypoleuca*
Line block–relief
30.5 x 22 cm

Sargent was one of the founders and the "conductor" of this journal (published 1888–1897) while he was director of the Arnold Arboretum and Botanic Garden, Harvard University (1872–?). He also was the author of the 14-volume *Silva of North America* [see Charles Faxon]. It was edited by William A. Stiles (1837–1897), who also was a journalist for the *New York Tribune* and often wrote about the necessity of protecting the urban parks in New York. Because of Sargent's connections with notable figures in landscape architecture and design, botany, horticulture, conservation and forestry management, authoritative articles were written on this vast array of subject matter.

Schafer, Alice P. (1899–1980)
79. (page 126) Gooseberries *[Ribes]*, ca. late 1940–1950s
Linocut, color
Image: 15 x26.5 cm   Paper: 22 x 33 cm   Edition: 5/20
Schafer graduated *cum laude* (1919) from the School of Fine Arts Albany.
She was an active member of the Print Club of Albany, Society of Ameri-
can Graphic Artists (SAGA), and the National Association of Women
Artists (NAWA). She exhibited regularly at the Print Club of America
(1945–1958), SAGA (1947–1958), NAWA (1951–1958), and the Chicago
Society of Etchers (1950–1958), as well as in various printmaking exhib-
its in the northeastern United States and overseas in Holland, England
and Switzerland. Her work is in the collection of the Metropolitan Museum of Art, Pennsylvania Academy of Fine Arts, Butler Institute of
American Art, and the Print Club of Albany. The Hunt Institute included
her etchings in the *3rd and 4th International Exhibition of Botanical Art &
Illustration* (1972/73, 1977/78)

Schutt, Ellen I. (active 1900–1914)
80. (page 87) Pecan varieties
Chromolithograph
22.5 x 14.5 cm
Publication: *Yearbook of the United States Department of Agriculture.*
1905. Pl. LXV.

Schutt, born in Virginia, was an artist for the United States Department
of Agriculture, Division of Pomology, providing illustrations for the
Yearbook and *Contributions from the United States National Herbarium.*

Senefelder Lithographic Co. [see Swett, Moses]

Sharp, Michelin & Co. [see Mattson, Morris, Moody, William, and Sharp
William]

Sharp, Philip T. [see Sharp, William]

Sharp, William (ca.1802–after 1862) [see also Allen, John Fisk]
81. (page 22) *Victoria Regia* [*Victoria amazonica* (Poepp.) Sowerby]
Lithograph, color
55.5 x 73.5 cm
Printmaker: Sharp and Son
Publication: Allen, John Fisk, *Victoria Regia.* Boston, 1854.

Sharp was born in Ramsey, near Peterborough, England. He exhibited
engravings at the Royal Academy between 1819 and 1831 and worked as
a lithographer in London by 1832. *The Literary Blue Book ... for 1830*
(London, 1830) applauded Sharp for "the beauty and delicacy of his tints,
and the fidelity of his delineations." Two portfolios of his lithographic
work are held by the Boston Public Library and include about 250

lithographs—proofs and published prints—done by Sharp in England. Many were printed by the famous C. J. Hullmandel ... dated prints range from 1829. Perhaps he had been trained by or worked for Hullmandel. By the time he emigrated he was competent in many lithographic drawing techniques, e.g., shading, tonal contrast, hatching, stopping out.

Sharp emigrated to Boston (1838 or 1839) with his wife and six children. He was the first, and first commercially successful, chromolithographer in America. Sharp had brief partnerships with Francis Michelin and Ephraim W. Bouvé before establishing his own business. He took his son, Philip T. Sharp, into partnership by 1852, forming W. Sharp & Son. He produced the 110 color plates for Charles Mason Hovey's *The Fruits of America* (Boston, 1847–1856), 12 chromolithographs for Anna Dinnies *Floral Year* (1847), as well as the six large plates for *Victoria Regia.* [See Groce, G. and D. Wallace. 1957. *The New-York Historical Society's Dictionary of Artists in America, 1564–1860.* New Haven: Yale University Press. P. 571]. The plant shown in Sharp's print was one of the earliest grown in North America. Allen's *Victoria Regia* folio was modeled on W. H. Fitch's *Victoria Regia; or, Illustrations of the Royal Water Lily*, with descriptions by Sir W. J. Hooker (London, 1851). Allen's adaptation, with the text somewhat shortened, was taken almost word for word from Hooker. He dropped two of Fitch's plates and added a new one. It was the first American horticultural treatment of water-lilies and inspired a fad for growing them.

Shecut, John Linnaeus Edward Whitridge (1770–1836)
Flora Carolinaeensis. Vol. 1 [A–Fus]. Charleston, Printed for the author, by J. Hoff, 1806. P. iv.
82. (page 10) [Variety of shapes and arrangements of leaves and parts of a flower]
Line engraving
21 x 12.5 cm

The engraver of this early American botanical plate is not recorded. It is a most unusual illustration, presenting a fanciful plant that bears various forms of leaves by way of illustrating descriptive terms. Since it clearly shows the kind of attachment to the stem it has some advantage over the usual practice of illustrating leaf forms as separate illustrations.

Shecut was born in Beaufort, South Carolina, received a medical education at the College of Philadelphia (1791), and was a physician in Charleston, South Carolina (1791–1836). He founded the Antiquarian Society of Charleston (1813) [now the Literary and Philosophical Society of South Carolina]. He also was the author of *Shecut's Medical and Philosophical Essays* (1819), *Elements of Natural Philosophy* (1826), and the novels *The Eagle of the Mohawks* (1841, 2 vols.) and *The Scout; or, The Fast of St. Nicholas* (1844).

T. Sinclair and Son [see Rothrock, Joseph Trimble]

Thomas S. Sinclair established a lithographic business in Philadelphia in 1839. His first foray into chromolithography was in 1847, and the firm continued to produce color work for 40 more years. Sinclair's did much good work for scientific books and many government publications, and the *Report upon United States Geographical Surveys West of the One Hundredth Meridian....* (Washington, 1878) is a typical example of the high standard of their work.

Smith, Sir James Edward (1759–1828) [see also Doolittle, Isaac]

A Grammar of Botany, Illustrative of Artificial, as Well as Natural Classification. By the late Henry Muhlenberg. New York, J. V. Seaman, 1822. P. [230].

Drawing: Arthur Stansbury

Printmaker: (William Armand) Barnet and (Isaac) Doolittle, New York.

83. (page 31) Table III, Fig. 41. Stamens and pistil of *Ulex europaeus,* Furze; 42. Stamens and style of *Pisum maritimum,* Sea-side pea; 43. Calyx of the same; 44. Standard; 45. A wing; 46. One petal of the keel; 47. Pistil; 48. Stamens and pistil of *Hypericum elodes,* Marsh St. John's-wort; 49. Calyx magnified; 50. Back of the whole flower; 51. *Stuartia pentagyna;* 52. A petal separate, with part of the stamens, a. pistils; 53. *Melaleuca thymifolia;* 54. Bundles of stamens; 55. Calyx and pistil; 56. Separate petal.

Lithograph

22.5 x 13.5 cm

This is an American edition of a work by Sir James Edward Smith, who was born in Norwich and studied botany as part of medical courses at Edinburgh and Leiden. He purchased the Linnaean herbarium (1784) and was one of the founders and presidents of the Linnaean Society (1788–1828). Included among Smith's numerous writings are *English Botany* (London, 1790–1014, 36 vols.), *Compendium Florae Britannicae* (London, 1800–1804, 4 vols.), and *English Florae* (London, 1824–1828, 4 vols.). After the death of the English botanist John Sibthorp (1758–1796), Smith prepared text from Sibthorp's notes and specimens for six volumes of *Flora Graeca* (1806–).

Sprague, Isaac (1811–1895) [see also, Gray, Asa; Prestele, Joseph; and Charles Armstrong & Co.]

84. (page 24) *Gaillardia amblyodon*

Lithograph, hand-colored

Image: 22.5 x 16.5 cm   Paper: 29 x 23 cm

Publication: Asa Gray, Chloris Boreali-Americana. *Memoirs of the American Academy of Arts and Science,* n.s. 1848. Vol. 3, pp. 1–56, pl. 4.

Printmaker: Hall & Mooney exc, Buffalo, New York

Lithograph drawn on stone by Joseph Prestele (1796–1867) Bavaria/
United States
[See Charles Van Ravenswaay, *Drawn from Nature: The Botanical Art of
Joseph Prestele and His Sons*, Washington, D.C., Smithsonian Institution
Press, 1984]

85. (page 25) *Thermopsis mollis*
Lithograph, hand-colored
Image: 22.5 x 16.5 cm   Paper: 24 x 23 cm
Publication: Asa Gray, Chloris Boreali-Americana. *Memoirs of the Ameri-
can Academy of Arts and Science*, n.s. 1848. Vol. 3, pp. 1–56, pl. 9.
Printmaker: Hall & Mooney exc, Buffalo, New York
Lithograph drawn on stone by Joseph Prestele (1796–1867) Bavaria/
United States

86. (page 2) *Magnolia auriculata*, Ear-lobed umbrella tree
Lithograph
27 x 24.5 cm

87. (page 50) White bay, *Gordonia pubescens* L'Hér.
Chromolithograph
34 x 26.5 cm   Artist's proof
Publication: George L. Goodale, *The Wild Flowers of America*. Boston,
Bradlee Whidden, 1886, or subsequent edition. Pl. 47.

88. (page 96) Canadian rock-rose, *Helianthemum canadense* Michx.
Chromolithograph
34 x 26.5 cm   Artist's proof
Publication: George L. Goodale, *The Wild Flowers of America*. Boston,
Bradlee Whidden, 1886, or subsequent edition. Pl. 29.

89. (page 78) Indian turnip, *Arisaema triphyllum* Torrey
Chromolithograph
31 x 23 cm
Printmaker: Armstrong and Co.
Publication: George L. Goodale, *The Wild Flowers of America*. Boston,
Bradlee Whidden, 1886, or subsequent edition. Pl. 28.

90. (page 79) *Symplocarpus foetidus* Salisbury
Chromolithograph
30 x 22.5 cm   Artist's proof
Publication: George L. Goodale, *The Wild Flowers of America*. Boston,
Bradlee Whidden, 1886, or subsequent edition. Pl. 27.

Sprague was born in Hingham, Massachusetts, and apprenticed with his
uncle as a carriage painter. He was a self-taught landscape, botanical
and ornithological painter. Sprague served as one of the assistants to
John James Audubon on an ornithological expedition up the Missouri
River (1843), taking measurements and making sketches. His diary of
this expedition is in the Boston Athenaeum. In 1844 he met Asa Gray
(1810–1888) of Harvard College, and over many years illustrated several

of his works including Gray's *Botanical Text-book* (1842), *Manual of the Botany of the Northern United States* (1848), several *Geographical Surveys of the South West*, and the two published volumes of *Genera Florae Americae Boreali-Orientalis* (discontinued because of lack of financing), containing 186 plates. He also illustrated Emerson's *Report on the Trees and Shrubs Growing Naturally in the Forests of Massachusetts* (1875) and George Goodale's *Wild Flowers of America* (1882). He wrote and illustrated *Flowers from Field and Forest* (1848–1849). The Houghton Library, Harvard University exhibited approximately 100 of Sprague's paintings, drawings and illustrations from books (1960).

Stansbury, Arthur [see Smith, Sir James Edward and Doolittle, Isaac]

Stowell, Louisa Maria Reed (1850–1932)
91. (page 68) *Sonchus oleraceus*, Sow thistle
Wood engraving
23 x 14.5 cm
Publication: *Report of the Botanist, U.S. Department of Agriculture.* 1889 (t.l.). Pl. IV (t.r.)

Stowell was born in Grand Blanc, Michigan, married Charles Henry Stowell (1878) and was an illustrator for the United States Department of Agriculture (active 1890).

Strong, Asa B. (fl.1850) [see also Moody, William]
The American Flora. Vol. 1. New York, Strong and Burdick, 1847. P. opp. 59.
92. (page 14) *Anemone pratensis*, Pasque flower
Chromolithograph
24.5 x 18.5 cm
Lithographer: William Moody

According to *Taxonomic Literature* (Stafleu and Cowan, Utrecht [etc.], 1986, vol. 6), Strong was a physician and author of popular works on natural history.

Swett, Moses (active 1826–1837) [see also Pendleton, William S.]
93. (page 88) [Flowers]
Lithograph, hand-colored
39.5 x 48.5 cm
Printmaker: Endicott and Swett, Graphic-Hall, Baltimore, 1831

This lithographer began working in Boston (1826) with the Pendletons and Annin & Smith, and he was superintendent of the Senefelder Lithographic Company (1828–1829). Swett was with George Endicott in New York City (1830–1836), and he worked in Washington, D.C. (1837). [See G. Groce and D. Wallace, *The New York Historical Society's Dictionary of Artists in America, 1564–1860*, New Haven, Yale University Press, 1957. Pp. 616–617]. Endicott and Swett were well known at the time for the 18 plates they printed for Natah R. Smith's 1832, *Surgical Anatomy of the Arteries*. Endicott's firm continued for many years producing unremarkable lithographed plates for topographical and other illustrated books down to the end of the century. This chalk-style lithographic image was probably one of the earliest pieces produced for display in the home.

Troth, Henry (1863–1948) [see also Blanchan, Neltje]
Troth was an early American plant photographer whose naturalistic images, shot against plain backgrounds with vivid clarity, were excellently reproduced in Neltje Blanchan's progressively illustrated flower book, *Nature's Garden* (1900).

vander Meijden (formerly Michas), Tjelda (1942–)
94. (page 143) Oriental poppy *[Papaver]*, 1980
Serigraph
Image: 53 x 67 cm   Paper: 62.5 x 76 cm   Edition: 123/225

Michas was born in New Jersey of Dutch parents and was educated in New York and the Netherlands (studying with her uncle, the artist, Jan Muller in Holland). She studied painting, drawing and intaglio at the National Academy of Design and Fine Art, New York (1988–1991), privately studied with printmaker Sergei Tsvetkov (1991–1992), took drawing and painting classes at the New York Studio School of Drawing, Painting and Sculpture (2001), and received a B.A, Visual Arts, from the Vermont College of Union University (2003). Her paintings and prints have been included in numerous one-person and group exhibitions including the American Museum of Natural History, New York; MacCulloch Hall Historical Museum, Morristown, New Jersey; and the Jekyll Island Museum, Jekyll Island, Georgia. Her works are part of numerous public and private collections including the Newark Art Museum, Reader's Digest, Visa International, and the Sloane Kettering Institute. Her serigraphs were included in the Hunt Institute's exhibit *Northeast Folio* (1979) and the *5th International Exhibition of Botanical Art & Illustration* (1983). She currently lives in Charleston, South Carolina, continues her work as a *plein air* painter in the Netherlands and the United States, and teaches painting and gives workshops in monotype and intaglio.

Vogel, Donella Reese (1942–)
95. (page 111) Plants *[Aloe, Areca, Philodendron, Sansevieria]*, 1970
Etching, color
Image: 55 x 47 cm   Paper: 66 x 61 cm   Artist's proof

Vogel was born in Milwaukee, Wisconsin, and received a B.S. in design from the University of Michigan, Ann Arbor (1964). She is a freelance artist, a former co-owner of the Klein-Vogel Gallery, Royal Oak, Michigan (1970–1976), and faculty member of the Birmingham-Bloomfield Association, Birmingham, Michigan (1974–1976). She has exhibited in numerous group printmaking exhibitions and her work is included in many corporate collections. Vogel's etching was included in the Hunt Institute's *4th International Exhibition of Botanical Art & Illustration* (1977/78).

Volpe, Richard (1926–)

96. (page 102) Wheat, ca. late 1960s.

Etching, color

Image size 14x 62.5 cm   Paper: 27.5 x 77.5 cm   Edition: 55/60

Volpe was born in Latrobe, Pennsylvania, received a B.A. from the University of New Mexico (1958), and studied at Ohio Wesleyan University, Denver University and the University of Nevada, Las Vegas. He was a playwright, actor and watercolorist who switched to printmaking in 1965. His prints have won many awards and have been exhibited at various museums and galleries in the South and Midwest. His work is in the collections of the University of Nevada, Las Vegas Art League, and the Academic Artists Association. This etching was included in the Hunt Institute's *3rd International Exhibition of Botanical Art & Illustration* (1972/73) and is notable for the artist's interesting use of a roulette to make the marks on the plate. Volpe currently works in Laguna Beach, California.

Walpole, Frederick Andrews (1861–1904)

97. (page 70) *Erica* ?

Wood engraving

12.5 x 10 cm

98. (page 70) *Vaccinium ovalifolium*

Wood engraving

12 x 10 cm

99. (page 71) *Vaccinium membranaceum*

Wood engraving

12.5 x 10 cm

100. (page 71) *Vaccinium parvifolium*, Red huckleberry

Wood engraving

12.5 x 19.5 cm

101. (Not shown in catalogue) *Tsuga*

Line engraving, collotype, halftone of same image

25 x 18 cm

102. (page 82) *Nymphaea polysepala [Nuphar]*

Heliotype

Printmaker Heliotype Co

Publication: Frederick V. Coville, Wokas: A primitive food of the Klamath Indians. *Annual Report of the United States National Museum.* 1902. Pl. 1.

Image: 24.5 x 17 cm   Paper: 30.5 x 24 cm

All of these works are on indefinite loan from the Smithsonian Institution.

Born in New York state, Frederick Walpole had art training in Chicago and moved to Oregon in the 1880s. There, in 1896, a Department of Agriculture botanist doing field research saw Walpole's work and helped him get an appointment as artist for the Division of Botany. In his short career he worked in Washington, D.C., and made several field trips to the Northwest, including Alaska. His unpublished notebooks give a vivid account of his work and adventures in the field. Walpole's many plant studies were done mostly in watercolor, but he also made remarkable ink drawings, using a single-hair brush instead of a pen.

Ward, Virginia (1917–)
103. (page 127) *Aesculus hippocastanum,* ca.1970s
Linocut, color
Image: 19 x 21 cm   Paper: 27 x 27.5 cm

Ward was born in Wavery, New York, and educated at the University of Albany night school (1955–1960). She also studied graphics under Alice Pauline Schafer [who also is represented in this exhibit] (1964–1968). Ward was a freelance artist and private nurse and an active member of the Print Club of Albany, Southern Vermont Art Center, Miniature Painters and Sculptors, the Engravers Society, and National Association of Women Artists, among others. She had a one-person exhibit at the Chaffee Art Gallery in Rutland, Vermont (1976), and participated in numerous group printmaking exhibitions in the northeastern United States. Her work is in the collection of the Print Club of America, the Southern Vermont Art Center, and many private collections. Her work was included in the Hunt Institute's *4th International Exhibition of Botanical Art & Illustration* (1977/78). The artist, now retired, lives in Montour Falls, New York.

Whitefield, Edwin (1816–1892) [see also Lewis & Brown]
104. (page 47) *Aquilegia canadensis,* Wild columbine
Lithograph, hand-colored
24.5 x 18.5 cm
Publication: Emma C. Embury, *American Wild Flowers in Their Native Haunts.* New York, D. Appleton, 1845. Opposite p. 75.
Printmaker: Lewis & Brown
105. (page 73) *Uvularia perfoliata,* Bellwort
Lithograph, hand-colored
24.5 x 18.5 cm
Publication: Emma C. Embury, *American Wild Flowers in Their Native Haunts.* New York, D. Appleton, 1845. Opposite p. 61.
Printmaker: Lewis & Brown

Whitefield was an English landscape and flower painter who came to the United States between 1837 and 1840 and is known chiefly for his lithographic prints of city views. The series of views in this publication were titled *North American Scenery*, and the drawings of wildflowers for these lithographs, according to the author, contain pencil backgrounds of "landscape views of their localities, from drawings on the *spot*." He also provided some of the illustrations for John B. Newman's *The Illustrated Botany of New York* (1846) and A. B. Strong's *American Flora* (1847–?). In 1856 he was artist and publicity agent for the Whitefield Exploration Association, which was involved in the exploration and development of the Kandiyohi Lakes region of Minnesota. From 1879 to 1889, Whitefield published his drawings of historic buildings of Massachusetts, Rhode Island and Connecticut, Maine, New Hampshire and Vermont, and a comparison of historic structures in Boston, England and Massachusetts. Seventy of Whitefield's paintings and two of his hand-drawn maps are in the collection of the Minnesota Historical Society.

Williams, Keith Shaw (1906–1951)
106. (page 108) Two brothers *[Quercus]*, ca.1940s
Etching
Image: 25 x30 cm   Paper: 30 x 35.5 cm   Edition: 6/80

Shaw was born in Marquette, Michigan. He studied at the National Academy of Design and was a member of the Chicago Society of Etchers. His works are included in the permanent collections of the National Academy of Design, the Library of Congress and the New York Historical Society.

Ziemann, Richard Claude (1932–)
107. (page 104) Grasses, 1956
Line engraving with etching
Image: 11 x13 cm   Paper: 31 x 32 cm   Edition: 23/25

Born in Buffalo, New York, Ziemann received a B.F.A. (1956) and M.F.A. (1958) from Yale University, where he studied with Bernard Chaet and Gabor Peterdi. He taught printmaking at Yale's School of Fine Art and Hunter College and has been a visiting critic and artist-in-residence at various universities. His work has been included in numerous one-person and group exhibitions in galleries and museums and has received many awards, including a Fulbright Grant to the Netherlands (1958–1959) and a Tiffany Foundation Grant (1960–1961). He is a member of the Print Council of America. His work was included in two Hunt Institute exhibitions, *Northeast Folio* (1979) and the *7th International Exhibition of Botanical Art & Illustration* (1992). A major retrospective, *Richard Claude Ziemann: Prints and Drawings, 1956–1979*, was exhibited at the Brooklyn Museum of Art (1979). His work is in their permanent collection as well as the Cincinnati Museum of Art, Metropolitan Museum of Art, Yale University Art Gallery, Philadelphia Museum of Art, the Minneapolis Art Institute, and the Library of Congress.

— Compiled by Lugene B. Bruno

THE

AMERICAN VEGETABLE PRACTICE,

OR A

NEW AND IMPROVED

GUIDE TO HEALTH,

DESIGNED

FOR THE USE OF FAMILIES.

IN SIX PARTS.

Part I. Concise View of the Human Body, with engraved and wood-cut illustrations. Part II. Glance at the Old School Practice of Physic. Part III. Vegetable Materia Medica, with colored illustrations. Part IV. Compounds. Part V. Practice of Medicine, based upon what are deemed correct Physiological and Pathological Principles. Part VI. Guide for Women, containing a simplified treatise on Childbirth, with a description of the Diseases peculiar to Females and Infants.

BY MORRIS MATTSON,

PHYSICIAN TO THE REFORMED BOSTON DISPENSARY, LECTURER ON PHYSIOLOGY, THE PRACTICE OF MEDICINE, ETC. ETC.

Do not counteract the living principle.—*Napoleon.*

"It is contrary to the dictates of common sense, to suppose that a POISON, either *mineral* or *vegetable*, can be a MEDICINE."

IN TWO VOLUMES.

VOL. I.

BOSTON:
PUBLISHED BY DANIEL L. HALE,
Blackstone St....Seven doors W. of Hanover St.
1841.

Title page of Morris Mattson's *American Vegetable Practice*, 1841 (see pages 176–177).

In order to assemble a balanced selection of items for this exhibition, and in the absence of any other such list, it was necessary to quickly assemble this provisional list. It includes all kinds of printed illustrations from the largest scientific monograph to the humblest children's book. It was based, in the first instance, on the Institute's own resources and was augmented by information gleaned from a number of reference works. A number of entries lack information on page and plate counts and types of illustrations, etc. It is offered here as a working tool for the interested reader until such time as a comprehensive list can be completed.

Nineteenth-century American illustrated botanical and other plant books

Anonymous. 1835. Language of Flowers. Philadelphia: Carey, Lea & Blanchard. 6 pls. {Ed. 2, Philadelphia: Carey, Lea & Blanchard, 1835; The Language of Flowers: With Illustrative Poetry, to Which Is Now First Added, The Calendar of Flowers, American ed. 3. Revised by the editor of "Forget me not" [i.e., Frederic Shoberl]. Philadelphia [etc.], 1836. 360 pp., 5 eng. pls. (col.).; American ed. 5, Philadelphia [etc.], 1839. 360 pp., 4 eng. pls. (col.); American ed. 6, rev. [etc.], Philadelphia [etc.], 1843. 6 pls. New pls. for this ed.}

Anonymous. 1836. Book of Flowers. Flora and Thalia; or, Gems of Flowers and Poetry: Being an Alphabetical Arrangement of Flowers with Appropriate Poetical Illustrations. Embellished with colored plates. By a lady. Philadelphia: Carey, Lea & Blanchard. 240 pp. & 24 eng. pls. (col.).

Anonymous. 1836? Conversations on the Botany of the Scriptures. New York: Protestant Episcopal Sunday Union. 250 pp. & 13 eng. pls.

Anonymous. 1841. Queen of Flowers; or, Memoirs of the Rose, [ed. 2]. With coloured plates. Philadelphia: Lea & Blanchard. 219 pp. & 4 eng. pls. (col.). {First pub. as: Memoirs of the Rose.}

Anonymous. 1842. Popular Treatise on Vegetable Physiology. Published under the auspices of the Society for the Promotion of Popular Instruction. With numerous cuts. Philadelphia: Lea & Blanchard. 301 pp., wood-eng. illus.

Anonymous. [1844.] Flowers by the Way-Side. Philadelphia: American Sunday-School Union. Frontis. 107 pp., pls.

Anonymous. 1845. The Bouquet see "A Lady."

Anonymous. [1840s?] About Plants. With many engravings. Worcester: Published by J. Grout, Jr. [24] pp., wood-eng. illus.

Anonymous. [1840s.] Wonders of Vegetation. Prepared for the American Sunday-School Union, and revised by the Committee of Publication. Philadelphia: American Sunday-School Union. 51 pp., wood-eng. illus.

Anonymous. [1852.] American Rose Culturist; Being a Practical Treatise on the Propagation, Cultivation, and Management of the Rose in All Seasons; with a List of Choice and Approved Varieties, Adapted to the Climate of the United States; to Which Are Added Full Directions for the Treatment of the Dahlia. Illustrated by engravings. New York: C. M. Saxton. 96+11+[11] pp., wood-eng. illus. [Saxton's Cottage and Farm Library.]

Anonymous. 1854. Floral Forget-Me-Not. Philadelphia: H. F. Anners. Illus.

Anonymous. 1857. The Illustrated Pear Culturist see "An Amateur."

Anonymous. 1857. Pond Lily Stories. Philadelphia: American Sunday School Union. 262 pp., pls. (chromoliths.).

Anonymous. 1859. Songs of the Woodland, the Garden, and the Sea. New York. Frontis., 189 pp. & 5 chromolith. pls.

Anonymous. 1864. Phantom Flowers: A Treatise on the Art of Producing Skeleton Leaves. Boston: J. E. Tilton & Co. 96 pp. & 6 eng. pls. {Also, Boston: J. E. Tilton & Co., 1866.}

Anonymous. 1864. Thoughts among Flowers. New York: Leavitt and Allen. Wood-eng. illus.

Anonymous. [ca.1865.] Examples for Drawing and Colouring Flowers. Philadelphia: Janentzky & Co. 8 pls.

Anonymous. 1894. Wild Flowers of America. Flowers of Every State in the American Union. By a Corps of Special Artists and Botanists. New York: Published weekly by G. H. Buek & Co., 22 May–11 Sept. 1894. 18 pts. [304] pp., 288 chromolith. illus. {Title page headed "Botanical fine art weekly."}

Abbott, J. M., W. G. Baker, et al. 1900. The Book of Gardening: A Handbook of Horticulture. W[illiam]. D. Drury, ed. New York: C. Scribner's Sons; London: L. Upcott Gill. vii+1198 pp., illus.

Abbott, Jacob and John S. C. Abbott. [1850s.] Common School Drawing Cards. Flower Set No. 1. Designed by J[ames]. A. Cleveland. New York: R. B. Collins.

Allen, Charles Linnaeus. 1893. Bulbs and Tuberous-Rooted Plants: Their History, Description, Methods of Propagation, and Complete Directions for Their Successful Culture in the Garden, Dwelling, and Greenhouse. New York: Orange Judd & Co. vi+311 pp., illus.

Allen, John Fisk. 1847. The Culture of the Grape, Embracing Directions for the Treatment of the Vine, in the Northern States of America, in the Open Air, and under Glass Structures, with and without Artificial Heat. Boston: Dutton & Wentworth, Printers. 55 pp., illus. {Ed. 2, enl., Boston [etc.], 1848. Frontis. & 247 pp., illus.; Ed. 3, enl. & rev. as A Practical Treatise on the Culture and Treatment of the Grape Vine; Embracing Its History, with Directions for Its Treatment, in the U.S. New York: C. M. Saxton, 1853, Frontis., 330 pp. & 3 pls.; 1856.}

Allen, John Fisk. 1854. Victoria Regia; or, The Great Water Lily of America. With a Brief Account of Its Discovery and Introduction into Cultivation. With illustrations by Wm. Sharp from specimens grown at Salem, Mass., U.S.A., by John Fisk Allen. Boston: Pr. & pub. for the Author by Dutton & Wentworth. 18 pp. & 6 chromolith. pls.

Allen, Richard Lamb. 1856. The American Farm Book; or Compend of American Agriculture; Being a Practical Treatise on Soils, Manures, Draining Irrigation, Grasses, Grain, Roots, Fruits, Cotton, Tobacco, Sugar Cane, Rice and Every Staple Product of the United States. With the Best Methods of Planting, Cultivating, and Preparation for Market. Illustrated by more than 100 engravings. New York: C. M. Saxton & Co. 325+10 pp., 100+ wood-eng. illus. {Also, New York: A. O. Moore, 1858. 325 pp., illus.}

Allen, Timothy F. [1880]. The Characeae of America. With colored illustrations from the original drawings by the author. Part. [1–2]. 2 vols. Boston: S. E. Cassino [etc.]. 6 pls. (col.). {Entirely distinct from his larger work published of the same title.}

Allen, Timothy F. 1888. The Characeae of America, Pt. 1: Introduction, Morphology and Classification. New York.; 1894. ... Pt. 2, Fasc. 1. Boston: Cassino. 14 pls. (liths. & photos); 1894. ... Pt. 2, Fasc. 2. Boston: Cassino. 8 lith. pls.; 1896. ... Pt. 2, Fasc. 3. 9 eng. pls.

"An Amateur." 1857. The Illustrated Pear Culturist; Containing Plain, Practical Directions for Planting, Budding, Grafting, Pruning, Training and Dwarfing the Pear Tree; also Instructions Relating to the Propagation of New Varieties etc. etc. A List of the Most Valuable Varieties for Dwarf or Standard Culture. New York: A. O. Moore & Co ; [New] London: Starr & Co. 33 lith. pls. (col.). {Ed. 2, New York and New London: C. M. Saxton, Starr & Co., 1858; New York: O. A. Moore & Co., 1859; New London: Starr & Co., 1859.}

Andrews, James. 1852. Studies in Flower Painting; a Series of Plates for Instruction in Drawing and Coloring Flowers, from Designs by James Andrews, Drawn on Stone by G. W. Lewis, and Colored by E. J. Perry. New York: Robert B. Collins. 8 lith. pls. (in col. & uncol. versions).

Apgar, Austin Craig. [1892.] Trees of the Northern United States: Their Study, Description and Determination. For the Use of Schools and Private Students. New York: American Book Co. 224 pp., illus.

Apgar, Ellis A. and Austin Craig Apgar. 1874. Apgar's Plant Analysis: Adapted to Gray's

Botanies. New York and Chicago: Ivison, Blakeman, Taylor. 12 pp., illus., & 122 blank forms.

Apgar, Ellis A. and Austin Craig Apgar. [1892.] Apgar's New Plant Analysis. New York [etc.]: American Book Co. 128 pp., illus.

Atkinson, George Francis. 1898. Elementary Botany. New York: H. Holt & Co. Frontis., xxiii+444 pp., illus. {Ed. 2, New York [etc.], 1899.}

Atkinson, George Francis. 1900. Lessons in Botany. New York: H. Holt & Co. xv+365 pp., illus.

Atkinson, George Francis. 1900. Studies of American Fungi. Mushrooms, Edible, Poisonous, etc. With a chapter on recipes for cooking mushrooms, by Mrs. Sarah Tyson Rorer; on the chemistry and toxicology of mushrooms, by J. F. Clark; on the structural characters of mushrooms, by H. Hasselbring. With 200 photographs by the author, and colored plates by F. R. Rathbun. Ithaca: Andrus & Church. Frontis. (col.) & vi+275 pp., 76 pls., illus. {Ed. 2, With 230 photographs by the author [etc.], Ithaca [etc.], 1901. Frontis. (col.)., vi+322 pp., 81 pls., illus.}

B., H. 1857. Leaf and Flower Pictures and How to Make Them. New York: Anson D. F. Randolph. 58 pp., 8 lith. pls. (col.). {New & enl. ed., New York: A. D. F. Randolph, 1868. 69 pp. & 7 pls. (col.).}

Badger, Mrs. C. M. 1859. Wild Flowers, Drawn and Colored from Nature. With an introduction by Mrs. L. H. Sigourney. New York: C. Scribner; London: Sampson Low, Son & Co. Frontis., vii+43 pp. & 21 lith. pls. (col.).

Badger, Mrs. C. M. 1867. Floral Belles from the Green-House and Garden. Painted from nature by Mrs. C. M. Badger [etc.]. New York: C. Scribner & Co. 66 pp. & 16 lith. pl. (col.). {Poems and illustrations.}

Bailey, Alice Ward. 1889. Flower Fancies. Illustrated by Lucy J. Bailey, Eleanor Ecob Morse [& others]. Boston: L. Prang & Co. 24 ff., chromolith. t.p. & illus.

Bailey, Liberty Hyde. 1898. First Lessons with Plants: Being an Abridgement of "Lessons with Plants": Suggestions for Seeing and Interpreting Some of the Common Forms of Vegetation. With delineations from nature by W. S. Holdsworth. New York: The Macmillan Co. x+117 pp., line illus.

Bailey, Liberty Hyde. 1898. Lessons with Plants: Suggestions for Seeing and Interpreting Some of the Common Forms of Vegetation. With delineations from nature by W. S. Holdsworth. New York: The Macmillan Co. xxxi+491 pp., illus.

Bailey, Liberty Hyde. 1898. Sketch of the Evolution of Our Native Fruits. New York: The Macmillan Co. Port., xiii+472 pp., line & half-tone illus.

Bailey, Liberty Hyde. 1900. Botany: An Elementary Text for Schools. New York: The Macmillan Co. xiv+355 pp., line & half-tone illus. {Ed. 2, New York [etc.], 1901.}

Bailey, Liberty Hyde, ed. 1900–1902. Cyclopedia of American Horticulture; Comprising Suggestions for Cultivation of Horticultural Plants, Descriptions of the Species of Fruits, Vegetables, Flowers and Ornamental Plants Sold in the United States and Canada, Together with Geographical and Biographical Sketches and a Synopsis of the Vegetable Kingdom. By ... assisted by Wilhelm Miller and many expert cultivators and botanists. 4 vols. New York: The Macmillan Co. xiv+xv+xxx+2016 pp., 50 half-tone pls., 2,800 text illus.

Bailey, William Whitman. [1895.] Among Rhode Island Wild Flowers. Providence: Preston & Rounds. Frontis., xi+105 pp. & pls. {Ed. 2, Providence, 1896.}

Baker, Charles R. 1866. Practical and Scientific Fruit Culture. Boston: Lee & Shepard. 533 pp., illus.

Baldwin, Henry Ives. 1884. The Orchids of New England: A Popular Monograph. New York: J. Wiley & Sons. 158 pp., illus.

Barry, Patrick. 1851. The Fruit Garden: A Treatise Intended to Explain and Illustrate the Physiology of Fruit Trees, the Theory and Practice of All Operations Connected with the Propagation, Transplanting, Pruning and Training of Orchard and Garden Trees, as Standards, Dwarfs, Pyramids, Espaliers, etc., the Laying Out and Arranging of Suitable Varieties for Different Purposes and Localities [etc.]. Illustrated with upwards of 150 figures, representing different parts of trees, all practical operations, forms of trees, designs for plantations, implements, etc. New York: Charles Scribner. Frontis. & xiv+398 pp., wood-eng. illus. {Also, New York: Charles Scribner, 1852; Auburn [etc.], 1853; Auburn and Rochester: Alden & Beardsley, 1855; Auburn; Rochester, 1857; New York: A. O. Moore (later C. M. Saxton & Co.) Agricultural Book Publisher, 1858; New York, 1862; Rochester: The Author, 1863.}

Barton, Benjamin Smith. 1803. Elements of Botany; or, Outlines of the Natural History of Vegetables. Illustrated by thirty plates. Philadelphia: Pr. for the Author. Pub. in 2 pts. xii+302+168+38 pp. & 30 eng. pls. {Ed. 2, corr. & greatly enl., illustrated by forty plates. Philadelphia: Pr. for the Author, 1812 [-14]. 39 [sic] eng. pls.; Ed. 3, corr. & greatly enl. 2 vols. Philadelphia: E. Desilver, 1827. 39 [sic] eng. pls.; New ed., rev. & condensed, with an account of the life and writings of the author, by William P. C. Barton [etc.]. Philadelphia: Robert Desilver, 1835. 325 pp. & 39 [sic] eng. pls.; Philadelphia, 1836. 39 [sic] pls.}

Barton, William Paul Crillon. 1817–1818. Vegetable Materia Medica of the United States; or, Medical Botany, Containing a Botanical, General and Medical History of Medicinal Plants Indigenous to the United States. Illustrated by coloured engravings, made after original drawings from nature, done by the author. 2 vols. Pub. in 7 pts. Philadelphia: M. Carey & Son. 50 eng. pls. (col.).

Barton, William Paul Crillon. 1820–1823. A Flora of North America. Illustrated by coloured figures, drawn from nature. 3 vols. Pub. in 36 pts. Philadelphia: M. Carey & Sons; [vols. 2–3] H. C. Carey & I. Lea. 106 eng. (partly col.-pr.) pls. (70 col.).

Bartram, William. 1791. Travels through North and South Carolina, Georgia, East and West Florida, the Cherokee Country, the Extensive Territory of the Muscogulges or Creek Confederacy and the Country of the Choctaws. Containing an Account of the Soil and Natural Productions of Those Regions, Together with Observations on the Manners of the Indians. Embellished with copper-plates. Philadelphia: Pr. by James & Johnson. xxiv+520+[12] pp. & 8 eng. pls. (col.).

Bastin, Edson Sewell. 1887. Elements of Botany, Including Organography, Vegetable Histology, Vegetable Physiology, and Vegetable Taxonomy, and a Glossary of Botanical Terms. Illustrated by nearly five hundred engravings from drawings by the author. Chicago: G. P. Englehard & Co. Frontis. & xv+282 pp., illus.

Bastin, Edson Sewell. 1889. College Botany, Including Organography, Vegetable Histology, Vegetable Physiology and Vegetable Taxonomy. With a Brief Account of the Succession of Plants in Geologic Time, and a Glossary of Botanical Terms. Being a revised and enlarged edition of the "Elements of botany," with nearly six hundred illustrations, largely from drawings by the author. Chicago: G. P. Engelhard & Co. Frontis. & xv+451 pp., illus.

Bastin, Edson Sewell and Henry Trimble. 1897. Some North American Coniferae. A Series of Papers Reprinted from the American Journal of Pharmacy, Jan. 1896 to July 1897. Philadelphia. 2 pls.

Beach, Spencer Ambrose, Nathaniel Ogden Booth and Orrin Morehouse Taylor. 1905. The Apples of New York. 2 vols. Albany: State of New York, Department of Agriculture. 136 tri-chromatic and 77 half-tones pls. [Report of the New York Agricultural Experiment Station for the Year 1903, 2.]

Beal, William James. 1887–1896. Grasses of North America for Farmers and Students [etc.]. 2 vols. Lansing and New York: The Author [vol. 1]; New York: H. Holt [vol. 2]. illus.

Beal, William James. 1898. Seed Dispersal. Boston: Ginn & Co. vii+87 pp., illus.

Bentley, Robert. 1886. Physiological Botany: An Abridgement of The Students' Guide to Structural, Morphological, and Physiological Botany. Prepared as a sequel to "Descriptive botany" by Eliza A. Youmans. New York: D. Appleton & Co. xiv+292 pp., illus.

Bergen, Joseph Young. 1896. Elements of Botany. Boston: Ginn & Co. 2 pts. viii+275+57 pp., illus. Part II: Key and Flora. Embracing a Few of the Commonest Spring Flowers of the Northern and Middle States. {Also, Boston [etc.], 1897.}

Bergen, Joseph Young. 1899. Elements of Botany. Boston: Ginn & Co. 2 pts., illus. Part II: Key and Flora. Rocky Mountain Edition. Prepared by Alice Eastwood.

Bessey, Charles Edwin. 1880. Botany for High Schools and Colleges. New York: Henry Holt & Co. x+611 pp., line illus. [American Science Series 5.]

Bickley, George W. L. 1853. Principles of Scientific Botany; Being a Concise Treatise on Structural and Systematical Botanical Science, as

Adapted by Modern Botanists, Simplified and Carefully Arranged for the Use of Colleges and Private Students. Cincinnati: H. W. Derby. 209 pp. & 20 pls. (col.), illus.

Bigelow, Jacob. 1817–1820. American Medical Botany; Being a Collection of the Native Medicinal Plants of the United States, Containing Their Botanical History and Chemical Analysis, and Properties and Uses in Medicine, Diet and the Arts, with Coloured Engravings. 3 vols. Pub. in 6 half-vols. Boston: Cummings & Hilliard; University Press, Hilliard & Metcalf. 20+20+20 eng. (col.-pr.) pls.

Biggle, Jacob. 1894. Biggle Berry Book: A Condensed Treatise on the Culture of Berries, with Leaves from the Experience of Many Practical Berry Growers in All Parts of the United States. Philadelphia: W. Atkinson Co. Frontis., 126 pp. & 20 pls. (col.). [Biggle Farm Library, no. 2.]

Blanchan, Neltje [i.e., Mrs. Nellie Blanchan Doubleday]. 1900. Nature's Garden: An Aid to Knowledge of Our Wild Flowers and Their Insect Visitors, with Colored Plates and Many Other Illustrations Photographed Directly from Nature by Henry Troth and A. R[adclyffe]. Dugmore. New York: Doubleday, Page & Co. xvi+415 pp. & half-tone & 3-col. pls.

Bourne, Hermon. 1833. Flores Poetici: The Florist's Manual: Designed as an Introduction to Vegetable Physiology and Systematic Botany for Cultivators of Flowers, with More Than Eighty Beautifully-Coloured Engravings of Poetic Flowers. Boston: Munroe & Francis; New York: Charles S. Francis. 288 pp., 80+ wood-eng. illus. (col.).

Brackenridge, William Dunlop. 1854–1855. Botany. Cryptogamia. With a folio atlas of plates. In: Charles Wilkes et al. 1845–1876. United States Exploring Expedition. During the Years 1838, 1839, 1840, 1841, 1842. Under the Command of Charles Wilkes, U.S.N. 19 vols. Philadelphia. Vol. 16. 46 eng. pls.

Breck, Joseph. 1833. The Young Florist; or, Conversations on the Culture of Flowers, and on Natural History. With numerous engravings, from original designs. Boston: Russell, Odiorne & Co. Frontis., 168 pp., & 2? pls.

Breck, Joseph. 1866. New Book of Flowers. Newly electrotyped and illustrated. Boston. 480 pp., illus. {Also, New York: Orange Judd & Co., N.d. 480 pp., illus.}

Bridgeman, Thomas. 1867. The American Gardener's Assistant. New ed., rev., enl. & illus. by S[ereno]. E[dwards]. Todd. New York: W. Wood & Co. 152+ 9–211+9–166 pp., illus. {Also, Philadelphia [etc.], 1870; New York [etc.], 1873.}

Brincklé, William Draper. 1860. Hoffy's North American Pomologist, Containing Numerous Finely Colored Drawings, Accompanied by Letter Press Descriptions etc. of Fruits of American Origin. William D. Brincklé, etc., ed. Book No. 1. Philadelphia: The Author. Frontis., vi pp.+36 ff. & 36 lith. pls. (col.).

Britten, Nathaniel Lord and Hon. Addison Brown. 1896–1898. An Illustrated Flora of the Northern United States, Canada and the British Possessions from Newfoundland to the Parallel of the Southern Boudary of Virginia, and from the Atlantic Westward to the 102d Meridian. ... The descriptive text chiefly prepared by Professor Britton ... the figures also drawn under his supervision. 3 vols. New York: C. Scribner's Sons. 4163 line illus.

Browne, Daniel Jay. 1832. The Sylva Americana; or, A Description of the Forest Trees Indigenous to the United States, Practically and Botanically Considered. Illustrated by more than one hundred engravings. Boston: W. Hyde & Co. Frontis. & 408 pp., wood-eng. illus.

Browne, Daniel Jay. 1843. The Trees of America, Native and Foreign, Pictorially and Botanically Delineated, and Scientifically and Popularly Described; Being Considered Principally with Reference to Their Geography and History; Soil and Situation; Propagation and Culture [etc.], Illustrated by Numerous Engravings. New York: Harper. xii+520 pp., wood-eng. illus. {Also, New York [etc.], 1844; New York: Harper & Bros., 1846; New York, 1857.}

Bryant, Arthur, Sr. 1871. Forest Trees for Shelter, Ornament, and Profit: A Practical Manual for Their Culture and Propagation. New York: Henry T. Williams. 274 pp. & 12 pls.

Bryant, William Cullen. [1874.] Among the Trees. Illustrated from designs by Jervis McEntee; engraved by Harley. New York: G. P. Putnam's Sons; Boston: Lee & Shepard. Illus. t.p. & 39 pp., 18 wood-eng. illus.

Buist, Robert. 1844. The Rose Manual; Containing Accurate Descriptions of All the Finest Varieties of Roses, Properly Classed in Their Respective

Families, Their Character, and Mode of Culture with Directions for Their Propagation, and the Destruction of Insects [etc.]. Philadelphia: The Author. 182 pp. & 1 pl., illus. {Ed. 3, with additions, Philadelphia: The Author [etc.], 1851. 188 pp., illus.; Ed. 4, with additions, Philadelphia [etc.], 1854; Philadelphia, 1859.}

Buist, Robert. 1847. The Family Kitchen Gardener, Containing Plain and Accurate Descriptions of All the Different Species and Varieties of Culinary Vegetables; with Their Botanical, English, French, and German Names, Alphabetically Arranged, and the Best Mode of Cultivating Them, in the Garden or under Glass; with a Description of Implements and Medicinal Herbs in General Use. Also, Descriptions and Characters of the Most Select Fruits, Their Management, Propagation, and Culture. New York: J. C. Riker. 216 pp., illus. {Also, New York: C. M. Saxton, 1851; ... Illustrated with twenty-five engravings. New York [etc.], 1854; New York: A. O. Moore, 1858.}

Burr, Fearing, Jr. 1863. Field and Garden Vegetables of America; Containing Full Descriptionas of Nearly Eleven Hundred Species and Varieties; with Directions for Propagation, Culture, and Use. Boston: Crosby & Nichols. xv+674, illus. {Also, Boston: J. E. Tilton & Co., 1865.}

Burr, Fearing, Jr. 1866. Garden Vegetables, and How to Cultivate Them. Boston: J. E. Tilton & Co. xii+355 pp., wood-eng. illus.

Bush & Son & Meissner, Nursery. 1875. Illustrated Descriptive Catalogue of American Grape-Vines, with Brief Directions for Their Culture. St. Louis. Frontis. (col.) & [ii]+80 pp., illus. {Ed. 3 as Illustrated Descriptive Catalogue of American Grape Vines: A Grape Growers' Manual. St. Louis, 1883. 153 pp. & 2 chromolith. pls.; Ed. 4, St. Louis [etc.], 1895. Frontis. & [iii]+208 pp., illus.}

California State Vinicultural Association. 1877. Grapes and Grapevines of California. Published under the auspices of The California State Vinicultural Association. Oleographed by Wm. Harring from original water color drawings by Miss Hannah Millard. San Francisco: E. Bosqui & Co. 17 ff. & 10 chromolith. pls.

Campbell, Douglas Houghton. 1889. Lectures on the Evolution of Plants. New York: The Macmillan Co. viii+319 pp., illus.

Campbell, Douglas Houghton. 1890. Elements of Structural and Systematic Botany. Boston: Ginn & Co. ix+253 pp., illus.

Campbell, Douglas Houghton. 1897. A Morphological Study of Naias and Zannichellia. San Francisco: [The University]. 61 pp. & 5 double pls.

Card, Fred Wallace. 1898. Bush-Fruits: A Horticultural Monograph of Raspberries, Blackberries, Dewberries, Currants, Gooseberries, and Other Shrub-Like Fruits. New York: The Macmillan Co. xii+537 pp., illus. [Rural Science Series.]

Carson, Joseph. 1847. Illustrations of Medical Botany, Consisting of Colored Figures of the Plants Affording the Important Articles in Materia Medica, with Descriptive Letterpress. With 100 superb color plates drawn on stone by J. H. Colen. 2 vols., pub. in 5 pts. Philadelphia: R. P. Smith. 100 lith. pls. (col.).

Carter, Sarah C. 1853. Lexicon of Ladies' Names, with Their Floral Emblems: Containing One Hundred and Thirty-Eight Names with Their Significations; also One Hundred and Thirty-Two Flowers with Their Symbolic Language. Boston: J. Buffum. 208 pp. & 6 chromolith. pls.

Church, Ella. 1881. The Home Garden. New York: D. Appleton & Co. 121 pp., many illus. [Appleton's Home Books.]

Church, Ella. [1885.] Flower Talks at Elmridge. Philadelphia: Presbyterian Board of Publication. 320 pp. & 4 pls., illus.

Clarkson, Louise, see Whitelock, Louise Clarkson.

Clute, Willard Nelson. [1901.] Our Ferns in Their Haunts: A Guide to All the Native Species. Illustrated by William Walworth Stilson. New York: F. A. Stokes. xii+332 pp. & 8 3-col. pls., half-tone illus.

Coe, Benjamin Hutchins. 1841. Drawing Book of Trees: Exhibiting the Whole Process of Sketching and Shading the Different Kinds of Foliage in the Most Familiar Manner. Hartford: E. B. & E. C. Kellogg. [4] pp. & 8 lith. pls. {Also, New York: Saxton & Miles, 1843; Boston: Saxton, Pierce & Co., 1843.}

Coe, Benjamin Hutchins. 1853. Coe's New Drawing Lessons, Series 3: Landscapes with Instructions in Foliage. New York: G. P. Putnam. 48 pls.

Cole, Samuel W. 1849. A Book for Every Body. The American Fruit Book; Containing Directions for

Raising, Propagating, and Managing Fruit Trees, Shrubs, and Plants; with a Description of the Best Varieties of Fruit, Including New and Valuable Kinds. Embellished and illustrated with numerous engravings of fruits, trees, insects, grafting, budding, training, &c., &c. Boston: John P. Jewett; New York: C. M. Saxton. Frontis. (double-sided) & 288 pp., many wood-eng. illus. {Another ed. Boston and Cleveland: John P. Jewett and H. P. B. Jewett, 1857.}

Colling, James Kellaway. 1873. Art Foliage, for Sculpture and Decoration; with an Analysis of Geometric Form; and Studies from Nature, of Buds, Leaves, Flowers, and Fruit. First American from the latest English edition. Boston: J. R. Osgood & Co. 3 pts. vi+136 pp. & 72 lith. pls. {Also, Boston, 1877.}

Colling, James Kellaway. 1880. Art Foliage, for Sculpture and Decoration; with an Analysis of Geometric Form; and Studies from Nature, of Buds, Leaves, Flowers, and Fruit. From the latest English edition. Boston: J. R. Osgood & Co. 80 lith. pls.

Comstock, John Lee. 1832. An Introduction to the Study of Botany; in Which the Science is Illustrated by Examples of Native and Exotic Plants, and Explained by Means of Numerous Woodcuts; Designed for the Use of Schools and Private Students. Hartford: D. F. Robinson & Co. 260 pp., wood-eng. illus. {Many eds., e.g., Ed. 2, Hartford [etc.], 1833; Ed. 3, New York: Robinson, Pratt & Co., 1835; Ed. 4, New York [etc.], 1837. 404 pp., illus.; Ed. 5, New York [etc.], 1839; Ed. 15, New York: Pratt, Woodford & Co., 1847; Ed. 25, New York [etc.], 1852; Ed. 32, New York: Pratt, Woodford, Palmer, & Brace, 1854; etc.}

Comstock, John Lee. 1835. The Young Botanist: Being a Treatise on the Science, Prepared for the Use of Persons Just Commencing the Study of Plants. New York: Robinson, Pratt & Co. Frontis. (col.) & x+259 pp., wood-eng. illus. {Ed. 2, New York [etc.], 1836; Ed. 3, New York: Pratt, Woodford, 1850; Ed. 4, New York [etc.], 1851.}

Comstock, John Lee. [1840s.] The Flora Belle; or, Gems from Nature. New York: T. L. Magagnos. Frontis. (col.) & 352 pp. & 8 pls. (col.). {Pls. actually numbered #27–#34, apparently re-used from vol. 2 of The Illustrated Botany.}

Comstock, John Lee, ed. 1847. The Illustrated Botany, see Newman, John B.

[Corsa, William Pinckney, comp.] 1896. Nut Culture in the United States. Embracing Native and Introduced Species. Washington: Department of Agriculture, Division of Pomology. 144 pp. & 16 pls. (2 col.).

Coultas, Harland. 1853. The Principles of Botany, as Exemplified in the Cryptogamia. For the Use of Schools and Colleges. Philadelphia: Lindsay & Blakiston. 94 pp., wood-eng. illus.

Coultas, Harland. 1854. The Principles of Botany, as Exemplified in the Phanerogamia. Philadelphia: King & Bird Printers. 230 pp., wood-eng. illus.

Coultas, Harland. 1855. The Plant: An Illustration of the Organic Life of the Animal. Philadelphia: Perry & Erety. 180 pp., illus.

Coultas, Harland. 1859. What May Be Learned from a Tree. New York: For sale by John Alexander. viii+190 pp. & 5 pls., illus. {Also, New York: D. Appleton & Co., 1860; Ed. 2, New York, 1863.}

Coulter, John Merle. 1899. Plant Relations: A First Book of Botany. New York: D. Appleton & Co. vii+264 pp., line & half-tone illus. [Twentieth Century Text-Books.] {Ed. 2, New York [etc.], 1903.}

Coulter, John Merle. 1900. Plant Structures: A Second Book of Botany. New York: D. Appleton & Co. ix+348 pp., line & half-tone illus. [Twentieth Century Text-Books.]

Coville, Frederick Vernon. 1903. Botany of the Death Valley Expedition. Washington: U.S. Department of Agriculture, Division of Botany, United States National Herbarium. vii+317 pp. & 21 lith. pls. [Contributions from the United States National Herbarium, vol. 4.]

Coxe, William. 1817. A View of the Cultivation of Fruit Trees, and the Management of Orchards and Cider; with Accurate Descriptions of the Most Estimable Varieties of Native and Foreign Apples, Pears, Peaches, Plums, and Cherries, Cultivated in the Middle States of America. Illustrated by cuts of two hundred kinds of fruits of the natural size; intended to explain some of the errors which exist relative to the origin, popular names, and character of many of our fruits; to identify them by accurate descriptions of their properties, and correct delineations of the full size and natural formation of each variety [etc.]. Philadelphia:

Pr. by D. Allinson, for M. Carey & Son. 77 wood-eng. pls. (each with two or more figures).

Creevey, Mrs. Caroline Alathea (Stickney). 1893. Recreations in Botany. New York: Harper & Bros. xiii+216 pp. & 10 eng. pls., 61 illus.

Creevey, Mrs. Caroline Alathea (Stickney). 1897. Flowers of Field, Hill, and Swamp. Illustrated by Benjamin Lander. New York: Harper & Bros. Frontis. & viii+568 pp., illus.

Dame, Lorin Low. 1890. Typical Elms and Other Trees of Massachusetts. Introductory chapter by Oliver Wendell Holmes. Plates by Henry Brooks. Boston: Little, Brown & Co. 89 pp. & 58 collotype pls.

Dame, Lorin Low and Henry Brooks. 1902. Handbook of the Trees of New England, with Ranges throughout the United States and Canada. Plates from original drawings by Elizabeth G. Bigelow. Boston: Ginn & Co. xv+196 pp., incl. 86 pls.

Dana, Mrs. William Starr. 1893. How to Know the Wild Flowers: A Guide to the Names, Haunts, and Habits of Our Common Wild Flowers. Illustrated by Marion Satterlee. New York: C. Scribner's Sons. xv+298 pp., incl. 158 line pls., (some col.). {Rev. & enl. ed., 39th thousand, New York [etc.], 1898. xvii+373 pp., illus.; New ed., New York [etc.], 1900. 158 pls., (some col.).}

Dana, Mrs. William Starr. 1902. According to Season: Talks about Flowers in the Order of Their Appearance in the Woods and Fields. New & enl. ed. With thirty-two plates in color by Elsie Louise Shaw. New York: C. Scribner's Sons. Frontis. (col.) & xiv+197 pp. & 31 pls. (col.). {Ed. 1, 1894, not illustrated.}

Darby, John. 1841. A Manual of Botany, Adapted to the Productions of the Southern States; in Two Parts: Part I: Vegetable Anatomy and Physiology; Part II: Descriptive Botany, Arranged on the Natural System, Preceded by an Analysis. Macon: Benjamin F. Griffin. 156+xx+344 pp., wood-eng. illus. {Also, Savannah, 1847.}

Darby, John. 1855. Botany of the Southern States; in Two Parts [etc.]: Part 1: Structural and Physiological Botany and Vegetable Products; Part 2: Descriptions of Southern Plants; Arranged on the Natural System; Preceded by a Linnaean and Dicotomous Analysis. New York: A. S. Barnes & Co.; Cincinnati: H. W. Derby; Savannah: John M. Cooper. 612 pp., wood-eng.

illus. {Also, 1856; 1857; New York [etc.], 1885. 612 pp., illus.}

Darlington, E. Dillwyn. 1888. How and What to Grow in a Kitchen Garden of One Acre. Philadelphia: W. A. Burpee & Co. 198 pp., illus.

Darlington, E. Dillwyn. 1895. Rare Flowers from Seed; How to Grow Tuberous Begonias, Calceolarias, Cinerarias, Chinese Primroses, Coleus, Cyclamens, Single and Double Petunias, Fuchsias, and Other Rare Flowers. Philadelphia: W. A. Burpee & Co. 37 pp., illus. {Ed. 8, Philadelphia, 1898. 37 pp., ? illus.}

Darlington, William. 1826. Florula Cestrica: An Essay towards a Catalogue of the Phaenogamous Plants, Native and Naturalized, Growing in the Vicinity of the Borough of West-Chester, in Chester County, Pennsylvania: With Brief Notices of Their Properties, and Uses, in Medicine, Rural Economy, and the Arts. To Which is Subjoined an Appendix of the Useful Cultivated Plants of the Same District. West-Chester: Pr. for the Author by S. Siegfried. xv+152 pp. & 3 eng. pls. (col.).

Darlington, William. [1859.] American Weeds and Useful Plants: Being a Second and Illustrated Edition of Agricultural Botany: An Enumeration and Description [etc.]. Rev., with additions, by George Thurber. New York: A. O. Moore & Co. Frontis., xvi+460 pp., 277 wood-eng. illus. {Also, New York, 1869; New York: Orange Judd & Co., 1879.}

Darwin, Erasmus. 1798. The Botanic Garden. A Poem, in Two Parts. Part I. Containing the Economy of Vegetation. Part II. The Loves of the Plants. With Philosophical Notes, American ed. 1. New York. [15]+viii–xi+[5]+256+x+12–146 pp. & 17 eng. pls. (some botanical). {American ed. 2, New York, 1807. 2 vols. 22 eng. pls.}

Davis, Lucius Daniel. 1899. Ornamental Shrubs for Garden, Lawn, and Park Planting with an Account of the Origin, Capabilities, and Adaptations of the Numerous Species and Varieties, Native and Foreign, and Especially of the New and Rare Sorts, Suited to Cultivation in the United States. New York: G. P. Putnam's Sons, The Knickerbocker Press. vi+338 pp., wood-eng., line & half-tone illus.

Deane, Fannie A. [1891.] National Flowers. Boston: D. Lothrop Co. Frontis. & 28 pp., illus.

Delmès, L. F. [1850s.] Collection of Flowers, Coloured. Drawn from nature by L. F. Delmès;

for the use of schools and amateurs. Philadelphia: Sold by L. F. Delmès, & Mrs. Cantelo's Corset Shop. 3? pts. 10 pls.

De Longpré, Paul. 1897. Facsimiles of Watercolors. New York: Frederick A. Stokes Co. 18 ff & 18 pls.(col.).

Dinnies, Mrs. Anna Peyre. 1847. The Floral Year. Embellished with bouquets of flowers drawn and colored from nature. Illustrated. Boston: B. B. Mussey. T.p., 256 pp. & 12 chromolith. pls.

Dix, Dorothea Lynde. 1829. The Garland of Flora. Boston: S. G. Goodrich & Co., & Carter & Hendee. Frontis. & 188 pp.

Downing, Andrew Jackson. 1845. The Fruits and Fruit Trees of America; or, The Culture, Propagation, and Management, in Garden and Orchard, of Fruit Trees Generally; with Descriptions of All the Finest Varieties of Fruit, Native and Foreign, Cultivated in this Country. Illustrated with many engravings. New York and London: Wiley & Putnam. xix+594 pp., wood-eng. illus. {Also, New York [etc.], 1846; ... Illustrated with colored engravings. New York: J. Wiley, 1847. (N.B., the 70 lith. pls. (col.) were drawn, printed and col. in Paris.) Wood-eng. illus.; Ed. 8, rev., New York & London: Wiley & Putnam, 1848. xiv+594 pp., illus.; Rev. & corr. by Charles Downing. New York: Wiley & Halsted, 1857. xix+760 pp.; 2nd revision & correction, with large additions, by Charles Downing. New York: J. Wiley & Son, 1869. xxiv+1008 pp.}

Downing, Andrew Jackson. 1859. A Treatise on the Theory and Practice of Landscape Gardening, Adapted to North America, with a View to the Improvement of Country Residences [etc.], ed. 6, enl., rev., and newly illustrated. With a supplement, containing some remarks about country places, and the best methods of making them; also, an account of the newer deciduous and evergreen plants, lately introduced into cultivation, both hardy and half-hardy, by Henry Winthrop Sargent. New York: A. O. Moore & Co. 576 pp., 51 lith. pls. (col.).; 11+3 wood-eng. illus. {Ed. 7, enl., rev. and newly illustrated. With a supplement [etc.]. New York: Orange Judd, 1865; New ed., New York [etc.], [1875].}

Doyle, Martin [i.e., William Hickey.] 1835. The Flower Garden; or, Monthly Calendar of

Practical Directions for the Cultivation of Flowers. By Martin Doyle [pseud.]. First American edition. Adapted to the climate of the United States, with notes and observations by L. D. Gale [etc.]. New York: Moore & Payne. 180 pp. & 4 lith. pls. (col.).

Draper, John William. 1844. A Treatise on the Forces Which Produce the Organization of Plants. With an Appendix, Containing Several Memoirs on Capillary Attraction, Electricity, and the Chemical Action of Light. New York: Harper & Bros. Frontis. (col.), xvi+108+216 pp. & 3 pls. {Also, New York, [etc.], 1845.}

Dreer, Henry A. 1897. Dreer's Grasses and Clovers. Philadelphia: H. A. Dreer. 121 pp., illus.

Dreer, Henry A. 1897. Dreer's Open-Air Vegetables. Philadelphia: H. A. Dreer. 148 pp., illus.

Dumont, Henrietta. 1851. The Language of Flowers: The Floral Offering: A Token of Affection and Esteem; Comprising the Language and Poetry of Flowers [etc.]. Philadelphia: H. C. Peck & Theo Bliss. Frontis. (col.) & 300 pp. & 5 lith. pls. (col.). {Re-pub. as, The Floral Offering: A Token of Affection and Esteem; Comprising the Language and Poetry of Flowers [etc.]. Philadelphia [etc.], 1862. 6 pls.; Philadelphia [etc.], 1856; Philadelphia, 1860.}

Dunning, M. O. B., see Lorimer, Mary.

Durand, Elias and Theodore Charles Hilgard. 1856 [1858]. Botanical report. Report of explorations in California for railroad routes, to connect with the routes near the 35th and 32nd parallels of north latitude by Lieutenant R. S. Williamson, ... 1853. In: U.S. War Department. 1855–1860. Reports of Explorations and Surveys, to Ascertain the Most Practicable and Economical Route for a Railroad Route from the Mississippi River to the Pacific Ocean. Made under the Direction of the Secretary of War, in 1853–[1856]. 12 vols. in 13. Washington: B. Tucker. Vol. 5. 18 lith. pls.

Eastman, Mrs. Elaine and Dora Read Goodale. 1879–1880. In Berkshire with the Wild Flowers. By Elaine and Dora Read Goodale. New York: G. P. Putnam's Sons. 92 pp., 24 illus.

Eastwood, B. 1856. A Complete Manual for the Cultivation of the Cranberry, with a Description of the Best Varieties. New York: C. M. Saxton & Co. 120 pp. & 10 lith. pls. {Also, New York: C. M. Saxton, Barker & Co., 1860; New York: Orange Judd & Co., 1865.}

Eaton, Daniel Cady. 1878–1880. The Ferns of North America. Colored Figures and Descriptions, with Synonymy and Distributions of the Ferns (Including the Ophioglossaceae) of the United States of America and the British North American Possessions. The drawings by J[ames]. H[enry]. Emerton and C[harles]. E[dward]. Faxon. 2 vols. (Pt. 1, Lond., Hardwick, 1878); Salem, Boston: S. E. Cassino, 1879–1880. 81 chromolith. pls. {Also, Boston [etc.], 1882; Boston: Bradlee Whidden, 1893; Troy: Nims & Knight, 1887.}

Eaton, Daniel Cady. 1882. Beautiful Ferns. From original water color drawings after nature, by C. E. Faxon and J. H. Emerton. Descriptive text by [etc.], Professor of Botany in Yale College. Boston: S. E. Cassino. 19 chromolith. pls. {Also, Troy: Nims & Knight, 1887. 10 chromolith. pls.}

Eaton, Daniel Cady. 1884. American Wild Flowers and Ferns. Boston: D. Lothrop Co. 24 chromolith. pls.

Eley, James Norman. 1845. The American Florist; or, A Guide to the Management and Cultivation of Plants in Conservatories, Greenhouses, Rooms, and Gardens; to Which Are Added, Directions for the Culture of Annual, Biennial, and Perennial Flowers, Trees, Shrubs, Bulbs, etc., etc. Hartford: Pr. by E. Geer. 183 pp., some illus.

Elliott, Franklin Reuben. 1854. Elliott's Fruit Book; or, The American Fruit-Grower's Guide in Orchard and Garden. Being a Compend of the History, Modes of Propagation, Culture, &c. of Fruit Trees and Shrubs, with Descriptions of Nearly all the Varieties of Fruits Cultivated in this Country: Notes of Their Adaptation to Localities and Soils, and also a Complete List of Fruits Worthy of Cultivation. New York: C. M. Saxton. 503 pp., illus. {Also, New York [etc.], 1855; New York [etc.], 1856. Re-issued as, The Western Fruit Book; or, The American Fruit-Grower's Guide for the Orchard and Fruit Garden: [etc.]. New York: A. O. Moore & Co., 1859. 528 pp., illus.; New York: Orange Judd Co., n.d.; Ed. 4, New York [etc.], 1856; Ed. 4, rev., enl. & improv, New York: A. O. Moore & Co., 1859.}

Elliott, Franklin Reuben. 1868. Popular Deciduous Evergreen Trees and Shrubs, for Planting in Parks, Gardens, Cemeteries, etcs. New York: F. W. Woodward. 125 pp., 64 wood-eng. illus.

Elliott, Franklin Reuben. 1876. Hand-Book for Fruit Growers. Rochester: D. M. Dewey. 128 pp., illus.

Elliott, Stephen. [1816–]1821–1824. A Sketch of the Botany of South-Carolina and Georgia. In two volumes. 2 vols. Pub. in 13 pts. Charleston: J. R. Schenk. 12 eng. pls.

Ellis, Job Bricknell and Benjamin Matlack Everhart. 1892. The North American Pyrenomycetes. A Contribution to Mycologic Botany. With original illustrations by F. W. Anderson. Newfield: Ellis & Everhart. iii+793 pp. & 41 pls. (col.).

Embury, Mrs. Emma Catherine Manley. 1845. American Wild Flowers in Their Native Haunts. With twenty plates of plants, carefully colored after nature; and landscape views of their localities, from drawings on the spot by E[dwin]. Whitefield. New York: D. Appleton & Co.; Philadelphia: G. S. Appleton. Illus. t.p., 256 pp. & 19 lith. pls. (col.). {Ed. 2, New York [etc.], 1845.}

Embury, Mrs. Emma Catherine Manley. 1846. Love's Token-Flowers. New York: J. C. Riker. 128 pp., 1 pl., illus.

[Emerson, George Barrell.] 1846. A Report on the Trees and Shrubs Growing Naturally in the Forests of Massachusetts. Published agreeably to an order of the Legislature, by the Commissioners on the Zoological and Botanical Survey of the State. Boston: Dutton & Wentworth, State Printers. xv+547 pp. & 17 pls. {Also, Boston: Little & Brown, 1850; Ed. 2, Boston, 1875. 2 vols., xxxii+624 pp. & 149 (i.e., 147) pls. (incl. 35 chromolith. pls.); Ed. 3, Boston: Little, Brown & Co., 1878; Ed. 4, Boston, 1887. 2 vols.}

Emmons, Ebenezer. 1849. Natural History of New York. Part V. Agriculture of New York. Vol. II. Containing Analyses of Plants, Food of Cattle, Leguminous Plants, Exculent Vegetables, Miscellaneous Analyses, and Fruit and Forest Trees. Albany. viii+343+50 pp. & 42 pls. (some col.).

Emmons, Ebenezer. 1851. Natural History of New York. Part V. Agriculture of New York. Vol. III. Containing Chapters on the Fruit of the State, Varieties of Apples, General Remarks on Pears, the Quince, the Peach, the Plum, the Cherry, the Grape, Gooseberries, the Currant, the Raspberry, Theoretical and Practical Husbandry, the Food of Animals, and Cultivation of Fruit Trees and Fruit. 2 vols. Albany. 81 pls. (col.).

Engelmann, George and J. M. Bigelow. 1856. Description of the cactaceae. Route near the thirty-fifth parallel, explored by Lieutenant A. W. Whipple, ... in 1853 and 1854. Report of the botany of the expedition. In: U.S. War Department. 1855–1860. Reports of Explorations and Surveys, to Ascertain the Most Practicable and Economical Route for a Railroad Route from the Mississippi River to the Pacific Ocean. Made under the Direction of the Secretary of War, in 1853–[1856]. 12 vols. in 13. Washington. Vol. IV, no. 3. 24 lith. pls.

Engelmann, George. 1859. Cactaceae of the boundary. In: W. H. Emory et al. 1857–1859. Report on the United States and Mexican Boundary Survey, Made under the Direction of the Secretary of the Interior, by William H. Emory, Major [etc.]. 2 vols. in 3. Washington: C. Wendell. Vol. II. 76 lith. pls. [34th Congress, 1st Session, House of Representatives, Ex. Doc. no. 135.]

Engelmann, George. 1887. Botanical Works, Collected for Henry Shaw. William Trelease and Asa Gray, eds. Cambridge: Wilson. 102 lith. pls. (Including reprints of the 75 original plates from his 1859 Cactaceae).

Esling, Catharine Harbeson Waterman. 1839. Flora's Lexicon. An Interpretation of the Language and Sentiment of Flowers: With an Outline of Botany and a Poetical Introduction. Philadelphia: Hooker & Claxton. 252 pp., & 4 lith. pls. (col.). {Also, Philadelphia: H. Hooker, 1840. 252 pp. & 4 pls.; Philadelphia: Hooker & Agnew, 1841; Philadelphia [etc.], 1842; Boston, 1858. 4 chromolith. pls.}

Fernald, Charles Henry. 1885. Grasses of Maine. Designed for the Use of Students of the Maine State College, and the Farmers of the State. C. D. Fernald, Orono, May, 1885. Augusta: Sprague & Son. 70 pp. & 42 pls.

Field, Thomas Warren. 1858. Pear Culture: A Manual for the Propagation, Planting, Cultivation, and Management of the Pear Tree. With Descriptions and Illustrations of the Most Productive of the Finer Varieties, and Selections of Kinds Most Profitably Grown for Market. New York: A. O. Moore. Frontis. & 286 pp., 115 wood-eng. illus. {Also, 1859.}

Flagg, Wilson. 1872. The Woods and By-Ways of New England. Boston: James R. Osgood & Co. xviii+442 pp. & 22 heliotype pls.

Flagg, Wilson. 1881. A Year Among the Trees; or, The Woods and By-Ways of New England. Boston: Estes & Lauriat. xvii+335 pp., illus. {Also, Boston: Educational Publishing Co., [1889]; Boston, 1890. [vi]+308 pp., illus. An abridged version of his The Woods and By-Ways of New England.}

Flint, Charles Louis. 1857. A Practical Treatise on Grasses and Forage Plants, Comprising Their Natural History, Comparative Nutritive Value, Methods of Cultivation, Cutting, and Curing; and the Management of Grass Lands. New York: G. P. Putnam & Co., [etc.]. Frontis., iv+236 pp., illus. {Ed. 2, New York [etc.], 1858.}

Flint, Charles Louis. 1859. Grasses and Forage Plants. A Practical Treatise, Comprising Their Natural History; Comparative Nutritive Value; Methods of Cultivation, Cutting, and Curing; and the Management of Grass Lands in the United States and British Provinces, ed. 4, rev. & enl. With one hundred and seventy illustrations. Boston: Phillips, Sampson. Frontis., viii+398 pp., & pls. {Ed. 5, rev. & enl., Boston: Crosby, Nichols, Lee & Co., 1860; Ed. 6, Boston, 1864; Boston: J. E. Tilton & Co., 1867; Rev. ed., Boston: Lee & Shepard, 1888. Frontis. & 398 pp., illus.}

Forsyth, William. 1803. A Treatise on the Culture and Management of Fruit Trees; in Which a New Method of Pruning and Training Is Fully Described. Together with Observations on the Diseases, Defects and Injuries in All Kinds of Fruit and Forest Trees, as also, an Account of a Particular Method of Cure, Made Public by Order of the British Government. To Which Are Added, an Introduction and Notes, Adapting the Rules of the Treatise to the Climates and Seasons of the United States of America. By William Cobbett. Albany: Pr. for & sold by D. & S. Whiting, at the Albany Bookstore; Boston [etc.]. 13 eng. pls.

Forsyth, William. 1803. An Epitome of Mr. Forsyth's Treatise on the Culture and Management of Fruit Trees. Also Notes on American Gardening and Fruits; with Designs for Promoting the Ripening of Fruits, and Securing Them as Family Comforts: And Further, of Economical Principles in Building Farmers' Habitations. By

An American Farmer. Philadelphia: John Morgan. 13 eng. pls. (Same plates as in preceding.) {Also, Philadelphia, 1804.}

[Francia, François Louis T.] 1818. A Series of Progressive Lessons, Intended to Elucidate the Art of Flower Painting in Water Colours. Philadelphia: M. Thomas. 32 pp. & 12 aquat. pl. (10 col.). {Cover title: Art of Flower Painting in Water Colours. Aquatinted, Printed, and Coloured by J. Hill. (First published in London by T. Clay in 1815, and re-published anonymously in America; this cover title misled many libraries into ascribing authorship to John Hill.) Also, Philadelphia: Thomas Desilver, 1820; New ed., Philadelphia [etc.], 1835; Philadelphia: Desilver, Thomas & Co., 1836.}

Frémont, Brevet Capt. J. C. and John Torrey. 1845. Report on the plants. In: Report of the Exploring Expedition to the Rocky Mountains in the Year 1842, and to Oregon and Northern California in the Years 1843–44, under the Orders of Col. J. J. Abert, Chief of the Topographical Bureau. Printed by order of the Senate of the United States. Washington: Blair & Rives, Printers. 4 (botanical) lith. pls.

Fuller, Andrew Samuel. 1862. The Illustrated Strawberry Culturist; Containing the History, Sexuality, Field and Garden Culture of Strawberries, Forcing or Pot Culture, How to Grow from Seed, Hybridizing, Results of Extensive Experiments with Seedlings ... With Receipts for Different Modes of Preserving, Cooking, and Preparing Strawberries for the Table. New York: Orange Judd & Co. Frontis. & 48 pp., illus. {Also, New York [etc.], 1867. 55 pp., 16 illus.}

Fuller, Andrew Samuel. 1864. The Grape Culturist: A Treatise on the Cultivation of the Native Grape. New York: For the Author, by Davies & Kent. 262 pp., 105 wood-eng. illus. {New & enl. ed., New York: Orange Judd & Co., 1867. vi+286 pp., illus.}

Fuller, Andrew Samuel. 1866. The Forest Tree Culturist: A Treatise on the Cultivation of American Forest Trees, with Notes on the Most Valuable Foreign Species. New York: G. E. & F. W. Woodward. 188 pp., 50 wood-eng. illus.

Fuller, Andrew Samuel. [1867.] The Small Fruit Culturist. New York: Orange Judd Co. 276 pp., 117 wood-eng. illus. {New, re-written & enl. ed., beautifully illustrated, New York [etc.], 1881;

New York [etc.], 1885; With an appendix, New York [etc.], 1887. 297 pp., 125 illus.}

Fuller, Andrew Samuel. [1884.] Practical Forestry: A Treatise on the Propagation, Planting, and Cultivation, with a Description, and the Popular Names of All the Indigenous Trees of the United States. New York: Orange Judd Co. 299 pp., illus.

Fuller, Andrew Samuel. 1887. The Illustrated Strawberry Culturist. New York: Orange Judd & Co. 59 pp., illus.

Fuller, Andrew Samuel. 1896. The Nut Culturist: A Treatise on the Propagation, Planting and Cultivation of Nut-Bearing Trees and Shrubs Adapted to the Climate of the United States, with the Scientific and Common Names of the Fruits Known in Commerce as Edible or Otherwise Useful Nuts. New York: Orange Judd & Co. viii+289 pp., port., illus.

Fulton, James Alexander. [1870.] Peach Culture. New York: Orange Judd & Co. 190 pp., 29 illus. {New, rev. & enl. ed., New York [etc.], 1882; New, rev. & greatly enl. ed., New York [etc.], 1889. 204 pp., 29 illus.}

Gibson, William Hamilton. 1887. Happy Hunting-Grounds: A Tribute to the Woods and Fields. Illustrated by the author. New York: Harper & Bros. 202 pp., wood-eng. illus.

Gibson, William Hamilton. 1895. Our Edible Toadstools and Mushrooms and How to Distinguish Them. A Selection of Thirty Native Food Varieties Easily Recognizable by Their Marked Individualities, with Simple Rules for the Identification of Poisonous Species, With thirty colored plates, and fifty-seven other illustrations by the Author. New York: Harper & Bros. x+337 pp. & 37 lith. pls. (30 col.). {Also, New York [etc.], 1899; New York [etc.], 1903.}

Goadby, Henry. 1858. A Text-Book of Vegetable and Animal Physiology. Designed for the Use of Schools, Seminaries, and Colleges in the United States. New York: D. Appleton & Co. xxxix+313 pp., illus. (part col.). {Also, New York [etc.], 1859.}

Going, Ellen Maud. [1894.] With the Flowers from Pussy-Willow to Thistledown: A Rural Chronicle of Our Flower Friends and Foes, Describing Them under Their Familiar English Names. By E. M. Hardinge [pseud.]. New York: The Baker & Taylor Co. xii+271 pp. & pls., illus. {Rev. ed., illustrated with many line and half-tone engravings, New York: The Baker & Taylor Co., [c1901]. xiv+271 pp., illus. ["Originally published, for the most part, in Demorest's Family Magazine and the New York Evening Post."]}

Going, Ellen Maud. [1903.] Field, Forest, and Wayside Flowers; with Chapters on Grasses, Sedges, and Ferns. Untechnical Studies for Unlearned Lovers of Nature. Illustrated in part with drawings from life by S. G. Porter and photographs by Edwin H. Lincoln. New York: The Baker & Taylor Co. 411 pp. & pls., illus.

Going, Ellen Maud. [1903.] With the Trees. Illustrated from photographs by Edwin H. Lincoln and C. B. Going. New York: The Baker & Taylor Co. x+335 pp., illus.

Good, Peter Peyto. [1845–1854.] Family Flora & Materia Medica Botanica, Containing the Botanical Analysis, Natural History and Medical Properties of Plants. Illustrated by colored engravings of original drawings copied from nature. 2 vols. Pub. in 96 quarterly pts. Elizabethtown: The Author. 98 lith. pls. (col.). (i.e., pls. 1–96, 99–100). {Also, New York: The Author, 1845+; also pub. as: Materia Medica Botanica, Containing the Botanical Analysis, Natural History and Medical Properties of Plants. Illustrated by colored engravings of original drawings copied from nature. New York: J. K. Wellman, 1845. 2 vols.; Elizabethtown, 1847; Cambridge, 1854.}

Goodale, George Lincoln. [1876–]1882. The Wild Flowers of America. With fifty colored plates, from original drawings by Isaac Sprague. Text by ..., M.D., Professor of Botany in Harvard University. Boston: S. E. Cassino. 25 pts. 50 chromolith. pls. {Boston: H. O. Houghton & Co. [etc.], c1876–1877. 2 vols.; Boston: Bradlee Whidden, 1886 [or later]. iv+210 pp. & 51 chromolith. pls.}

Goodale, George Lincoln. 1885. Physiological Botany; I. Outlines of the Histology of Phaenogamous Plants; II. Vegetable Physiology. New York: Ivison, Blakeman, Taylor. vii+194 pp., line illus. [Gray's Botanical Textbook, ed. 6. Vol. II.] {Also, New York: Cincinnati [etc.], American Book Co., [1885].}

Goodrich, Samuel Griswold, see Parley, Peter.

Graham, Mrs. Elizabeth Turner. 1884. Buttercups & Daisies. Baltimore: D. W. Glass & Co. 2 pp. & pls. (col.).

Graham, Mrs. Elizabeth Turner. [1885.] Holly & Mistletoe. Songs across the Snow. Companion to Buttercups and Daisies. Written and illustrated by E. T. G. Baltimore: D. W. Glass & Co. 37 pp. & 7 pls. & 3 vign.

Grandville, J.-J. [i.e., Jean Ignace Isidore Gerard.] 1847–1849. The Flowers Personified. Being a translation of Grandville's "Les Fleurs Animées" by N. Cleaveland, Esq. Illustrated with steel engravings beautifully colored. 2 vols. Pub. in 9 pts. New York: R. Martin. 52 eng. pls. (col.). {Also, New York: Johnson, Fry & Co., c1847. 2 vols.}

Gray, Asa. Textbooks:

Gray, Asa. 1836. Elements of Botany. New York: G. & C. Carvill & Co. xiv+428 pp., wood-eng. illus.

Gray, Asa. 1842. The Botanical Text-Book for Colleges, Schools, and Private Students: Comprising Part I. An Introduction to Structural and Physiological Botany. Part II. The Principles of Systematic Botany; with an Account of the Chief Natural Families of the Vegetable Kingdom [etc.]. New York: Wiley & Putnam; Boston: Little & Brown. 413 pp., wood-eng. illus. {"The illustrations of this volume were drawn on wood by Miss Agnes Mitchell, and engraved by Mr. J. J. Butler." A revised ed. of Elements of Botany. Also, New York: Wiley, 1843; Ed. 2, Illustrated with more than a thousand engravings on wood, New York: Wiley & Putnam; Boston: Little & Brown, 1845; Ed. 3, rewritten & enl. Illus. with twelve hundred engravings in wood. New York: George P. Putnam, 1850. 520 pp., 1,200 illus.}

Gray, Asa. 1857. First Lessons in Botany and Vegetable Physiology. Illustrated by over 360 wood engravings from original drawings, by Isaac Sprague. To which is added a copious glossary, or dictionary of botanic terms. New York: G. P. Putnam & Co., and Ivison & Phinney. Wood-eng. illus. {Also, New York: G. P. Putnam & Co., 1858. xii+236 pp., illus.; Ed. 2, New York: Ivison & Phinney; Chicago: S. C. Griggs & Co., 1859; New York [etc.], 1862; New York [etc.], 1864; New York [etc.], 1866.}

Gray, Asa. 1858. Botany for Young People and Common Schools: How Plants Grow, a Simple Introduction to Structural Botany; with a Popular Flora, or an Arrangement and Description of Common Plants, Both Wild and Cultivated. Illus. by 500 wood engravings. New

York: Ivison, Blakeman, Taylor & Co. 237 pp., wood-eng. illus. {Spine title: How Plants Grow. Also, New York: Ivison & Phinney, 1858; New York: American Book Co., 1858; Ed. 3, New York: Ivison & Phinney, 1859; Ed. 5, New York [etc.], 1860; New York: Ivison, Phinney, Blakeman & Co.; Chicago: S. C. Griggs & Co., 1868; New York [etc.], 1869; New York, Cincinnati, [etc.]: American Book Co., [1900]. 46 pp., illus.}

Gray, Asa. 1858. Introduction to Structural and Systematic Botany, and Vegetable Physiology. Being a 5th & rev. ed. of The Botanical Textbook. Illus. with over thirteen hundred woodcuts. New York: Ivison and Phinney; Chicago: S. C. Griggs & Co. 555 pp., wood-eng. illus. {Also, New York: Ivison, Phinney, Blakeman & Co., 1869; New York and Chicago: Ivison, Blakeman, Taylor & Co., 1876.}

Gray, Asa. 1868. Gray's Lessons in Botany and Vegetable Physiology. Illustrated by over 360 wood engravings from original drawings. By Isaac Sprague. To which is added a copious glossary, or dictionary of botanic terms. New York and Chicago: Ivison, Blakeman, Taylor & Co. xii+236 pp., illus. {Also, New York [etc.], 1870; New York [etc.], 1875; New York [etc.], 1876; New York [etc.], 1878; New York and Chicago [etc.], 1879. xii+236 pp., illus.; Issued as an introduction to Gray's Manual [etc.], ed. 5, 8th issue, New York and Chicago, 1879, the two volumes in one, titled Gray's New Lessons and Manual of Botany.}

Gray, Asa. 1868. Gray's School and Field Book of Botany; Consisting of "First Lessons in Botany" and "Field, Forest, and Garden Botany"; Bound in One Volume. New York: Ivison, Blakeman, Taylor & Co. 2 pts. (each with it's part title). Wood-eng. illus. {Also, New York: Ivison, Phinney, Blakeman & Co.; Chicago: S. C. Griggs & Co., 1869; New York: Ivison, Blakeman, Taylor & Co., 1879.}

Gray, Asa. [1872.] Botany for Young People. Part II. How Plants Behave: How They Move, Climb, Employ Insects to Work for Them, &c. New York and Chicago: Ivison, Blakeman, Taylor & Co. Wood-eng. illus. [Gray's Botanical Series.] {Also, New York and Chicago: Ivison, Blakeman, Taylor & Co., 1875.}

Gray, Asa. [1879.] Structural Botany; or, Organography on the Basis of Morphology. To Which Is Added the Principles of Taxonomy and Phytography, and a Glossary of Botanical Terms. New York, Cincinnati [etc.]: American Book Co. 442 pp., wood-eng. illus. [Gray's Botanical Textbook, ed. 6, vol. 1.]

Gray, Asa. 1887. The Elements of Botany for Beginners and for Schools. New York: Chicago, Ivison, Blakeman & Co. 226 pp., illus. {"Takes the place of the author's Lessons in Botany and Vegetable Physiology and is a kind of new and much revised edition of that ... work." Preface. Also, New York: Chicago, Ivison, Blakeman & Co., [1890].}

Manual:

Gray, Asa. 1856. A Manual of the Botany of the Northern United States, ed. 2. Including Virginia, Kentucky, and All East of the Mississippi: Arranged According to the Natural System. (The mosses and liverworts by William Starling Sullivant.) With fourteen plates, illustrating the genera of the Cryptogamia. New York: G. P. Putnam & Co. xviii+739 pp. & 14 eng. pls. {Ed. 1 was not illustrated. Later eds. appeared in many issues, sometimes combined with his Lessons in Botany, including, Rev. ed. [3], With fourteen plates illustrating the genera of the Cryptogamia. New York: Ivison & Phinney, 1859. xxviii+739 pp. & 14 lith. pls.; Rev. ed. [3], (School & college ed.) With six plates illustrating the genera of ferns, etc. New York: Ivison, Phinney & Co, 1862. 606 pp. & 6 lith. pls.; Ed. 4 rev., To Which Is Added Garden Botany, an Introduction to the Knowledge of the Common Cultivated Plants. With twenty-two plates, illustrating the genera of the grasses, ferns, mosses, etc. New York: Ivison, Phinney, & Co.; Chicago: S. C. Griggs & Co., 1863. i–xviii, xviiia–xviiid, xxix–ci+743 pp. & 14+8 lith. pls.; Ed. 5, With twenty plates, illustrating the sedges, grasses, ferns, etc. New York: Ivison, Blakeman, Taylor & Co., [1867]. 703 pp. & 20 lith. pls.; Ed. 6, Rev. & extended westward to the 100th meridian, by Sereno Watson & John M[erle]. Coulter. With twenty-five plates, illustrating the sedges, grasses, ferns, etc. New York and Chicago: Ivison, Blakeman & Co., 1890. [iii]+760 pp. & 25 pls.}

Scientific works:

Gray, Asa. [1846.] 1848. Chloris Boreali-Americana. Illustrations of New, Rare, or Otherwise Interesting North American Plants, Selected

Chiefly from Those Recently Brought into Cultivation at the Botanic Garden of Harvard University. Decade I. Cambridge: Metcalf & Co. 10 lith. pls. (8 col.). [Memoirs of the American Academy of Arts and Sciences, n.s., vol. 3.]

Gray, Asa. 1848–1849. Genera Florae Americe Boreali-Orientalis Illustrata. The Genera of the Plants of the United States, Illustrated by Figures and Analyses from Nature. By Isaac Sprague ... Superintended, and with descriptions, &c. by Asa Gray. 2 vols. Boston: J. Munroe & Co.; New York: John Wiley; New York: Wiley & Putnam (vol. 2). 186 lith. pls.

Gray, Asa. 1852–1853. Plantae Wrightianae. Texano-Neo Mexicanae. An Account of a Collection of Plants Made by Chas. Wright, A.M., in an Expedition from Texas to New Mexico in the Summer and Autumn of 1849, with Critical Notes and Characters of Other New or Interesting Plants from Adjacent Regions, &c. Washington: Smithsonian Institution. 14 lith. pls. [Smithsonian Contributions to Knowledge, vol. 3, art. 5, 1852; vol. 5, art. 6, 1853.]

Gray, Asa. 1854–1857. Botany. Phanerogamia. With a folio atlas of one hundred plates. In: Charles Wilkes et al. 1845–1876. United States Exploring Expedition. During the Years 1838, 1839, 1840, 1841, 1842. Under the Command of Charles Wilkes, U.S.N. 19 vols. Philadelphia: C. Sherman. Vol. 14. 100 eng. pls.

Gray, Asa. 1891. Plates Prepared between the Years 1849 and 1850, to Accompany a Report on The Forest Trees of North America. [By Isaac Sprague.] Washington: Smithsonian Institution. 4 pp. & 23 lith. pls. (col.).

Green, Charles A. [1885.] How to Propagate and Grow Fruit. [Rochester: Union & Adv. Co.'s Print.]. 64 pp. & 2 pls. (col.).

Green, Frances Harriett Whipple and Joseph Whipple Congdon. 1855. Analytical Class-Book of Botany, Designed for Academies and Private Students. In two parts. Part I. Elements of Vegetable Structure and Physiology. By Frances H. Green. Part II. Systematic Botany: Illustrated by a Compendious Flora of the Northern States. By Joseph W. Congdon. New York and London: D. Appleton & Co. vi+228 pp., wood-eng. illus. {Also, New York [etc.], 1857. vi+228 pp., illus.}

Green, Samuel. 1894. Amateur Fruit Growing. A Practical Guide to the Growing of Fruit for Home Use and the Market. Written with Special Reference to Colder Climates. Minneapolis: Farm, Stock & Home Publishing Co. 138 pp., 107 illus.

Green, Samuel. 1896. Vegetable Gardening: A Manual on the Growing of Vegetables for Home Use and Marketing. Prepared Especially for the Classes of the School of Agriculture of the University of Minnesota. St. Paul: Webb Publishing Co. 224 pp., illus.

Greene, Edward Lee. 1889–1890. Illustrations of West American Oaks. From drawings by the late Albert Kellogg, M.D. The text by Edward L. Greene. Published from funds provided by James M. McDonald, Esq. San Francisco. 2 pts. xii+84 pp. & 37 lith. pls.

Gregg, Thomas. [1857.] Fruit Culture for the Million. A Hand-Book of Fruit Culture: Being a Guide to the Cultivation and Management of Fruit Trees; with Condensed Descriptions of Many of the Best and Most Popular Varieties in the United States. Illustrated with ninety engravings. With an appendix. New York: Fowler & Wells. 163 pp., illus.

Gregg, Thomas. 1877. How to Raise Fruits; A Hand-Book of Fruit Culture. Being a Guide to the Proper Cultivation and Management of Fruit Trees, and of Grapes and Small Fruits. New York: Wells. 183 pp., 75 illus. {Also, New York, 1880.}

Griffin, Mary M. 1846. Drops from Flora's Cup; or, The Poetry of Flowers, with a Floral Vocabulary. Boston: O. L. Perkins, [c.1845]. Frontis. & half-title (chromolith.) & 160 pls. {Also, Boston, [1848].}

Griffith, Robert Eglesfeld. 1847. Medical Botany; or, Descriptions of the More Important Plants Used in Medicine, with Their History, Properties, and Mode of Administration. With upwards of three hundred illustrations. Philadelphia: Lea & Blanchard. 704 pp., wood-eng. illus.

Griswold, Norman W. 1883. Beauties of California. Including Big Trees. Yosemite Valley, Geysers, Lake Tahoe, Donner Lake, S.F. '49 & '83, etc. San Francisco: H. S. Crocker & Co. [44] pp. & 13 pls. (col.). {Also, San Francisco [etc.], 1884. [58] pp. & 19 pls. (col.).}

Guillet, Peter, l'aîné. 1823. The Timber Merchant's Guide. Also a Table, Whereby, at One View, May Be Seen the Solid and Superficial Measure of Any Square or Unequal Hewed Logs or Plank, from One to Forty-Seven Inches. Also, plates representing the figures of the principal pieces of timber, used in building a seventy-four gun ship of the line, in standing trees. Baltimore: J. Lovegrove. 24 pp. & 30 lith. pls. (col.).

Hackel, Eduard. 1890. The True Grasses. Translated from Die natürlichen Pflanzenfamilien. By F. Lamson-Scribner and Effie A. Southworth. Copiously illustrated. New York: Henry Holt & Co. Frontis. & viii+228 pp., line illus.

Haité, George Charles. [1883?] Haité's Plant Studies for Artists, Designers, and Art Students, Complete in Two Volumes of 25 Lithographic Plates Each, with Letter Press. New York: J. O'Kane. 2 pts. 50 pls.

Hale, Gertrude Elisabeth. 1887. Little Flower-People. Boston: Ginn & Co. xiii+85 pp., wood-eng. illus.

Hale, Sarah Josepha Buell. 1832. Flora's Interpreter; or, The American Book of Flowers and Sentiments, ed. 2, improv. Boston: Marsh, Capen & Lyon. 262 pp. & 2 eng. pls. (col.). {Several eds. including, Ed. 3, Boston [etc.], 1834; Ed. 6, improv., Boston [etc.], 1838; Ed. 9, Boston: Marsh, Capen, Lyon and Webb, 1840; Ed. 10, Boston [etc.], 1841; Ed. 11, Boston [etc.], 1842; Ed. 14, Boston: T. H. Webb & Co., [184??]; also as, Flora's Interpreter, and Fortuna Flora. Boston: Sanborn, Carter, Bazin & Co., 1848. 288 pp. & 2 chromolith. pls.; Boston: Bazin & Ellsworth, [c1848]; Boston: Benjamin B. Mussey & Co., 1853.; 3rd revision. Enlarged by 160 new interpretations, with new illustrations. Boston: Chase, Nichols & Hill, [c1860]. 288 pp. & 2 chromolith. pls.}

Hall, Abbie G. 1887. Botany: Lessons in Botany and Analysis of Plants. Chicago: George Sherwood & Co. 276 pp., illus. {Cover title: Botany for public schools.}

Halliday, Robert J. 1880. Practical *Azalea* Culture: A Treatise on the Propagation and Culture of the *Azalea indica*. Illustrated. Baltimore. 114 pp., illus.

Halliday, Robert J. 1880. Practical *Camellia* Culture: A Treatise on the Propagation and Culture of the *Camellia japonica*. Illustrated.

Baltimore. 141 pp. & 5 lith. pls. (col.).

Hammond, Thomas W. [1881?] Flowers and Plants from Nature. By Emile Favart [pseud.]. Complete in sixty plates. New York: J. O'Kane. [ii] pp. & 60 pls.

Harriman Alaska Expedition. 1901. Alaska. Vol. I: Narrative [etc.]; Vol. II: History [etc.]. Harriman Alaska Expedition, with cooperation of Washington Academy of Sciences. New York: Doubleday, Page, & Co. Pls., incl. some botanical chromoliths. & heliotypes.

Harris, Amanda Bartlett. 1882. Wild Flowers and Where They Grow. [Illus. by Miss. L[izbeth]. B[ullock]. Humphrey.] Boston: D. Lothrop & Co. Frontis., 160 pp., illus.

Hart, Mary E. 1893. Stray Violets. Gathered and pictured by [etc.]. New York: G. M. Allen. Frontis. & 16 pls.

[Hawks, Francis Lister.] 1834. The American Forest; or, Uncle Philip's Conversations with the Children about the Trees of America. New York: Harper & Bros. 6 wood-eng. illus. (of trees). {Also, New York [etc.], 1839; New York, 1841.}

Heinrich, Julius J. 1880. The Window Flower Garden. New York: Orange Judd & Co. 93 pp., 73 illus.

Heller, Amos Arthur. 1895. Botanical Explorations in Southern Texas during the Season of 1894. Lancaster: Herbarium of Franklin and Marshall College. 116 pp. & 9 line-block pls. [Contributions from the Herbarium of Franklin and Marshall College, no. 1.]

Heller, Amos Arthur. 1897. Observations on the Ferns and Flowering Plants of the Hawaiian Islands. Minneapolis. Pp. 760–922, & 28 pls. {First pub. in Bulletin, no. 9, Minnesota Botanical Studies.}

Hemsley, William Botting. 1873. Handbook of Hardy Trees, Shrubs, and Herbaceous Plants. Containing Descriptions, Native Countries, etc. … Based on the French work of Messrs. Decaisne and Naudin entitled "Manuel de l'amateur des jardins," and including the original woodcuts by Riocreux and Leblanc. With an introduction by Edward S. Rand, Jr. With nearly 300 illustrations. Boston: Estes & Lauriat. viii+xdiii+687 pp. wood-eng. illus.

Henderson, Peter. [1869.] Practical Floriculture: A Guide to the Successful Cultivation of Florist's Plants, for the Amateur and Professional Florist. New York: Orange Judd & Co. 249 pp., wood-eng. illus. {Also, New York [etc.], [1874]. 288 pp., 69 wood-eng. illus.; Ed. 3, greatly enl. New York [etc.], 1879. 311 pp., 72 wood-eng. illus.; 1882; New York [etc.], 1883; New & enl. ed. New York [etc.], 1887. 325 pp., 58 illus.}

Henderson, Peter. [c1875.] Gardening for Pleasure: A Guide to the Amateur in the Fruit, Vegetable, and Flower Garden, with Full Directions for the Greenhouse, Conservatory, and Window Garden. New York: Orange Judd Co. 250 pp., 134 wood-eng. illus. {Also, New York [etc.], 1880; New York [etc.], 1884; New enl. ed. New York [etc.], (c1887) 1888. 404 pp., 203 illus.; New York [etc.], 1899.}

Henderson, Peter. 1884. Garden and Farm Topics. New York: Peter Henderson & Co. Frontis. (port.) & 244+[8] pp., wood-eng. illus.

Henderson, Peter. 1889. Henderson's Handbook of Plants and General Horticulture, new ed. New York: P. Henderson & Co. 526 pp., illus. {Earlier eds. not illustrated.}

Henry, Samuel. 1814. A New and Complete American Medical Family Herbal, Wherein Is Displayed the True Properties and Medical Virtues of the Plants, Indigenous to the United States of America; Together with Lewis' Secret Remedy, Newly Discovered, Which Has Been Found Infallible in the Cure of That Dreadful Disease Hydrophobia; Produced by the Bite of a Mad Dog. ... With an Appendix, of Many Choice Medical Secrets, Never Made Known to the World Before. New York: [by E. Low] for Samuel Henry. 393 pp., wood-eng. illus.

Herrick, Mrs. Sophie M'Ilvaine Bledsoe. 1883. The Wonders of Plant Life under the Microscope. New York: G. P. Putnam's Sons. [iii]+248 pp., illus.

Hervey, Alpheus Baker. 1882. Sea Mosses: A Collector's Guide and an Introduction to the Study of Marine Algae. Illustrated with twenty full-page engravings in color, from photographs of actual specimens. Boston: S. E. Cassino. 281 pp. & 20 eng. pls (col.). {Also, Boston: Bradlee Whidden, 1893.}

Hervey, Alpheus Baker. 1886. Fairy Flowers from Ocean Bowers. Boston: S. E. Cassino. 17ff, illus. (Poetry.)

Hickey, William, see Doyle, Martin.

Hill, Mrs. Ann. [1830s/40s?] Drawing-Book of Flowers. Baltimore: F. Lucas, Jr. 15 pls.

Hill, Mrs. Ann. 1844. The Drawing Book of Flowers and Fruit: With Beautifully Colored Illustrations. For the Use of Seminaries, Private Pupils and Amateurs. Philadelphia: E. C. Biddle. 18 lith. pls. (col.).

Hill, Mrs. Ann. 1845. Progressive Lessons in Painting Flowers and Fruit. Comprising Twenty-Four Lessons or Studies, on Six Sheets. Designed for the Use of Schools and Private Pupils. Philadelphia: E. C. Biddle. 6 lith. pls. (col.).

Hillhouse, Lizzie Page. 1897. House Plants and How to Succeed with Them. A Practical Handbook. New York: A. T. De La Mare Printing & Publishing Co. Ltd. Frontis. & ix+220 pp., line & half-tone illus.

Hills, William H. 1886. Small Fruits; Their Propagation and Cultivation, Including the Grape. Boston: Cupples, Upham & Co. 138 pp., illus.

Himes, Charles Francis. 1868. Leaf Prints; or, Glimpses at Photography. Philadelphia: Benerman & Wilson. Frontis. (photo) & 38 pp.

Hooper, Edward James. 1857. Hooper's Western Fruit Book: A Compendious Collection of Facts from the Notes and Experience of Successful Fruit Culturists, Arranged for Practical Use in Orchard and Garden. Cincinnati: Moore, Wilstach, Keys & Co. 333 pp. & 5 pls. (4 chromoliths.).

Hooper, Lucy, ed. 1842. The Lady's Book of Flowers and Poetry, to Which Are Added a Botanical Introduction, a Complete Floral Dictionary and a Chapter on Plants in Rooms. New York: J. C. Riker. 263 pp. & 9 lith. pls. (col.) {Also, New York [etc.], 1843; New York, [etc.], 1846; New York, [etc.], 1847; N.p., 1848; New York: Derby & Jackson, 1858. 275 pp., 9 pls. (col.).; New York [etc.], 1860; Philadelphia: J. B. Lippincott, 1864. Frontis., 275 pp. & 5 lith. pls. (col.).; Philadelphia: Claxton, Remsen & Haffelfinger, 1868. Frontis., 275 pp. & lith. pls.}

Hoopes, Josiah. 1868. The Book of Evergreens: A Practical Treatise on the Coniferae, or Cone-Bearing Plants. New York: Orange Judd & Co. 435 pp., 65 wood-eng. illus.

Hopkins, John Henry. [ca.1846.] The Burlington Drawing Book of Flowers, Progressively Arranged, from a Single Leaf up to Large Groups; Accurately Drawn and Coloured from Nature; for the Use of Amateurs, Families And Schools. New York: Pr. by R. Craighead for the Author. 20 lith. pls. (10 in uncol. & col.

versions). {Re-pub. as: The Vermont Drawing Book of Flowers Progressively Arranged from a Single Leaf up to Large Groups; Accurately Drawn and Colored from Nature. [Burlington]: Hopkins, 1847.}

Hovey, Charles Mason. [1847–]1852–1856. The Fruits of America. Containing Richly Coloured Figures, and Full Descriptions of All the Choicest Varieties Cultivated in the United States. Boston: Hovey & Co.; New York: D. Appleton & Co.; Boston: C. C. Little & James Brown. Pub. in 12+12+3 pts. 1856 (complete pub. in 2 vols.) 48+48 chromolith. pls. (incl. ports. of Hovey and Sharp). Sponsored by the Massachusetts Horticultural Society.

Howe, Marshall A. 1899. The Hepaticae and Anthocerotes of California. New York. 208 pp. & 35 heliotype pls. (i.e., # 88–#122) [Memoirs of the Torrey Botanical Club, vol. 7.]

Hunt, Myron A. 1893. How to Grow Cut Flowers. A Practical Treatise on the Cultivation of the Rose, Carnation, Chrysanthemum, Violet, and Other Winter Flowering Plants. Also Green-house Construction. Terre Haute: The Author. [ii]+vii+228 pp., 41 illus.

Huntington, Annie Oakes. 1902. Studies of Trees in Winter: A Description of the Deciduous Trees of Northeastern America. With an introduction by C. S. Sargent. Boston: Knight & Millet. xviii+198 pp. & 79 half-tone pls. (12 col.).

Hutchings, J. M. 1860. Scenes of Wonder and Curiosity in California. Illustrated by Ninety-Two Well Executed Engravings, Including the Mammoth Trees of Calveras; Caves and Natural Bridges of the Yosemite Valley; the Mammoth Trees of Mariposa and Fresno, Mount Shasta; the Quick-Silver Mines of New Almaden and Hemriqueta; the Farallone Islands; the Geyser Springs, etc. San Francisco: Hutchings & Rosenfield. 236 pp., illus. {Also, San Francisco [etc.], 1861. 267 pp., illus.; San Francisco [etc.], 1865; New York and San Francisco: A. Roman, 1870. 292 pp., illus.; New York [etc.], 1871; New York [etc.], 1872; New York [etc.], 1875.}

Hutchins, Rev. William Tucker. [1892.] All about Sweet Peas: An Art Monograph. Philadelphia: W. A. Burpee & Co., [1892]. 24 pp., illus. {Ed. 2 as: All about Sweet Peas: A Complete Epitome of the Literature of This Fragrant Annual. Philadelphia [etc.], 1894. Frontis. & 131 pp., illus.}

Hutchins, Rev. William Tucker. 1897. Sweet Peas Up-To-Date. With a Complete Description of All Known Varieties, Including Novelties for 1897. Philadelphia: W. A. Burpee & Co. 72 pp., illus.

Irving, Christopher. 1822. A Catechism of Botany: Containing a Description of the Most Familiar and Interesting Plants, Arranged According to the Linnaean system. With an Appendix, on the Formation of an Herbarium. Adapted to the Use of Schools in the United States. With engraved illustrations. American ed. 1, improv. and enl. New York: F. & R. Lockwood. Frontis. (etc) & [vi]+85 pp. {American ed. 2, enl. New York: F. & R. Lockwood, 1824; American ed. 3, improv. & enl. New York: Collins & Hannay, 1826; Another ed. New York: Collins & Hannay, 1829.}

Jerome, Irene Elizabeth. 1888. A Bunch of Violets. Boston: Lee & Shepard. Illus. t.p. & 22 pp., wood-eng. illus.

Johnson, George William. 1847. A Dictionary of Modern Gardening. With one hundred and eighty wood cuts. Ed, with numerous addi-tions, by David Landreth, of Philadelphia. Philadelphia: Lea & Blanchard. 635 pp., 180 wood-eng. illus.

Johnson, Laurence. 1884. A Manual of the Medical Botany of North America. New York: William Wood & Co. Frontis. (col.), xi+292 pp. & 9 chromolith. pls., wood-eng. illus. [Wood's Library of Standard Medical Authors.]

Johnson, Mrs. S. O. ["Daisy Eyebright."] [c1871.] Every Woman her Own Flower Gardener. A Handy Manual of Flower Gardening for Ladies. New York: H. T. Williams. Illus {Ed. 6, New York [etc.], 1876. Frontis. & 148 pp., illus.}

Johnson, W. W. 1884. Forest Leaves. A Practical Work on the Propagation and Management of Trees for Forest and Ornamental Planting. With a Descriptive List of Varieties. Snowflake [Mich.]: The Author. 7 chromolith. pls. {Ed. 2, Chicago: J. J. Spalding & Co., printers, 1884. Frontis. (col.), 60 pp. & 5 chromolith. pls.}

Joslyn, Mary E. [1885.] Flower Studies for Water-Color Painting, Showing Lights and Shadows, with Directions for Coloring. Boston: S. W. Tilton & Co. Nos. 1–3. [36] pls.

Kearney, Thomas Henry. 1898. Studies on American Grasses. Washington: Government Printing Office. 62 pp., 17 pls., illus.

Keeler, Harriet Louise. 1900. Our Native Trees and

How to Identify Them: A Popular Study of Their Habits and Their Peculiarities. With 178 illustrations from photographs and with 162 illustrations from drawings. New York: C. Scribner's Sons. xxiii+533 pp., illus. {Ed. 5, New York: C. Scribner's Sons, 1905.}

Keese, John, ed. [1850s?] The Floral Keepsake. With thirty engravings elegantly colored from nature. New York: Leavitt & Allen. 111 pp. & 30 lith. pls. (col.). {Half-title as: The Floral Keepsake and Language of Flowers. Also, New York, 1854.}

Keese, John, ed. 1850. The Floral Keepsake for 1850. With forty-six beautiful colored engravings. New York: Leavitt & Co. Frontis., illus. t.p., 112 pp. & 44 pls. (col.)

Kellerman, William Ashbrook. [1883.] The Elements of Botany, Embracing Organography, Histology, Vegetable Physiology, Systematic Botany and Economic Botany ... Together with a Complete Glossary of Botanical Terms. Philadelphia: J. E. Potter & Co. 358 pp., illus.

Kellogg, Lavinia S. 1882. Twelve Original Designs of Flowers for Painting in Water Colors. New York: E. L. Kellogg. 12 lith. pl. Prize art cards.

Klippart, John Hancock. 1860. The Wheat Plant: Its Origin, Culture, Growth, Development, Composition, Varieties, Diseases, etc. etc. Together with a Few Remarks on Indian Corn, Its Culture, etc. One hundred illustrations. Cincinnati: Moore, Wilstach, Keys & Co. 706 pp., 100 wood-eng. illus.

Knobel, Edward. 1894. A Guide to Find the Names of All Wild-Growing Trees and Shrubs of New England by Their Leaves. Boston: L. Barta & Co. 48 pp., 211 leaf figs. on 15? illus.

Knobel, Edward. 1899. The Grasses, Sedges and Rushes of the Northern United States, Illustrated; an Easy Method of Identification. Boston: B. Whidden. 78 pp., illus.

Koehler, August. 1876. Practical Botany, Structural and Systematic, the Latter Portion Being an Analytical Key to the Wild Flowering Plants, Trees, Shrubs, Ordinary Herbs, Sedges and Grasses of the Northern and Middle United States East of Mississippi. New York: H. Holt & Co. 400 pp. & 14 pls. {Also, New York, 1877.}

"A Lady." 1845. The Bouquet: Containing the Poetry and Language of Flowers. Boston: Benjamin B. Mussey. Chromolith. t.p. {Also, Boston: O. L. Perkins, 1845. Frontis. (col.), & 128 pp.; Boston [etc.], 1846.}

Lamborn, Levi Leslie. 1887. Carnation Culture. Dianthus caryophyllus semperflorens; Its Classification, History, Propagation, Varieties, Care, Culture, etc. Alliance: [L. L. Lamborn]. 151 pp., 2 chromolith. pls., illus. {Also, Alliance, 1890.}

Lamborn, Levi Leslie. 1901. American Carnation Culture. The Evolution of Dianthus caryophyllus semperflorens, ed. 4. Rewritten & brought completely up to date. Alliance: Lo Ra L. Lamborn. 176 pp., illus.

Lamson-Scribner, Frank, see Scribner, Frank Lamson-.

Larcom, Lucy. 1886. Easter Messengers: A New Poem of the Flowers by Lucy Larcom, with designs of lilies; white daisies and grasses ... by Susie Barstow Skelding. New York: White, Stokes, & Allen. 24 pp., & 4 pls. (col.).

Lelong, Byron Martin. 1888. The Olive in California; Varieties, Budding, Grafting, New Methods, and General Observations. Sacramento: J. D. Young. 21 pp. & 14 pls. {Also, 1889.}

Lelong, Byron Martin. 1888. A Treatise on Citrus Culture in California; with a Description of the Best Varieties Grown in the State, and Varieties Grown in Other States and Foreign Countries, Gathering, Packing, Curing, Pruning, Budding, Diseases, etc. Sacramento: J. D. Young, Supt. State Printing. 96 pp. & 1 pl. (col.), illus.

LeMaout, Emmanuel. 1873. Flower Object Lessons; or, First Lessons in Botany. A Familiar Description of a Few Flowers. From the French of [etc. by A. L. Paige]. New York: W. J. Read. 55 pp., 99 line illus.

Lemmon, John Gill. 1892. Handbook of West-American Cone-Bearers. Approved English names with brief descriptions of the cone-bearing trees of the Pacific slope north of Mexico and west of Rocky Mountains., ed. 2. Oakland: Printed by the Pacific Press Publishing Co. 24 pp. & 2 pls. {Ed. 3, Oakland, 1895. Frontis., 104 pp. & 16 pls.; Ed. 4 (pocket edition), Oakland, 116 pp. & 17 pls.}

Lesquereux, Leo. 1874–1883. Contribution to the Fossil Flora of the Western Territories. 3 vols. Washington. 155 lith. pls. [Report of the United States Geological Survey of the Territories, vols. 6–8.]

Lesquereux, Leo. 1879–1884. Description of the Coal Flora of the Carboniferous Formation in Pennsylvania and throughout the United

States. 3 vols. in 2. Harrisburg. [2]+xvi+977+lxiii pp., 26 pls., & atlas of 37 lith. pls. [Report of the Progress of the 2nd Geological Survey of Pennsylvania.]

Lesquereux, Leo. 1891. Flora of the Dakota Group. A posthumous work by [etc.]. F. H. Knowlton, ed. Washington: U.S. Geological Survey. 400 pp. & 66 pls. [Monograph, vol. 17.]

Lesquereux, Leo and Thomas Potts James. 1884. Manual of the Mosses of North America. With six plates illustrating the genera. Boston: S. E. Cassino & Co. v+447 pp. & 6 lith. pls. {Pls. I–V were first published in Asa Gray, Manual of the Botany of the Northern United States, rev. ed. New York, 1856.}

Lincoln, Mrs. Almira Hart, see Phelps, Almira Hart Lincoln.

Lloyd, John Uri and Curtis Gates Lloyd, eds. 1884–1887. Drugs and Medicines of North America: A Publication Devoted to the Historical and Scientific Discussions of Botany, Pharmacy, Chemistry and Therapeutics of the Medical Plants of North America, Their Constituents, Products and Sophistications. Vol. I. Ranunculaceae. 2 vols. Cincinnati: J. U. & C. G. Lloyd. Pls., illus.

Locke, John. 1819. Outlines of Botany, Taken Chiefly from Smith's Introduction; Containing an Explanation of Botanical Terms and an Illustration of the System of Linnaeus. Also, Some Account of Natural Orders, and the Anatomy and Physiology of Vegetables. Illustrated by engravings. For the use of schools and students. Boston: Cummings & Hilliard, for the Author. xiii+161 pp. & 16 eng. pls.

Long, Elias. 1885. The Home Florist: A Treatise on the Cultivation, Management and Adaptability of Flowering and Ornamental Plants, Designed for the Use of Amateur Florists, ed. 7, rev. & enl. Springfield: C. A. Reeser. 319 pp., numerous illus.

Lorimer, Mary [i.e., M. O. B. Dunning]. 1869. Among the Trees: A Journal of Walks in the Woods and Flower-Hunting through Field and by Brook. By Mary Lorimer. New York: Hurd & Houghton. 153 pp., wood-eng. illus.

Lounsberry, Alice. [1899.] A Guide to the Wild Flowers. With sixty-four colored and one hundred black-and-white plates and fifty-four diagrams by Mrs. Ellis Rowan. With an

introduction by Dr. N. L. Britton. New York: Frederick A. Stokes. xviii+347 pp. & 3-col. pls., illus.

Lounsberry, Alice. [1900.] A Guide to the Trees. With sixty-four coloured and one hundred and sixty-four black-and-white plates and fifty-five diagrams, by Mrs. Ellis Rowan. With an introduction by N. L. Britton. New York: F. A. Stokes Co. Frontis., xx+313 pp. & pls. (col.), illus.

Lounsberry, Alice. [1901.] Southern Wild Flowers and Trees, Together with Shrubs, Vines and Various Forms of Growth Found through the Mountains, the Middle District and the Low Country of the South. ... with ... plates ... vignettes and diagrams by Mrs. E[llis]. Rowan. With an introduction by C. D. Beadle. New York: F.A. Stokes Co. xxxi+570 pp. & 3-col. pls., half-tone illus.

McIlvaine, Charles and Robert K. Macadam. [c1900.] Toadstools, Mushrooms, Fungi, Edible and Poisonous. One Thousand American Fungi. How to Select and Cook the Edible. How to Distinguish and Avoid the Poisonous. Giving Full Botanic Descriptions. Indianapolis: Bowen-Merrill Co. xxxvii+704 pp. & 171 pls. (3-col.), line & half-tone illus. {Revised ed. with Supplement. Indianapolis: The Bowen-Merrill Co., c1902. xxxvii+729 pp. & 171+1 pls. 3-col.}

Macloskie, George. 1883. Elementary Botany with Students' Guide to the Examination and Description of Plants. New York: Henry Holt & Co. Frontis. & viii+373 pp., line illus.

McMahon, Bernard. 1857. American Gardener's Calendar; Adapted to the Climate and Seasons of the United States, ed. 11. With a memoir of the author; rev. and illus. under the supervision of J. Jay Smith. Philadelphia: J. B. Lippincott & Co. Frontis. & wood-eng. illus. {In this ed. "woodcuts have been inserted to add interest to the work."}

Maisch, John Michael. 1882. A Manual of Organic Materia Medica: Being a Guide to Materia Medica of the Vegetable and Animal Kingdoms for the Use of Students, Druggists, Pharmacists, and Physicians. With 242 illustrations. Philadelphia: H. C. Lea's Son & Co. 459 pp., wood-eng. illus. (few of plants). {Ed. 2, Philadelphia: Lea Brothers & Co., 1885; Ed. 3, Philadelphia [etc.], 1887; Ed. 4, Philadelphia [etc.], 1890; Ed. 5, Philadelphia [etc.], 1892;

Ed. 6, Philadelphia [etc.], 1895; Ed. 7, Philadelphia [etc.], 1899.}

Mann, Mary Tyler Peabody. 1846. The Flower People: A Token of Friendship. Hartford: H., T. Wells. 228 pp., 12 wood-eng. pls.

Manning, Robert. 1838. Book of Fruits, Being a Descriptive Catalogue of the Most Valuable Varieties of the Pear, Apple, Peach, Plum & Cherry, for New England Culture. To Which Is Added the Gooseberry, Currant, Raspberry, Strawberry, and the Grape; with Modes of Culture. Also Hardy Ornamental Trees and Shrubs. With plates. First series for 1838. Salem: Ives & Jewett. Frontis., 120 pp. & 3 lith. pls., text illus. {Ed. 2, enlarged, Salem and Boston, 1844.}

Manning, Robert. 1844. New England Book of Fruit; Containing an Abridgement of Manning's Descriptive Catalogue of the Most Valuable Varieties of the Pear, Apple, Peach, Plum, and Cherry, for New England Culture. To Which Are Added the Grape, Quince, Gooseberry, Currant, and Strawberry; with Outlines of Many of the Finest Pears, Drawn from Nature; with Directions for Pruning, Grafting, and General Modes of Culture, ed. 2, enl. by John M. Ives. Salem: W. & S. B. Ives; Boston, B. B. Mussey. Frontis. (col.), 133 pp., illus. {Ed. 3, rev. & enl. by John M. Ives. Salem: W. & S. B. Ives; Boston: W. J. Reynolds & Co.; B. B. Mussey & Co., [etc.], 1847. Eng. t.p. & frontis. (col.), viii+144 pp., wood-eng. illus.}

[Marcet, Mrs. Jane Haldimand.] 1830. Conversations on Vegetable Physiology; Comprehending the Elements of Botany with Their Application to Agriculture. Adapted to the use of schools by Rev. J. L. Blake, A. M. Boston: Crocker & Brewsater; New York: J. Leavitt. Frontis. (col.), 372 pp. & 9 pls. (4 eng., 5 lith. col.). {American ed. 3, Philadelphia: E. L. Carey & A. Hart; Baltimore: Carey, Hart & Co. and W. & J. Neal; Boston: Crocker & Brewster, Allen & Ticknor, Russell, Odiorne & Co. and Lilly, Wait & Co., 1833. 4 pls.; American ed. 4, Philadelphia: E. L. Carey & A. Hart, 1835; Philadelphia [etc.], 1836; American ed. 7, with engravings. Philadelphia [etc.], 1837.}

Marion, Fulgence. 1872. The Wonders of Vegetation. From the French of Fulgence Marion. Ed., with numerous additions, by Schele de Vere [etc.] With 61 illustrations. New York: Scribner.

Frontis., 283 pp., & pls. [Illustrated Library of Wonders, ser. 2.]

Martyn, Mrs. Sarah Towne, ed. [ca.1848.] The Golden Keepsake; or, Ladies' Wreath. A Gift for All Seasons. New York: J. C. Burdick. v+418+[2] pp., lith. pls. (col.). {Issued as monthly publications which were collected and re-issued as "annuals," Ladies' Wreath and Parlor Annual. 12 (flower) lith. pls. (col.), per vol. The text does not relate to plants and includes other unrelated "remainder" plates, views, portraits, etc.}

Marvin, Arthur Tappan. 1889. The Olive: Its Culture in Theory and Practice. San Francisco: Payot, Upham & Co. 146 pp. & 16 lith. pls.

Mason, Mrs. Mary. 1859. A Wreath from Woods of Carolina. Illustrated with colored engravings of native wild flowers. New York: General Protestant Episcopal Sunday School Union, & Church Book Society. 11 lith. [sic] pls. (col.).

Mathews, Ferdinand Schuyler, ed. 1890. The Golden Flower Chrysanthemum. Verses by Edith M. Thomas, Richard Henry Stoddard, Alice Ward Bailey, Celia Thaxter, Kate Upson Clark, Louis Carroll, Margaret Deland, Robert Browning & Oliver Wendell Holmes. Arranged and Embellished with Original Designs by F. Schuyler Mathews. Illustrated with Reproductions of Studies from Nature in Water Color by James & Sidney Callowhill, Alois Lunzer and F. S. M. Boston: Lithographed and printed by L. Prang & Co. [ii]+9 pp.+23 ff. & 15 chromolith. pls.

Mathews, Ferdinand Schuyler, ed. 1895. Familiar Flowers of Field and Garden. Described and illustrated by F. Schuyler Mathews. New York: D. Appleton & Co. vii+308 pp., illus. {Ed. 4, New York [etc.], 1897. Frontis. & x+320 pp., illus.; New ed., with orthochromatic photographs from nature by L[everett]. W. Brownell … and a systematical index and floral calendar. New York [etc.], 1901. xi+308 pp. & pls.}

Mathews, Ferdinand Schuyler, ed. 1896. Familiar Trees and Their Leaves. Described and illustrated by F. Schuyler Mathews. With over two hundred drawings by the author and an introduction by Prof. L. H. Bailey. New York: D. Appleton & Co. x+320 pp., illus. {Also, New York [etc.], 1897; New York [etc.], 1901.}

Mathews, Ferdinand Schuyler, ed. 1897. Familiar Features of the Roadside: The Flowers, Shrubs,

Birds, and Insects. With ... drawings by the author, and many of the songs of our common birds and insects. New York: D. Appleton & Co. xiv+269 pp., line & half-tone illus.

Mathews, Ferdinand Schuyler, ed. [c1899.] Wayside Trees. Illustrated with pen and ink drawings from nature by the author. Springfield: Taber-Prang Art Co. 4 pts. Illus.

Mathews, Ferdinand Schuyler, ed. 1902. Field Book of American Wild Flowers; Being a Short Description of Their Character and Habits, a Concise Definition of Their Colors, and Incidental References to the Insects Which Assist in Their Fertilization. With numerous reproductions of water colors and pen-and-ink studies from nature by the author. New York: Putnam. Frontis. (col.), xx+552 pp., pls. (col.), illus.

Mattson, Morris. 1841. The American Vegetable Practice; or, A New and Improved Guide to Health Designed for the Use of Families in Six Parts. Part I. Concise view of the human body ... Part III. Vegetable materia medica, with colored illustrations.... 2 vols. Boston: Dan'l L. Hale. 24 chromolith. pls., illus. {Ed. 2, Boston: W. Johnson, 1845. 2 vols. 26 pls., illus.}

Meech, William Witler. 1888. Quince Culture: An Illustrated Hand-Book for the Propagation and Cultivation of the Quince, with Descriptions of Its Varieties, Insect Enemies, Diseases and Their Remedies. New York: Orange Judd & Co. 143 pp., line-block & half-tone illus. {Rev. & enl. ed. New York [etc.], 1896. 180 pp., 148 illus.}

Meehan, Thomas. 1878–1880. The Native Flowers and Ferns of the United States in Their Botanical, Horticultural and Popular Aspects. Series 1 and 2. Philadelphia: American Natural History Publishing Co.; (later) Charles Robson & Co.; Boston: Louis Prang. 4 vols. 192 chromolith. pls. (from paintings by Alois Lunzer).

Meehan, Thomas. 1881. Wayside Flowers. Philadelphia: Ch. Robson. 128 pp. & 31 chromolith. pls.

Merrick, John Mudge, Jr. 1870. The Strawberry and Its Culture; with a Descriptive Catalogue of All Known Varieties. Boston: J. E. Tilton & Co. Frontis., 128 pp. & 4 pls.

Michaux, François André. 1841. The North American Sylva; or, A Description of the Forest Trees of the United States, Canada and Nova Scotia, Considered Particularly with Respect to Their Use in the Arts, and Their Introduction into Commerce; to Which Is Added a Description of the Most Useful of the European Forest Trees. Illustrated by 156 coloured engravings. Translated from the French of [etc.]. (With three additional volumes, containing all the forest trees discovered in the Rocky Mountains, the Territory of Oregon, down to the shores of the Pacific and into the confines of California, as well as in various parts of the United States. Illustrated by 122 finely coloured plates. By Thomas Nuttall. The whole forming six volumes, and comprising 278 plates.) Philadelphia: J. Dobson. 156 (+122) eng. pls. (col.). {Also, Cincinnati: W. Amphlett and Doolittle & Munson, 1842. 2 vols. (The pls. in earlier editions were printed in Paris.) [American ed. 2] Philadelphia: R. P. Smith; New York: G. P. Putnam, 1850[–1851]. 3 vols.; Philadelphia: R. P. Smith, 1852–1853; Philadelphia [etc.], 1853; Philadelphia [etc.], 1854; Philadelphia [etc.], 1855; Philadelphia, A. N. Hart, 1855; Philadelphia [etc.], 1856; [American ed. 3] Philadelphia: D. Rice & A. N. Hart, 1857; Philadelphia [etc.], 1859; Philadelphia, Rice, Rutter & Co., 1865; Philadelphia, Wm. Rutter & Co., 1871. [See Nuttall, Thomas for details of his 3-vol., 1842[–1849], supplement.]}

Millard, Hannah, see California State Vinicultural Association.

Miller, Ellen and Margaret Christine Whiting. 1895. Wild Flowers of the North-Eastern States: Being Three Hundred and Eight Individuals Common to the North-Eastern United States, Drawn and Described from Life by [etc.]. With three hundred and eight illustrations the size of life. New York: G. P. Putnam's Sons. Frontis. (col.)., xi+622 pp. & 307 line-block pls.

Miller, Thomas. 1848. The Poetical Language of Flowers. New York: J. C. Riker. Illus. {Another ed. as, The Romance of Nature; or, The Poetical Language of Flowers. New York: Ricker, Thorne & Co., [186–?]. Frontis. & xii+224 pp., pls. (col.).}

Millspaugh, Charles Frederick. [1882–1887.] American Medicinal Plants. An Illustrated and Descriptive Guide to the American Plants as Homeopathic Remedies. Their History, Preparation, Chemistry and Physiological Effects.

Illustrated by the Author. 2 vols., pub. in 6 pts. New York and Philadelphia: Boericke & Tafel. 180 lith. pls. (col.). {Another ed. as, Medicinal Plants. Philadelphia: J. C. Yorston, 1892. 2 vols.}

Miner, Harriet Stewart. 1885. Orchids, the Royal Family of Plants. With illustrations from nature by Harriet Stewart Miner. Boston: Lee & Shepard; New York: C. T. Dillingham. 90 pp. & 24 chromolith. pls.

Moore, Rev. Henry D., ed. 1850. The Winter Bloom. With nine brilliant illuminations, in oil colors. Philadelphia: Hogan & Thompson. 240 pp. & 9 chromoxylogr. pls.

Morley, Margaret Warner. 1891. A Song of Life. Chicago: A. C. McClurg & Co. 155 pp., illus. {Also, Illustrated by the author and Robert Forsyth. 15th thousand. Chicago [etc.], 1902. 155 pp. illus.}

Morley, Margaret Warner. 1897. A Few Familiar Flowers: How to Love Them at Home or in School. Boston: London, Ginn & Co. xiv+274 pp., illus.

Morley, Margaret Warner. 1897. Flowers and Their Friends. Boston: Ginn & Co. vi+255 pp. illus.

Morton, James. 1891. Chrysanthemum Culture for America: A Book about Chrysanthemums, Their History, Classification, and Care. New York: Rural Publishing Co. 126 pp., illus. (by A. Blanc). [Rural Library Series.]

Moser, Ferdinand. [1894?] Study of Ornamental Plants; Suggestions for Teachers and Pupils in Form and Word. New York: Hinsling & Spielmeyer. 30 pls.

Munson, Laura Gordon. 1864. Flowers from My Garden. Sketched and painted from nature by [etc.]. With an introductory poem by Mrs. L. H. Sigourney. New York: A. D. F. Randolph. 18 lith. pls. (col.).

Mure, Benoît Jules. 1854. Materia Medica; or, Provings of the Principal Animal and Vegetable Poisons of the Brazilian Empire: And Their Application in the Treatment of Disease. Transl. from the French and arranged according to Hahnemann's method by Charles J. Hempel. New York: W. Radde. 220 pp., few wood-eng. illus.

Neill, Patrick. 1855. The Practical Fruit, Flower and Vegetable Gardener's Companion, with a Calendar. Adapted to the United States. From the 4th ed. Rev. & improv. by the author. Ed.

by G[ouvernour]. Emerson. With notes and additions, by R[ichard]. G[ay]. Pardee. New York: C. M. Saxton & Co. Frontis. & 408 pp., illus.

Newell, Jane Hancox. 1889–1893. A Reader in Botany Selected and Adapted from Well-Known Authors. 2 vols. Boston: Ginn & Co. Illus.

Newell, Jane Hancox. 1889. Outlines of Lessons in Botany. For the Use of Teachers, or Mothers Studying with Their Children. Pt. I. From Seed to Leaf; 1892. ... Pt. II. Flower and Fruit. 2 vols. Boston: Ginn & Co. Illus. {Also, Boston [etc.], 1893. Pls.}

Newhall, Charles Stedman. 1890. The Trees of Northeastern America. Illustrations from original sketches by [etc.]. With introductory note by Nath. L. Britton. New York: G. P. Putnam's Sons. xiv+250 pp., 116 line illus. {Also, New York [etc.], 1891; New York [etc.], 1894; New York [etc.], 1897.}

Newhall, Charles Stedman. 1891. The Leaf-Collector's Hand-Book and Herbarium: An Aid in the Preservation and in the Classification of Specimen Leaves of the Trees of Northeastern America. New York: G. P. Putnam's Sons. xv+216 pp., line illus. {Also, New York [etc.], 1892; Ed. 2, New York [etc.], 1898.}

Newhall, Charles Stedman. 1893. The Shrubs of Northeastern America. New York: G. P. Putnam's Sons. 249 pp., line illus.

Newhall, Charles Stedman. 1897. The Vines of Northeastern America. Fully illustrated from original sketches by [etc.]. New York: G. P. Putnam's Sons. xxx+207 pp., line illus.

Newman, John B., ed. 1846. Boudoir Botany; or, The Parlor Book of Flowers, Comprising the History, Description and Colored Engravings of Twenty-Four Exotic Flowers, Twenty-Four Wild Flowers of America, and Twelve Trees and Fruits. With an Introduction to the Science of Botany. Illustrated with 250 engravings by Lewis and Brown. New York: Harper & Bros. 296 pp. & 65 lith. pls. (col.). {Also, New York [etc.], 1847.}

Newman, John B., ed. 1846–1847. The Illustrated Botany. Comprising the Most Valuable Native and Exotic Plants, with Their History, Medicinal Properties, etc. To Which Is Added an Introduction on Physiology, and a View of the Natural and Linnaean Systems. [Vol. 2, J. L. Comstock, ed.]. 2 vols. New York: J. K. Wellman.

Newman, John B., ed. 1848. Beauties of Flora, and Outlines of Botany with a Language of Flowers. A Perennial Offering. New York: E. Kerney. Frontis., 288 pp. & 34 lith. pls. (some col.).

Newman, John B., ed. 1850. Illustrated Botany, Containing a Floral Dictionary and a Glossary of Scientific Terms. New York: Fowlers & Wells. x+226 pp., wood-eng. illus.

Newman, John B., ed. 1854. Ladies Flora for 1854. London and New York. 11 lith. pls. (col.).

Newman, John B., ed. [1865?] The Ladies' Flora: Containing a Dictionary and Glossary of Botanical Names. With Fifteen Colored Illustrations. New York: T. L. Magagnos. 384 pp. & 17 pls. (col.).

Noll, Henry R. 1852. The Botanical Class-Book, and Flora of Pennsylvania, Designed for Seminaries of Learning and Private Classes. In two parts. Part I. Structural and physiological botany. Part II. Systematic botany. Comprising a brief sketch of the Linnaean and natural systems of botany; a glossary of technical terms; analytical tables, and the natural orders, illustrated by a flora of Pennsylvania, which embraces descriptions of nearly nine-tenths of the indigenous flowering plants of the northern United States. Lewisburg: O. N. Worden, Printer. 158+452 pp., wood-eng. illus.

Nuttall, Thomas. 1827. Introduction to Systematic and Physiological Botany. Cambridge: Hilliard & Brown; Boston: Hilliard, Gray, Little, & Wilkins; Richardson & Lord. xi+360 pp. & 12 lith. pls. {Ed. 2, with additions. Cambridge: Hilliard & Brown, 1830.}

Nuttall, Thomas. 1842[–1849]. The North American Sylva; or, A Description of the Forest Trees of the United States, Canada and Nova Scotia, not Described in the Work of F. A. Michaux, and Containing All the Forest Trees Discovered in the Rocky Mountains, the Territory of Oregon, down to the Shores of the Pacific and into the Confines of California, as well as in Various Parts of the United States. Illustrated by 122 fine plates. In three volumes. Being the fourth [fifth] [sixth] volume of Michaux and Nuttall's North American Sylva. 3 vols. Pub. in 6 half-vols. Philadelphia: J. Dobson (vol. 1); Townsend Ward (vol. 2); Smith & Wistar (vol. 3). 121 [sic] lith. pls. (col.), (pls. 30–31 omitted; extra pl. for no. 5 & 10). {Also, Philadelphia: Smith & Wistar, [etc.], 1849; Philadelphia: R. P.

Smith, 1852; Philadelphia [etc.], 1853; Philadelphia [etc.], 1854; Philadelphia [etc.], 1855; Philadelphia: A. N. Hart, 1855.}

Nutting, Benjamin F. 1860. Introduction to Tree Drawing with Full Instructions. Boston: Chase, Nichols & Hill. 18 pls.) {Plates in the form of cards with instructions accompanying each.}

Olcott, Henry Steel. 1860. How to Cultivate and Preserve Celery, see Roessle, Theophilus.

Osborn, Henry Stafford. 1860. Plants of the Holy Land, with their Fruits and Flowers, Beautifully Illustrated by Original Drawings, Colored from Nature. Philadelphia: Parry & McMillan. Frontis., 174 pp. & 5 chromolith. pls. {Also, Philadelphia: J. B. Lippincott & Co., 1861. 6 chromolith. pls.}

Osgood, Mrs. Frances Sargent Locke. [1841.] The Poetry of Flowers and the Flowers of Poetry, with a Simple Treatise of Botany. New York: Leavitt & Allen Bros. Lith. illus. (col.). {Also, New York: J. C. Riker, 1841. 276 pp. & 12 lith. pls. (col.); New York [etc.], 1843; New York [etc.], 1846; New York [etc.], 1851; New York [etc.], 1853; New York [etc.], 1859.}

Osgood, Mrs. Frances Sargent Locke. [1845.] The Flower Alphabet, in Gold and Colours. Boston: S. Colman. 31 ff., 24 chromolith. illus.

Osgood, Mrs. Frances Sargent Locke. 1847. The Floral Offering; a Token of Friendship. Illustrated with ten beautiful bouquets of flowers, elegantly coloured after nature, by J. Ackerman. Philadelphia: Carey & Hart. [123] pp. & 10 lith. pls. (col.)

Pardee, Richard Gay. 1854. A Complete Manual for the Cultivation of the Strawberry; with a Description of the Best Varieties. Also, Notices of the Raspberry, Blackberry, Currant, Gooseberry, and Grape. With Directions for Their Cultivation, and the Selection of the Best Varieties. New York: C. M. Saxton. 144 pp., illus. {New & rev. ed., New York: O. Judd & Co., [1856]. 157 pp., illus.; Rev. ed. 3, New York: C. M. Saxton, 1856; Ed. 6, New York: A. O. Moore, 1858; Ed. 6, New York: Saxton, Barker, 1858; New & rev. ed. [10], New York: C. M. Saxton, 1863.}

Parley, Peter [i.e., Samuel Griswold Goodrich]. 1838. Peter Parley's Cyclopedia of Botany, Including Familiar Descriptions of Trees, Shrubs and Plants. With numerous engravings. Boston: Weeks, Jordan & Co. civ+330 pp., wood-eng. illus. {Also, Boston: Otis, Broaders & Co., 1838; re-pub. as: Peter Parley's Illustrations of the Vegetable Kingdom; Trees, Plants and Shrubs. New York: W. Robinson, [c1840] 1844; Hartford: Pub. by H. H. Hawley & Co.; Utica: Hawley, Fuller & Co., 1849. civ+330 pp., wood-eng. illus.}

Parrish, Edward. 1864. The Phantom Bouquet: A Popular Treatise on the Art of Skeletonizing Leaves and Seed-Vessels and Adapting Them to Embellish the Home of Taste. Philadelphia: J. B. Lippincott. 47 pp. & 5 pls. {Also, Philadelphia [etc.], 1865.}

Parsons, Mrs. Frances Theodora, see Dana, Mrs. William Starr.

Parsons, Mary Elizabeth. 1897. The Wild Flowers of California: Their Haunts, Names and Habits. Illustrated by Margaret Warriner Buck. San Francisco: William Doxey. xlviii+410 pp., illus. (some col.). {Other eds. including, Ed. 4, San Francisco: Payot, Upham & Co., 1902.}

Parsons, Samuel Bowne. 1847. The Rose: Its History, Poetry, Culture, and Classification. New York: Wiley & Putnam. Frontis., 280 pp. & 1 pl. {Also, New York: J. Wiley, 1860. 282+36 pp. & 1 pl. Re-pub. as, Parsons on the Rose, a Treatise on the Propagation, History, and Culture of the Rose. New rev. & enl. ed. New York: Orange Judd & Co., 1883. 236 pp., illus.}

Peck, Charles Horton. 1897. Mushrooms. Annual Report, State Botanist of New York. Albany. 43 pls.

Peck, Charles Horton. 1900. Report of the State Botanist on edible fungi of New York 1895–1899. Albany: University of the State of New York. Pp. 133–234 & pls. 44–68, chromoliths. [Memoir of the New York State Museum, vol. 3(4).]

Phelps, Almira Hart Lincoln. 1829. Familiar Lectures on Botany. Including Practical and Elementary Botany, with Generic and Specific Descriptions of the Most Common Native and Foreign Plants and a Vocabulary of Botanical Terms. For the Use of Higher Schools and Academies. By Mrs. Almira H. Lincoln. Hartford: H. & F. J. Huntington; New York: G. & C. & H. Carvill; Boston: Richardson & Lord. 335+[4] pp., 13 eng. pls. (by Miss Lee). {Many eds. including, Ed. 2, Hartford: H. & F. J. Huntington, 1831. 428 pp. & 13 pls.; Ed. 3, Hartford: F. J. Huntington; New York: Collins &

Hannay, and G. & C. & M. Carvill [etc.]., 1832. 440 pp; Ed. 4, rev. & enl., Hartford [etc.], 1835. 307+190 pp. & 7 pls.; Ed. 5, rev. & enl., Hartford [etc.], 1836. 246+186 pp., incl. illus., & 8 pls.; Ed. 5, Raleigh: Turner & Hughes, 1836; Ed. 5, rev. & enl., New York: F. J. Huntington & Co., 1837; Ed. 6, rev. & enl., New York [etc.], 1838; Ed. 7, rev. & enl., New York [etc.], 1838; Ed. 8, rev. & enl., New York [etc.], 1839; Ed. 9, New York [etc.], 1839; Ed. 10, New York [etc.], 1840; Ed. 12, rev. & enl., New York [etc.], 1841; Ed. 13, rev. & enl., New York [etc.], 1841. 246+186 pp. & pls. (now in the text); Ed. 16, rev. & enl., New York [etc.], 1841; Ed. 17, rev. & enl. [etc.]. New York [etc.], 1838; Ed. 17, rev. & enl. [etc.], New York: Huntington [etc.], 1842; Ed. 18, New York, 1843; New ed., rev. & enl. Illustrated by many additional engravings. New York: Huntington & Savage, 1845; New ed., New York, [etc.], 1846; New ed., New York: F. J. Huntington & Savage, 1848. 246+220 pp., incl. illus., & 8 pls.; New ed., New York: Huntington & Savage, 1850; New ed., rev. & enl., New York: F. J. Huntington, and Mason and Law, 1852; New ed., rev. and enl., New York: Mason Brothers, 1856. Frontis., 8 pls., & 221wood-eng. illus.; New ed., New York [etc.], 1852; New ed., New York [etc.], 1854; New ed., New York [etc.], 1855; New ed., New York [etc.], 1858; New ed., New York [etc.], 1860. 316 pp., 8 pls.; New ed., New York [etc.], 1864. 514 pp. & 8 pls.}

Phelps, Almira Hart Lincoln. 1833. Botany for Beginners: An Introduction to Mrs. Lincoln's Lectures on Botany. For the Use of Common Schools, and Younger Pupils of Higher Schools and Academies. Hartford: F. J. Huntington. v+212 pp., wood-eng. illus. {Many eds. including, Ed. 2, Hartford [etc.], 1833; Ed. 3, Hartford [etc.], 1835; Ed. 3, Hartford [etc.], 1836; Ed. 3, New York: F. J. Huntington, 1837; Ed. 3, New York [etc.]., 1838; Ed. 4, New York [etc.]., 1838. 216 pp., wood-eng. illus.; Ed. 5, New York [etc.]., 1837; Ed. 6, New York [etc.]., 1840; Ed. 7, New York [etc.]., 1841; Ed. 8, New York [etc.]., 1841; Ed. 9, New York [etc.]., 1841; Ed. 10, New York [etc.]., 1842; Ed. 12, New York: Huntington & Savage, 1845; Ed. 13, New York, 1841; Another ed., New York [etc.]., 1846; Stereotype ed., New York [etc.]., 1847; Stereotype ed., New York [etc.]., 1848; New ed., New

York [etc.], 1852; New ed., New York [etc.], 1854; New ed., New York [etc.], 1855; New ed., New York [etc.], 1858; New ed., New York [etc.], 1860; New ed., New York [etc.], 1864.}

Phin, John. 1862. Open Air Grape Culture: A Practical Treatise on the Garden and Vineyard Culture of the Vine, and the Manufacture of Domestic Wine. To Which Is Added a Selection of Examples of American Vineyard Practice, and a Description of the Celebrated Thomery System of Grape Culture. New York: C. M. Saxton. 375 pp., illus. {Also, New York: G. E. Woodward & Co., 1876. 266 pp., 67 wood-eng. illus.}

Piper, Richard Upton. [1855–1858.]. The Trees of America. Boston: William White. 4 pts. (uncompleted work). Eng. t.p., 64 pp. & 14 lith. pls.

Pollard, Josephine. 1888. Flowers from Field and Woodland. New York: F. A. Stokes & Brother. 128 pp., illus. (col.).

Pratt, Anna M. 1890. Flower Folk. New illustrations in colors and monotint by Laura C. Hills. New verses by Anna M. Pratt. New York: Frederick A. Stokes. 37 ff., chromolith. illus.

Pratt, Mara Louise. 1890. The Fairyland of Flowers: A Popular Illustrated Botany, ed. 3. Boston: Education Publishing Co. 220 pp., many illus.

Prince, William Robert, aided by William Prince. 1830. Treatise on the Vine; Embracing Its History from the Earliest Ages to the Present Day, with Descriptions of Above Two Hundred Foreign, and Eighty American Varieties; Together with a Complete Dissertation on the Establishment, Culture, and Management of Vineyards. New York: T. & J. Swords [etc.]; Philadelphia [etc.]. Frontis. (lith.) & viii+9–355 pp. {Also, Charleston: Joseph Simmons, 1830.}

Quinn, Patrick T. 1869. Pear Culture for Profit. New York: The Tribune Association. Frontis. & 136 pp., 18 illus. {New ed., New York: Orange Judd & Co., 1883.}

Quinn, Patrick T. 1871. Money in the Garden; a Vegetable Manual Prepared with a View to Economy and Profit. New York: The Tribune Association. 268 pp., illus.

Rafinesque-Schmaltz, Constantine Samuel. 1828–1830. Medical Flora; or, Manual of the Medical Botany of the United States of North America. Containing a Selection of Above 100 Figures and Descriptions of Medical Plants, with Their Names, Qualities [etc.]. In two volumes. Vol. the first. A–H with 52 plates. Vol. the second, with 48 plates. 2 vols. Philadelphia: Atkinson & Alexander. 100 wood-eng.[?] pls. (printed in green).

Rafinesque-Schmaltz, Constantine Samuel. 1832. American Florist: Containing 36 Figures of Beautiful or Curious American and Garden Flowers, Plants, Trees, Shrubs and Vines; Natives of North America, or Cultivated in Gardens. "Let us teach by Pictures." Philadelphia. 36 illus. {Also, American Florist ...: Second Series. Philadelphia. 18 wood-eng. pls. (36 figures).}

Rafinesque-Schmaltz, Constantine Samuel. 1841. Manual of the Medical Botany of the United States, Containing a Description of 52 Medical Plants. Philadelphia. 52 wood-eng. pls. {A new ed. of vol. 1 of his: Medical Flora, [etc.]. Philadelphia, [etc.], 1828.}

Rand, Edward Sprague, Jr. 1863. Flowers for the Parlor and Garden. Illus. by John Andrew and A. C. Warren. Boston: J. E. Tilton. 411 pp., wood-eng. illus. {Several eds. including, Boston: J. E. Tilton & Co., 1868; Ed. 25, New York: Hurd & Houghton; Cambridge: Riverside Press, 1876. 444 pp., wood-eng. illus.}

Rand, Edward Sprague, Jr. 1866. Bulbs: A Treatise on Hardy and Tender Bulbs and Tubers. Boston: J. E. Tilton & Co. 306 pp., illus. {Various later eds., e.g., Ed. 10, Boston: Houghton, Mifflin & Co., 1884. 369 pp., illus.}

Rand, Edward Sprague, Jr. 1866. Garden Flowers; How to Cultivate Them. A Treatise on the Culture of Hardy Ornamental Trees, Shrubs, Annuals, Harbaceous and Bedding Plants. Boston: J. E. Tilton & Co. 384 pp., illus. {Also, New York: Hurd & Houghton [etc.], 1876.}

Rand, Edward Sprague, Jr. 1870. Seventy-Five Popular Flowers, and How to Cultivate Them. New York: J. E. Tilton & Co. Frontis., 208 pp., wood-eng. pls. {Also as, Popular Flowers, and How to Cultivate Them. New York: Hurd & Houghton; Cambridge: Riverside Press, 1876. Frontis., 230 pp., wood-eng. pls.}

Rand, Edward Sprague, Jr. 1872. The Window Gardener. Boston: Shepard & Gill. 6+132 pp., illus. {Also, Boston [etc.], 1873; New York: Hurd & Houghton; Cambridge: Riverside Press, 1876. 9+154 pp., illus.}

Rand, Edward Sprague, Jr. 1876. Bulbs: A Treatise on Hardy and Tender Bulbs and Tubers. Boston. 142 pp., illus.

Rand, Edward Sprague, Jr. 1876. Orchids: A Description of the Species and Varieties Grown at Glen Ridge, near Boston, with Lists and Descriptions of Other Desirable Kinds: Prefaced by Chapters on the Culture, Propagation, Collection, and Hybridization of Orchids [etc.]. New York: Hurd & Houghton. 476 pp., illus.

Randolph, Cornelia J. [1861.] The Parlor Garden; A Treatise on the House Culture of Ornamental Plants. Translated from the French and adapted to American use. Boston: J. E. Tilton & Co. Frontis., 158 pp. & 10 pls.

Rattan, Volney. 1880. A Popular California Flora; or, Manual of Botany for Beginners. Containing Descriptions of Exogenous Plants Growing in Central California, and Westward to the Ocean, ed. 2, rev. & enl. San Francisco: A. L. Bancroft & Co. xviii+138 pp., illus. {Ed. 1, unillustrated. Ed. 3, rev. & enl. With Illustrated Introductory Lessons, Especially Adapted to the Pacific Coast. San Francisco [etc.], 1882. xviii+138 [i.e., 146] pp., illus.; Ed. 4, rev. & enl., San Francisco [etc.], 1882; Rev. ed. 6, San Francisco [etc.], 1885; Rev. ed. 7, San Francisco [etc.], 1887; Ed. 8, Pt. 1: A Popular California Flora. Pt. 2. Analytical Key to West Coast Botany. San Francisco: Bancroft Co., 1891 (pt. 2 1888). xxvii+106 & 128 pp., illus.; Rev. ed. 9, To Which Is Added an Analytical Key to West Coast Botany. San Francisco: Whitaker & Ray, 1892 (pt. 2 1888). xxvii+106 & 128 pp., illus.; San Francisco, 1896.}

Rattan, Volney. 1897. Exercises in Botany for the Pacific States. San Francisco: Whitaker & Ray Co., 1897. iii+120 pp., illus.

Rattan, Volney. 1898. West Coast Botany: An Analytical Key to the Flora of the Pacific Coast in Which Are Described Over Eighteen Hundred Species of Flowering Plants Growing West of the Sierra Nevada and Cascade Crests, from San Diego to Puget Sound. San Francisco: Whitaker & Ray. 221 pp., illus.

Rees, Abraham. 1806–1818. The Cyclopaedia; or, Universal Dictionary of Arts, Sciences, and Literature, American ed. 1. Philadelphia: S. F. Bradford, and Murray, Fairman & Co. 41+5 vols. (text & pls.) Numerous line-eng. pls., incl. 14 botanical.

[Reid, Miss Anna Johnson, ed.] 1835–1836? The Passion Flower. New York: S. C. Reid [etc.], William Van Morden, No. 1–30–?, May 1835–1836–? Lith. pls. (col.).

Rennie, James and Arabella Clark. 1833. Alphabet of Botany for the Use of Beginners. By James Rennie. Revised and corrected for the use of American schools, by Arabella Clark. New York: Peter Hill. Wood-eng. illus. {Also, New York [etc.], 1835; Ed. 2, New York: Mahlon Day; Charleston: B. B. Hussey, 1837. 151 pp., wood-eng. illus.}

Rexford, Eben Eugene. 1887. Grandmother's Garden. Illustrated by Mary Cecilia Spaulding. Chicago: A. C. McClurg & Co. [4] pp. & 10? pls.

Rexford, Eben Eugene. 1890. Home Floriculture: A Familiar Guide to the Treatment of Flowering and Other Ornamental Plants in the House and Garden. Rochester: James Vick. xi+226 pp., 54 illus. {Also, Rochester, 1903.}

Richards, Thomas A. 1838. The American Artist; or, Young Ladies' Instructor, in the Art of Flower Painting, in Water Colours. Illustrated by Twenty-Three Progressive Studies, Drawn and Coloured by the Author. Baltimore: Batly & Burns. [23] pp. & 23 pl. (partly col.).

Rivers, Thomas. 1866. The Miniature Fruit Garden; or, The Culture of the Pyramidal and Bush Fruit Trees [etc.]. American ed. 1, from the English ed. 13. New York: Orange Judd & Co. x+133 pp. & 1 pl., 18 illus. {Also, Ed. 15, Boston: J. E. Tilton & Co., 1870. x+156 pp., illus.}

Robinson, John. 1878. Ferns in Their Homes and Ours. Salem: S. E. Cassino. Frontis., xvi+178 pp. & 22 pls. (8 chromolith.). [American Natural History Series.] {Ed. 5, Boston: Whidden, 1894. [American Natural History Series.]}

Roe, Edward Payson. 1880. Success with Small Fruits. New York: Dodd, Mead & Co. 313 pp., 11+1+11 wood-eng. illus. {Also, New York [etc.], 1886; 1898.}

Roessle, Theophilus. 1860. How to Cultivate and Preserve Celery. Ed. with a preface by Henry Steel Olcott. Albany: T. Roessle; New York: C. M. Saxton, Barker & Co. Frontis. (col.), 100 pp. & 3 pls. (2 col.). [Roessle's Gardener's Hand-Books, no.1.]

Rogers, Julia Ellen. 1902. Among the Green Trees; A Guide to Pleasant and Profitable Acquaintance with Familiar Trees. Chicago: A. W. Mumford. Frontis., xxii+202 pp. & 24 pls.

Rogers, Julia Ellen. 1905. The Tree Book: A Popular Guide to a Knowledge of the Trees of North America and Their Uses and Cultivation. With sixteen plates in colour and one hundred and sixty in black-and-white from photographs by A. Radclyffe Dugmore. New York: Doubleday, Page & Co. xx+589 pp., & 16 3-col. pls., half-tone illus. {Also, New York [etc.], 1907.}

Rose, N. Jönsson-. 1895. Window and Parlor Gardening; a Guide Book for the Selection, Propagation and Care of House Plants. New York: Scribner's. xi+164 pp., illus.

Rothrock, Joseph Trimble. [1878.] Reports upon the botanical collections made in portions of Nevada, Utah, California, Colorado, New Mexico and Arizona, during the years 1871, 1872, 1873, 1874, and 1875. By J. T. Rothrock ... and the following scientists: Sereno Watson, George Engelmann, Thos. C. Porter, M. S. Bebb, William Boott, George Vasey, D. C. Eaton, Thos. P. James [and] Edward Tuckerman. In: Engineer Department, U.S. Army. 1875–1889. Report upon United States Geographical Surveys West of the One Hundredth Meridian, in Charge of First Lieut. Geo. M. Wheeler [etc.]. 7 vols. in 8. [Washington: Government Printing Office]. Vol. VI. Botany. Frontis. (chromolith.), xx+404 pp. & 30 lith. pls.

Ruschenberger, William Samuel Waithman. 1844. Elements of Botany. Prepared for the Use of Schools and Colleges ... from the Text of Milne-Edwards, and Achille Comte. Philadelphia: Turner & Fisher. 161 pp., illus. [First Books of Natural History, vol. 7.] {Ed. 2, Philadelphia [etc.], 1845; Philadelphia [etc.], 1846.}

Rydberg, Per Axel. 1898. A Monograph of the North American Potentilleae. [Lancaster: New Era Printing House.] 223 pp. & 112 line pls. [Memoirs from the Department of Botany at Columbia College, vol. 2.]

St. Pierre, Jacques Henri Bernardin de. 1797. Studies of Nature. Translated by Henry Hunter, D.D. Illustrated with plates. 3 vols. Worcester: J. Nancrede. frontis. & 4 et. pls. (Rollinson sc.). {The eleventh study was also issued separately as: Botanical Harmony Delineated; or, Applications of Some General Laws of Nature to Plants. [etc.]. Worcester [etc.], 1797. 179 pp. &

3 et. pls. Pls. III–V are reversed etched copies by Rollinson of the line-eng. botanical plates in the original French ed.}

Sargent, Frederick Leroy. 1899. Corn Plants: Their Uses and Ways of Life. With numerous illustrations. Boston: Houghton, Mifflin & Co. v+106 pp., 32 line illus. {Also, New York and Boston, 1902.}

Sayre, Lucius Elmer. 1895. A Manual of Materia Medica and Pharmacognosy; an Introduction to the Study of the Vegetable Kingdom and the Vegetable and Animal Drugs [etc.]. Philadelphia: P. Blakiston's Son & Co., [c1894]. 555 pp., illus.

Schleiden, Matthias Jacob. 1853. Poetry of the Vegetable World; a Popular Exposition of the Science of Botany, and Its Relations to Man. Amer. ed. 1 from the London ed. of Henfrey. Alphonso Wood [etc.], eds. Cincinnati: Moore, Anderson, Wilstach & Keys; New York: Newman & Ivison. 360 pp. & 4 pls.

Schneider, Albert. 1897. A Textbook of General Lichenology, with Descriptions and Figures of the Genera Occurring in the Northeastern U.S. Binghamton: W. N. Clute & Co. xvii+230 pp. & 76 pls.

Schneider, Albert. 1898. A Guide to the Study of Lichens. Boston: B. Whidden. xii+234 pp. & 11 pls.

Schultz, Benjamin. 1795. An Inaugural Botanico-Medical Dissertation on the *Phytolacca decandra* of Linnaeus. Philadelphia: Thomas Dobson. 1 eng. pl.

Scribner, Frank Lamson-. 1869. Weeds of Maine: Affording Popular Descriptions and Practical Observations in Regard to the Habits, Properties and Best Methods of Extermination, of Nearly All the Weeds Found in the State. Augusta: Printed at the Kennebec Journal Office. 62 pp., illus.

Scribner, Frank Lamson-. 1875. The Ornamental and Useful Plants of Maine: Affording Popular Descriptions and Practical Observations on the Habits, Properties ... of Nearly All the Ornamental and Useful Plants Found Native in the State. [Part 1]. Augusta: Printed for the Author. Frontis. & 85 pp., illus. [All published.]

Scribner, Frank Lamson-. 1890. Fungus Diseases of the Grape and Other Plants and Their Treatment. Little Silver: J. T. Lovett Co. Frontis. (port.) & 134 pp., illus.

Scribner, Frank Lamson-. 1892–1894. Grasses of
Tennessee. Knoxville: Agricultural Experiment
Station of the University of Tennessee. 2 pts.
Illus. [Bulletin of the Agricultural Experiment
Station of the University of Tennessee, vol. 5,
no. 2; vol. 7, no. 1.]

Scribner, Frank Lamson- and C. L. Newman. 1888.
Preliminary Report on the Weeds of the Farm.
Knoxville: Agricultural Experiment Station of
the University of Tennessee. 44 pp. & 9 pls.
[Bulletin of the Agricultural Experiment Station
of the University of Tennessee, vol. 1, no. 3.]

Seelye, Charles W. 1874. The Language of Flowers
and Floral Conversation. Rochester, Union &
Advertiser Company's print. 119 pp., illus. {Ed.
2, Rochester: E. Hart, 1875. 142 pp., illus.}

Shecut, John Linnaeus Edward Whitridge. 1806.
Flora Carolinaeensis; or, A Historical, Medical,
and Economical Display of the Vegetable
Kingdom; According to the Linnaean, or Sexual
System of Botany. Being a Collection or
Compilation of the Various Plants Hitherto
Discovered and Made Known by the Several
Authors on Botany, &c. In two volumes. Vol. I.
Charleston: Pr. for the Author; by John Hoff.
All published. 579+[5] pp., 5 eng. pls.

Skelding, Mrs. Susie Barstow. 1883. Flowers from
Hill and Dale. Poems arranged and illustrated
by [etc.]. New York: White, Stokes & Allen.
Frontis. (col.), 132 pp., incl. chromolith. pls.

Skelding, Mrs. Susie Barstow. 1883. Maple Leaves
and Goldenrod: Poems of Maple Leaves, Golden
Rod, Harebells, Sweet Peas. New York: White,
Stokes & Allen. [16] pp. & 4 chromolith. pls.

Skelding, Mrs. Susie Barstow. 1883. Songs of
Flowers; Poems of Wood-Fringe, Pansies,
Columbine, Daisies and Ferns. New York:
White, Stokes & Allen. [126] pp. & chromolith.
pls.

Skelding, Mrs. Susie Barstow. 1884. A Bunch of
Roses, Designs of Pink Roses, Tulips, White
Roses, Heliotrope and Mignonette, Passion
Flowers. New York: White, Stokes & Allen. [15]
pp., & 4 chromolith. pls.

Skelding, Mrs. Susie Barstow. [1884.] Birthday
Flowers. New York: White, Stokes & Allen. 4
chromolith. pls.

Skelding, Mrs. Susie Barstow. 1884. Easter
Flowers, with Illustrations of Easter Lilies. New
York: White, Stokes & Allen. [16] pp. & 4
chromolith. pls.

Skelding, Mrs. Susie Barstow. 1884. Flowers from
Glade and Garden. Poems arranged and
illustrated by Susie Barstow Skelding. New
York: White, Stokes & Allen. Frontis. (col.),
8+[128] pp., & 11 chromolith. pls.

Skelding, Mrs. Susie Barstow. 1884. From Moor
and Glen. New York: White, Stokes & Allen.
[16] pp. & 4 chromolith. pls.

Skelding, Mrs. Susie Barstow. 1884. Heartsease:
Poems of Pansies. New York: White, Stokes &
Allen. 4 chromolith. pls.

Skelding, Mrs. Susie Barstow. 1884. Roses and
Forget-Me-Nots; a Valentine with Illustrations
of Moss-Roses and Forget-Me-Nots [etc.]. New
York: White, Stokes & Allen. [16] pp. & 4
chromolith. pls.

Skelding, Mrs. Susie Barstow. 1885. Flowers for
Winter Days. New York: White, Stokes & Allen.
[16] pp. & 4 chromolith. pls.

Skelding, Mrs. Susie Barstow. 1885. Flowers from
Here and There. Poems arranged and illustrated by Susie Barstow Skelding. New York:
White, Stokes & Allen. Frontis. (col.), 134 pp. &
11 chromolith. pls.

Skelding, Mrs. Susie Barstow. 1885. Flowers from
Sunlight & Shade. Poems arranged and
illustrated by [etc.]. New York: White, Stokes &
Allen. Frontis. (col.), 128 pp. & 11 chromolith.
pls.

Skelding, Mrs. Susie Barstow. 1885. Midsummer
Flowers; Designs of Maple Leaves; Clematis;
Wild Raspberry; Meadow Sweet, Berries and
Ferns. New York: White, Stokes & Allen. [16]
pp. & 4 chromolith. pls.

Skelding, Mrs. Susie Barstow. 1885. Spring
Blossoms. New York: White, Stokes & Allen. 4
chromolith. pls.

Skelding, Mrs. Susie Barstow. 1886. Flowers from
Dell and Bower. Poems illustrated by Susie
Barstow Skelding. New York: White, Stokes &
Allen. Frontis. (col.), 128 pp., & 11 chromolith.
pls.

Skelding, Mrs. Susie Barstow. 1886. Pansies and
Orchids; Designs of Pansies, Snow-Drops,
Heather, and Wild Rose, Orchids, Nasturtiums,
Geraniums; Poems by Prominent Authors. New
York: White, Stokes & Allen. [16] pp. & 4
chromolith. pls.

Small, John Kunkel. 1895. A Monograph of the
North American Species of the Genus
Polygonum. [Lancaster: New Era Printing

House]. 183 pp. & 85 pls. [Memoirs from the Department of Botany at Columbia College, vol. 1.]

Smith, Miss Ann, see Hill, Mrs. Ann.

Smith, Elisha. 1844. The Botanic Physician; Being a Compendium of the Practice of Physic, upon Botanic Principles, Containing All the Principal Branches Necessary to the Study of Medicine. Rev. ed., corr. & improv. by I. S. Smith. New York: Pr. by D. Adee. xii+508 pp. & 8 pls. (col.).

Smith, Emory Evans. 1902. The Golden Poppy. Palo Alto: San Francisco News Co., San Francisco, [c1901]. Frontis. (3-col. half-tone) & 230 pp., illus.

Smith, Sir James Edward. 1814. An Introduction to Physiological and Systematical Botany. First American, from the second English edition; with notes, by Jacob Bigelow, M.D. Boston: Published by Bradford and Read. 415 pp. & 15 eng. pls. {Also, Philadelphia, [by Munroe & Francis] for Anthony Finley; Boston: Bradford & Read, 1814.}

Smith, Sir James Edward. 1822. A Grammar of Botany, Illustrative of Artificial, as well as Natural Classification with an Explanation of Jussieu's System. To Which Is Added, a Reduction of All the Genera Contained in the Catalogue of North American Plants, to the Natural Families of the French Professor. By the late Henry Muhlenberg., D.D. New York: James V. Seaman. 284 pp. & 21 lith. pls. (col.).

Sprague, Isaac. 1881. Beautiful Wild Flowers of America. From original water-color drawings after nature, by [etc.]. Descriptive text by A[lpheus]. B[aker]. Hervey. With extracts from Longfellow, Whittier, Bryant, Holmes, and others. Boston: D. Lothrop & Co. 14 chromolith. pls. {Also, Boston: S. E. Cassino, 1882. 156 pp., incl. 14 chromolith. pls.; Boston: Estes & Lauriat, 1886. 86 pp. & 14 pls.; Troy: Nims & Knight, 1887. 10 chromolith. pls.}

Sprague, Isaac. 1883. Flowers of Field and Forest. From original water color drawings after nature by [etc.]. Descriptive text by Rev. A[lpheus]. B[aker]. Hervey. With extracts from Longfellow, Lowell, Bryant, Emerson and others. Boston: S. E. Cassino. 154 pp., incl. 14 chromolith. pls. {Also, Nims & Knight, 1888. 93 pp. & 10 pls.; Boston: L. C. Page, 1899.}

Sprague, Isaac. 1883. Wayside Flowers and Ferns. From original water-color drawings by [etc.]. With selections from the poets. Boston: S. E. Cassino. 14 chromolith. pls. {Also, Troy: Nims & Knight, 1887. 10 chromolith. pls.; Boston: L. C. Page, 1899. 10 chromolith. pls.}

Starr, William Martin. 1895. Medical Botany or Specific Remedies from Nature's Own Cures. Washington. Port. & 100 pp., illus.

Stewart, Homer. 1891. Celery Growing and Marketing: A Success. Tecumseh: The Blade Printing & Paper Co. Port. & 151 pp., 13 wood-eng. illus.

Stewart, Homer. 1893. The Pecan, and How to Grow It. Where They Grow Wild, Where They Are Being Cultivated, What Lands Are Best and All about It. Chicago: Woman's Temperance Publishing Association. Frontis. & 90 pp., illus.

Stiles, William Augustus. [1894.] Orchids. Illustrations by Paul de Longpré. [New York]. [14] pp., illus. {First printed in Scribner's Magazine, vol. 15, pp. 190–203, 1894.}

Strong, Asa B. 1846–1850. The American Flora; or, History of Plants and Wild Flowers, Containing a Systematic and General Description, Natural History, Chemical and Medicinal Properties of Over Six Thousand Plants, Accompanied with a Circumstantial Detail of the Medical Effects, and of the Diseases in Which They Have Been Most Successfully Employed. 4 vols. New York: Green & Spencer. 195 lith. pls. (col.). {Also, New York: String & Bidwell, 1846–1850; New York: J. C. Burdick, 1847; New York: Strong and Burdick, 1847; New York, 1849–1851; New York, 1851–1853; New York: Green & Spencer, 1853.}

Strong, Thomas W. [1840s?] Drawing without a Master: Animals & Flowers. Boston: G. W. Cottrell. 12 pls.

Sullivant, William Starling. 1846–1849. Contributions to the Bryology and Hepaticology of North America. Pts. I & II. Boston. [Memoirs of the American Academy of Arts and Sciences, ser. 2, vol. III(1), 1846, pp. 57–66 & pls. 1–5; and vol. IV(1), 1849, pp. 169–176, pls. 1–5.] {Re-pub., Cambridge, 1849. Lith. pls.}

Sullivant, William Starling. 1856. Description of the mosses and liverworts. Route near the thirty-fifth parallel, explored by Lieutenant A. W. Whipple, ... in 1853 and 1854. Report of the botany of the expedition. In: U.S. War Department. 1855–1860. Reports of Explorations and Surveys, to Ascertain the Most Practicable and Economical Route for a Railroad Route from the Mississippi River to the Pacific Ocean. Made under the Direction of the Secretary of War, in 1853–[1856]. 12 vols. in 13. Washington. Vol. IV, no. 5. Pp. 185–193. 10 lith. pls.

Sullivant, William Starling. 1856. The Musci and Hepaticae of the United States East of the Mississippi Contributed to the Second Edition of Gray's Manual of Botany. New York: G. P. Putnam & Co. 8 lith. pls. {A separate issue of this portion of the Manual.}

Sullivant, William Starling, et al. 1862. Botany. Lower Cryptogamia. With a folio atlas of plates. In: Charles Wilkes et al. 1845–1876. United States Exploring Expedition. During the Years 1838, 1839, 1840, 1841, 1842. Under the Command of Charles Wilkes, U.S.N. 19 vols. Philadelphia: C. Sherman. Vol. 17. 38 eng. pls.

Sullivant, William Starling. 1864. Icones Muscorum or Figures and Descriptions of Most of Those Mosses Peculiar to Eastern North America, Which Have Not Been Heretofore Figured. Cambridge: Sever & Francis. vii+216 pp. & 129 eng. pls.

Sullivant, William Starling. 1874. Icones Muscorum ...: Supplement. Cambridge [etc.]. 81 pls.

Sumner, George. 1820. A Compendium of Physiological and Systematic Botany. With plates. Hartford [etc.] xii+300 pp. 8 eng. pls.

Thayer, Mrs. Emma Homan. [1885.] Wild Flowers of Colorado. From original water color sketches drawn from nature by Emma Homan Thayer. New York: Cassell & Co. 54 pp. & 24 chromolith. pls.

Thayer, Mrs. Emma Homan. [1887?] Wild Flowers of the Pacific Coast. From original water color sketches drawn from nature by [etc.]. New York: Cassell Publishing Co. 64 pp. & 24 chromolith. pls.

Thayer, Mrs. Emma Homan. c1887. Wild Flowers of the Rocky Mountains. (formerly Wild Flowers of Colorado.) New York: Cassell & Co. 54 pp. & 24 chromolith. pls.

"Thinker, Theodore." [i.e., Francis Channing Woodworth]. 1847. First Lessons in Botany; or, The Child's Book of Flowers. Illustrated with engravings. For families and schools. By Theodore Thinker. New York: D. Austin Woodworth; Boston: Saxton & Kelt. Wood-eng. illus. {Also, [n.p.,] 1851.}

Thomas, John Jacobs. 1846. The Fruit Culturist, Adapted to the Climate of the Northern States; Containing Directions for Raising Young Trees in the Nursery, and for the Management of the Orchard and Fruit Garden. Illustrated with engravings. New York: Mark H. Newman. 30 wood-eng. illus. {Also, Auburn: J. C. Derby & Co.; Geneva: G. H. Derby & Co., 1846; Ed. 4, Buffalo, 1847. 216 pp., 36 wood-eng. illus.}

Thomas, John Jacobs. 1847. The American Fruit Culturist. Containing Directions for the Propagation and Culture of Fruit Trees in the Nursery, Orchard and Garden. With Descriptions of the Principal American and Foreign Varieties Cultivated in the United States. Illustrated with three hundred accurate figures. Auburn: Derby, Miller & Co. 410 pp., 300 wood-eng. illus. {Many other eds. including, Auburn [etc.], 1850. Also, 6th thousand. Auburn, Derby [etc.], 1851. 300 text illus.; 7th thousand. New York [etc.], 1852; New York: Miller, Orton & Mulligan, 1856. 424 pp.; New York: C. M. Saxton, 1859. 424+[6] pp., wood-eng. illus.; New York: C. M. Saxton, Barker & Co., 1860; New York: W. Wood & Co., 1867. 511 pp., illus.; New York [etc.], 1868; Thoroughly rev. ed., illus. with five hundred and eight accurate figures. New York [etc.], 1875. 576 pp., illus.; Ed. 20, rev. & enl. by William H. S. Wood. New York, [etc.], 1897. xv+758 pp., illus.; Ed. 21, New York, 1903. Nearly 800 text illus. "Probably no other horticultural work in America has been revised so often or published in such large editions. Why its popularity was so great is a little hard to understand, since its descriptions of varieties were largely compiled, often inaccurate, and not particularly well written." (Hedrick, U. P. 1950. History of Horticulture in America to 1860. New York.)}

Thomson, Samuel. 1841. The Thomsonian Materia Medica; or, Botanic Family Physician: Comprising, a Philosophical Theory, the Natural Organization and Assumed Principles of Animal and Vegetable Life; to Which Is Added the Description of Plants and Their Various Compounds; Together with Practical Illustrations Including Much Other Useful Matter.

With plates. Ed. 12, enl., corr., rev. & improv.
[John Thomson, ed.] Albany: Printed by
J. Munsell. 834 pp. & 12 (botanical) eng. pls.
(col.), many anatomical illus. {Ed. 13, Albany:
J. Munsell, 1841.}

Thornton, Robert John. 1818. A Grammar of
Botany; Containing an Explanation of the
System of Linnaeus, and the Terms of Botany,
with Botanical Exercises, for the Use of Schools
and Students. Illustrated by forty-five engravings. Multum in parvo. New York: James
Eastburn & Co. 317 pp. & 45 eng. pls.

Todd, Sereno Edwards. 1871. The Apple Culturist;
a Complete Treatise for the Practical Pomologist, to Aid in Propagating the Apple, and
Cultivating and Managing Orchards. New York:
Harper & Bros. 334 pp., illus.

Torrey, John. 1843. A Flora of the State of New
York, Comprising Full Descriptions of All the
Indigenous and Naturalized Plants Hitherto
Discovered in the State, with Remarks on Their
Economical and Medicinal Properties. 2 vols.
Albany: Carroll & Cook. 72+88 lith. pls.
[Natural History of New York, pt. 2.]

Torrey, John. 1848. [List of plants collected by
Major W. H. Emory.] In: W. H. Emory et al.
1848. Notes of a Military Reconnoissance, from
Fort Leavenworth in Missouri, to San Diego, in
California, Including Parts of the Arkansas, Del
Norte, and Gila rivers. By W. H. Emory ... Made
in 1846-7 [etc.]. Washington. 12 lith. pls. [30th
Congress. 1st Session [Senate] Executive no.
7.]

Torrey, John. 1852. Catalogue of plants collected by
the Expedition. In: Howard Stansbury et al.
1852. Exploration and Survey of the Valley of
the Great Salt Lake of Utah, Including a
Reconnaissance of a New Route through the
Rocky Mountains [1849–1850]. Philadelphia:
Lippincott, Grambo & Co. 9 lith. pls. [Special
Session March 1851, Senate, Executive vol. 2,
Serial no. 608, no. 3.]

Torrey, John. 1853. Botany. In: L. Sitgreaves et al.
1853. Report of an Expedition down the Zuni
and Colorado Rivers, by Captain L. Sitgreaves,
[etc.]. Washington: R. Armstrong. 21 lith. pls.
[32nd Congress, 2nd Session Senate. Executive, no. 59.]

Torrey, John. 1853. Description of plants collected
during the expedition. In: Randolph B. Marcy
et al. 1853. Exploration of the Red River of

Louisiana, in the Year 1852: by Randolph B.
Marcy, Captain ... Assisted by George B.
McClellan, Brevet Captain [etc.]. Washington:
R. Armstrong. 20 lith. pls. [32nd Congress, 2nd
Session Senate Executive, no. 54.]

Torrey, John. 1854. Plantae Frémontianae or
Descriptions of Plants Collected by Col. J. C.
Frémont in California. Washington. 10 lith. pls.
[Smithsonian Contributions to Knowledge, vol.
6, pt. 2.]

Torrey, John. 1856 [1857]. Description of the
general botanical collections. Route near the
thirty-fifth parallel, explored by Lieutenant A.
W. Whipple, ... in 1853 and 1854. Report of the
botany of the expedition. In: U.S. War Department. 1855–1860. Reports of Explorations and
Surveys, to Ascertain the Most Practicable and
Economical Route for a Railroad Route from
the Mississippi River to the Pacific Ocean.
Made under the Direction of the Secretary of
War, in 1853–[1856]. 12 vols. in 13. Washington: B. Tucker. Vol. IV, [no. 4]. 126 pp. & 25
lith. pls.

Torrey, John. 1854–1855 [1858]. Botanical report
... 1856. Routes in California to connect with
the routes near the thirty-fifth and thirty-
second parallels, and route near the thirty-
second parallel between the Rio Grande and
Pimas villages, explored by Lieutenant John G.
Parke, ... in 1854 and 1855. In: U.S. War
Department. 1855–1860. Reports of Explorations and Surveys, to Ascertain the Most
Practicable and Economical Route for a
Railroad Route from the Mississippi River to
the Pacific Ocean. Made under the Direction of
the Secretary of War, in 1853–[1856]. 12 vols.
in 13. [Washington]. [Vol. VII]. 8 lith. pls.

Torrey, John. 1856 [1858]. Description of plants
collected along the route, by W. P. Blake, and
at the mouth of the Gila. Report of explorations
in California for railroad routes, to connect
with the routes near the 35th and 32d parallels
of north latitude by Lieutenant R. S.
Williamson, ... 1853. In: U.S. War Department.
1855–1860. Reports of Explorations and
Surveys, to Ascertain the Most Practicable and
Economical Route for a Railroad Route from
the Mississippi River to the Pacific Ocean.
Made under the Direction of the Secretary of
War, in 1853–[1856]. 12 vols. in 13. Washington: B. Tucker. Vol. V. 10 lith. pls.

Torrey, John. 1859. Botany of the boundary. In: W. H. Emory et al. 1857–1859. Report on the United States and Mexican Boundary Survey, Made under the Direction of the Secretary of the Interior, by William H. Emory, Major [etc.]. 2 vols. in 3. Washington: C. Wendell. Vol. II. 61 lith. pls. [34th Congress, 1st Session, House of Representatives, Ex. Doc. no. 135.]

Torrey, John. 1862, 1874. Phanerogamia of Pacific North America. With a folio atlas of plates. In: Charles Wilkes et al. 1845–1876. United States Exploring Expedition. During the Years 1838, 1839, 1840, 1841, 1842. Under the Command of Charles Wilkes, U.S.N. 19 vols. Philadelphia: Printed by C. Sherman. Vol. 17. Pt II. 514 pp. & 29 eng. pls.

Torrey, John and Asa Gray. 1855 [1857]. Report on the botany of the expedition. Route on the forty-first parallel of north latitude, under the command of Lieut. E. G. Beckwith, ... and route near the thirty-eighth and thirty-ninth parallels of north latitude, under the command of Capt. J. W. Gunnison, ..., 1854. In: U.S. War Department. 1855–1860. Reports of Explorations and Surveys, to Ascertain the Most Practicable and Economical Route for a Railroad Route from the Mississippi River to the Pacific Ocean. Made under the Direction of the Secretary of War, in 1853–[1856]. 12 vols. in 13. Washington: B. Tucker. Vol. II. 10 lith. pls.

Torrey, John and Asa Gray. 1855 [1857]. Report on the botany of the expedition. Report of exploration of a route for the Pacific Railroad near the thirty-second parallel of north latitude from the Red River to the Rio Grande, by Brevet Captain John Pope, 1854. In: U.S. War Department. 1855–1860. Reports of Explorations and Surveys, to Ascertain the Most Practicable and Economical Route for a Railroad Route from the Mississippi River to the Pacific Ocean. Made under the Direction of the Secretary of War, in 1853–[1856]. 12 vols. in 13. Washington: B. Tucker. Vol. II. 10 lith. pls.

Turner, Mrs. Cordelia Harris.] 1891. The Floral Kingdom; Its History, Sentiment, and Poetry. Chicago: Standard Columbian Co. 5 chromolith. pls.

[Tyas, Robert.] 1840. The Sentiment of Flowers; or, A Language of Flora. Embracing an Account of Nearly Three Hundred Different Flowers, with Their Powers of Language. With coloured plates. Philadelphia: Lea & Blanchard. 276 pp. & 4 eng. pls. (col.).

Underwood, Lucien Marcus. 1899. Moulds, Mildews, and Mushrooms: A Guide to the Systematic Study of the Fungi and Mycetozoa and Their Literature. New York: H. Holt & Co. Frontis. (chromolith.), v+236 pp. & 9 heliotype pls.

University of Nebraska, Botanical Seminar. 1894–1895. Flora of Nebraska. Ed. by members of the Botanical Seminar of the University of Nebraska. Lincoln. Pts. 1 & 2. 128 pp. & 36 line-drawn pls.; pt. 21, Per Axel Rydberg. Rosales. 82 pp. & 11 line-drawn pls.

Vasey, George. 1884. The Agricultural Grasses of the United States. Also the chemical composition of American grasses. By Clifford Richardson. Washington: Government Printing Office. 144 pp. & 120 lith. pls. {New & rev. & enl. ed. Washington: G.P.O., 1889. 148 pp. & 114 pls.}

Vasey, George. 1886. Report of an Investigation of the Grasses of the Arid Districts of Kansas, Nebraska, and Colorado. Washington: Government Printing Office. 19 pp. & 13 pls.

Vasey, George. 1887. Grasses of the South: A Report on Certain Grasses and Forage Plants for Cultivation in the South and Southwest. Washington: Government Printing Office. 63 pp. & 16 pls.

Vasey, George. 1891–1893. Illustrations of North American Grasses. Vol. I. Grasses of the Southwest. Plates and Descriptions of the Grasses of the Desert Region of Western Texas, New Mexico, Arizona and Southern California. Vol. II. Grasses of the Pacific Slope, Including Alaska and the Adjacent Islands. Plates and Descriptions of the Grasses of California, Oregon, Washington, and the Northwestern Coast, Including Alaska. Washington. 200 lith. pls. [Bulletin, Division of Botany, U.S. Department of Agriculture, nos. 12–13.]

Vick, James, Seedsman. [1876.] Vick's Flower and Vegetable Garden. Rochester: J. Vick. 119 pp. & 6 chromolith. pls., wood-eng. illus. {Includes Vick's priced catalogue of seeds, bulbs and other plants for 1876.}

Vick, James. [1885.] Portfolio of Rare and Beautiful Flowers from Original Water Color Sketches, Painted from Nature [by John Walton].

Rochester: J. Vick. [11] pp. & 6 chromolith. pls.

Vick, James, [ca.1889.] Practical Garden Points. Rochester. [ii]+108 pp., illus.

Vischer, Edward. 1862. Vischer's Views of California: The Mammoth Tree Grove, Calveras County, California, and Its Avenues. San Francisco: "Published by Edward Vischer." Portfolio, t.p. & 12 pls. with 25 images. {This publication was suddenly interrupted when the stone broke on which the principal images were drawn.}

Vischer, Edward. ca.1862. The Mammoth Tree Grove, Calaveras Co., California, and Its Avenues. Drawn by [etc.]. San Francisco: Nagel, Fisbourne, & Kuchel, lithographers. 16 views on one sheet with legends and descriptive letterpress beneath.

Vischer, Edward. [1862?] The Forest Trees of California. *Sequoia gigantea.* Calaveras Mammoth Tree Grove. Photographs, from the original drawings of Edward Vischer, with contributions from various sources. San Francisco: Agnew & Deffebach, printer; Geo. W. Johnston, photo. [v]+14+iii pp. & 27 photo pls.

Vischer, Edward. [1870.] Vischer's Pictorial of California: Landscape, Trees, and Forest Scenes: Grand Features of California Scenery, Life, Traffic and Customs: Photographs from the Original Drawings. In five series of twelve numbers each, with a supplement, and contributions from reliable sources. [San Francisco: Printed by J. Winterburn & Co.] [v]+132+iii pp. & 169 photos.

Wailes, Benjamin Leonard Covington. 1854. Report on the Agriculture and Geology of Mississippi. Embracing a Sketch of the Social and Natural History of the State. Philadelphia: Lippincott, Grambo & Co. 371 pp. & 17 chromolith. pls.

Wakefield, Priscilla Bell. 1811. An Introduction to Botany, in a Series of Familiar Letters, with Illustrative Engravings. The first American from the fifth London edition. To which is added, an appendix, containing the celebrated Mr. Roscoe's address to the Proprietors of the Botanic Garden at Liverpool; A catalogue of the English names and Linnaean genera of the plants described in this volume; and A glossary of technical terms. Boston: J. Belcher; and J. W. Burditt & Co. xii+216 pp. & 12 eng. pls. {Also, Philadelphia: Pr. by Wm. Brown for Kimber & Conrad, 1811.}

Warder, John Aston. 1858. Hedges and Evergreens. A Complete Manual for the Cultivation, Pruning, and Management of All Plants for American Hedging; Especially the Maclura, or Osage orange ... To Which Is Added, a Treatise on Evergreens [etc.]. New York: A. O. Moore. 291 pp., & 12 pls., illus. {Also, New York: Orange Judd & Co., [1858]; New York: A. O. Moore, 1859.}

Warder, John Aston. [1867.] American Pomology. Apples. New York: Orange Judd & Co. 744 pp., illus.

Waring, William G. 1851. The Fruit Grower's Hand Book. A Concise Manual of Directions for the Selection and Culture of the Best Hardy Fruits in the Garden or Orchard. Boalsburg. Illus.

Waterman, Caleb H. 1857. Flora's Lexicon ... Outline of Botany. Boston. Illus.

Watson, Alexander. 1859. The American Home Garden. Being Principles and Rules for the Culture of Vegetables, Fruits, Flowers, and Shrubbery. To Which Are Added Brief Notes on Farm Crops. [etc.]. Illustrated. New York: Harper & Bros. ix+531 pp., 316 illus. {Also, New York [etc.], 1860.}

Watson, Sereno. 1871. Botany. Report of the Geological Exploration of the 40th Parallel ... Made by Clarence King, vol. 5. (Botany.) Washington. liii+525 pp. & 40 lith. pls.

Waugh, Frank Albert. 1901. Plums and Plum Culture. A Monograph of the Plums Cultivated and Indigenous in North America. With a Complete Account of Their Propagation, Cultivation, and Utilization. New York: Orange Judd & Co. xix+371 pp., half-tone illus.

Weed, Clarence Moores. 1894. Fungi and Fungicides: A Practical Manual Concerning the Fungous Diseases of Cultivated Plants and the Means of Preventing Their Ravages. New York: Orange, Judd. vii+228 pp., line illus. {Also, New York [etc.], 1896.}

Weed, Clarence Moores. 1898. Seed Travellers; Studies of the Methods of Dispersal of Various Common Seeds. Boston: Ginn & Co. Frontis. & iv+53 pp., illus.

Wellcome, Mrs. M. D. [1881.] Talks about Flowers. Yarmouth, Maine. Frontis. & 162 pp., illus.

White, Joseph J. [1870.] Cranberry Culture. New York: O. Judd & Co. 126 pp., illus. {New & enl. ed., 1885. 131 pp., 34 illus.}

White, William N. 1856. Gardening for the South; or, The Kitchen and Fruit Garden: With the Best Methods for Their Cultivation, Together with Hints upon Landscape and Flower Gardening. Containing Modes of Culture, and Descriptions of the Species and Varieties of the Culinary Vegetables; Fruit Trees and Fruits, and a Select List of Ornamental Trees and Plants, Found by Trial Adapted to the States of the Union South of Pennsylvania; with Gardening Calendars for the Same. New York: C. M. Saxton & Co.; Athens: W. N. White. 402 pp., some illus. {Also, New York [etc.], 1857; Rev. & newly stereotyped. With additions by Mr. J. Van Buren, and Dr. Jas. Camak. New York, 1868. Frontis. (port.) & 444 pp., 116 illus.; New York: Orange Judd & Co., 1885; Ed. 3, Richmond: B. F. Johnson Publishing Co., 1901. Frontis. & 683 pp., illus.}

Whitelock, Louise Clarkson. 1877. The Gathering of the Lilies. Illustrated by the Author, L. Clarkson. Colored plates and lithographic etchings. Philadelphia: J. L. Sibole & Co. 36 ff., 4 chromolith. pls.

Whitelock, Louise Clarkson. 1883. Indian Summer: Autumn Poems and Sketches. New York: E. P. Dutton & Co. [5] ff. & 12 lith. pls. (col.).

Whitner, J. N. 1885. Gardening in Florida: A Treatise on the Vegetables and Tropical Products of Florida. Jacksonville: C. W. Da Costa. 246 pp., illus.

Whittock, Nathaniel. 1852. The Oxford Drawing Book, Containing Progressive Information in Sketching, Drawing, and Coloring Landscape Scenery, Animals, and the Human Figure. With a New Method of Practical Perspective. To Which Is Added, Lessons in Flower Drawing, a Series of Plates by James Andrews. New York: R. B. Collins. 27+4 lith. pl. (col.).

Wickson, Edward James. 1889. The California Fruits and How to Grow Them; A Manual of Methods Which Have Yielded Greatest Success: With Lists of Varieties Best Adapted to the Different Districts of the State. San Francisco: Dewey & Co. Frontis. (col.) & 575 pp.,illus. {Ed. 2, rev. & enl., San Francisco [etc.], 1891. 599 pp., half-tone illus.; Ed. 3, largely rewritten, San Francisco: Pacific Rural Press, 1900. 477 pp., illus.}

Wickson, Edward James. 1897. The California Vegetables in Garden and Field; a Manual of Practice, with and without Irrigation, for Semitropical Countries. San Francisco: Pacific Rural Press. Frontis. & viii+336 pp., illus.

Wilkes, Charles. 1845–1876. United States Exploring Expedition. During the Years 1838, 1839, 1840, 1841, 1842 ..., see Brackenridge, Gray, Sullivant and Torrey.

Willement, Emily Elizabeth. 1841. A Bouquet from Flora's Garden. Norwich. Illus.

Williams, Henry T., ed. 1872. Window Gardening: Devoted Specially to the Culture of Flowers and Ornamental Plants for in door Use and Parlor Decoration. New York: H. T. Williams. 300 pp., 199 wood-eng. illus. {Several later eds., e.g., Ed. 10, 1874; Ed. 12, 1876; Ed. 13, New York: H. T. Williams, 1877; Ed. 14, 1878.}

Williams, Joseph Otis, comp. 1871. Mammoth Trees of California. Illustrated by a Comparison with Other Noted Trees, Ancient and Modern, with a Handbook in Brief for a Trip to the Calavaras Groves and Yosemite Valley. Boston: A. Mudge & Son, printers. 51 pp., wood-eng. illus.

Williamson, John. 1878. Ferns of Kentucky. With sixty full-page etchings and six wood-cuts, drawn by the author, illustrating structure, fertilization, classification, genera, and species. Louisville: Printed by J. P. Morton & Co. 154 pp., illus. {Also, Louisville, 1898. 60 pls.}

Willis, Oliver Rivington. 1894. A Practical Flora for Schools and Colleges. New York and Cincinnati: American Book Co. xvi+349 pp., many illus.

Wirt, Mrs. Elizabeth Washington Gamble. [1830?] Flora's Dictionary. By a Lady. Baltimore: Fielding Lucas, jun. [192] pp., & 6 lith. pls. (col.). {Other eds., some with more or less, or quite different pls., Baltimore: Fielding Lucas, jun., [1831]; Baltimore [etc.], 1832; Baltimore [etc.], 1833; Another ed. Embellished by Mrs. Anna Smith. Baltimore [etc.], 1835. Unpaged, 58 lith. pls. (col.).; Baltimore [etc.], [1837]; Baltimore: Lucas Bros., [c1855]. Eng. t.p., pres. leaf, & 6 lith. pls. (col.), numerous wood-eng. illus.}

Wolle, Rev. Francis. 1884. Desmids of the United States, and List of American Pediastrums. With Eleven Hundred Illustrations on Fifty-Three Colored Plates. Bethlehem: Moravian Publication Office. 168 pp. & 53 lith. pls. (col.).

[Report, United States Department of Agriculture, no. 32.]

Wolle, Rev. Francis. 1887. Fresh-water Alga of the United States (Exclusive of the Diatomacea). Complemental to Desmids of the United States. Bethlehem: The Comenius Press. 364 pp. & 157 lith. pls. (col.).

Wolle, Rev. Francis. 1890. Diatomacea of North America. Illustrated with twenty-three hundred figures from the author's drawings on one hundred and twelve plates. Bethlehem: The Comenius Press. 47 pp. & 112 lith. pls. (col.). {Also, 1894.}

Wolle, Rev. Francis. 1892. Desmids of the United States and List of American Pediastrums with Nearly Fourteen Hundred Illustrations on Sixty-Four Colored Plates. New & enl. ed. Bethlehem: Moravian Publication Office. 182 pp. & 64 lith. pls. (col.).

Wood, Alphonso. 1845. A Class-Book of Botany, Designed for Colleges, Academies, and Other Seminaries Where the Science Is Taught [etc.]. In two parts: Pt. I. The Elements of Botanical Science. Pt. II. The Natural Orders. Illustrated by a Flora of the Northern United States Particularly New England and New York. Boston: Crocker & Brewster. 124+474 pp., wood-eng. illus. {Ed. 2, rev. & enl. as, A Class-Book of Botany, ... Illustrated by a Flora of the Northern Middle, and Western States; Particularly of the United States North of the Capitol, lat. 38 3/48°. Claremont Manufacturing Co., S. Ide, agent, 1847. Illus. Many eds., incl., Ed. 10, Claremont, [etc.], 1848; Ed. 10, Boston: Crocker & Brewster, 1849; Ed. 17, Boston [etc.], 1851; Ed. 23, Claremont, [etc.], 1851; Ed. 35, Boston [etc.], 1854; Ed. 41, Claremont, [etc.], 1856; Class-book of Botany ... with a Flora of the United States and Canada. New York: A. S. Barnes & Burr, 1861. viii+832+xx+[8] pp., 5 pls., illus.; many more unnumbered eds., New York: A. S. Barnes & Co.; Troy: Moore & Nims [imprints vary], 1862 to 1881.}

Wood, Alphonso. 1856. First Lessons in Botany; Designed for Common Schools in the United States. Claremont, N.H.: Claremont Manufacturing Co., Samuel Ide, Agent; Boston: Crocker & Brewster. Frontis. & 255 pp., wood-eng. illus.

Wood, Alphonso. 1863. Leaves and Flowers; or, Object Lessons in Botany, with a Flora; Prepared for Beginners in Academies and Public Schools. New York: Barnes & Burr; Troy: Moore & Nims. Frontis. (col.) & 322 pp., illus. (part col.). {Also, New York: A. S. Barnes, 1867; New York [etc.], 1873; New York [etc.], 1877.}

Wood, Alphonso. 1870. The American Botanist and Florist; Including Lessons in the Structure, Life and Growth of Plants; Together with a Simple Analytical Flora, Descriptive of the Native and Cultivated Plants Growing in the Atlantic Division of the American Union. New York: A. S. Barnes. 441 pp., 560 line illus. {Also, New York [etc.], 1872; New York [etc.], 1873; New York [etc.], 1874; New York: A. S. Barnes, 1875; Rev. & ed. by Oliver R. Willis. New York and Chicago: A. S. Barnes & Co., [c1889]. vi+220+15–449 pp., illus.; also issued as, The New American Botanist and Florist [etc.]. Rev. & ed. by Oliver R. Willis. New York [etc.]: American Book Co., c1889.}

Wood, Alphonso. 1871. The Sedges and Grasses Growing in the Atlantic Division of the United States: Being an Addenda to the American Botanist and Florist. New York: A. S. Barnes. pp. 355–444, wood-eng. illus.

Wood, Alphonso. 1877. Wood's Illustrated Plant Record, with King's Check Tablets, for the Rapid and Systematic Analysis of Plants. Adapted to any American botany. New York, Chicago, [etc.]: A. S. Barnes & Co. 21+[155] pp., illus.

Wood, Alphonso. 1879. Flora Atlantica. Descriptive Botany: Being a Succinct Analytical Flora, Including All the Plants Growing in the United States from the Atlantic Coast to the Mississippi River. From the American Botanist and Florist. New York, Chicago, [etc.]: A. S. Barnes. iv+448 pp., wood-eng. illus. {Also, New York: American Book Co., [1879].}

Wood, Alphonso. 1882. How to Study Plants; or, Introduction to Botany, Being an Illustrated Flora. By ... to accompany the "Fourteen weeks series in natural science." New York: A. S. Barnes. 318 pp., wood-eng. & half-tone illus. [Steele's Series in Natural Science.] {Also, New York, Cincinnati, [etc.]: American Book Co., c1895. 308+53+3–30+38 pp., illus.}

Wood, Alphonso. [c1889.] Lessons in the Structure, Life, and Growth of Plants, for Schools and Academies. Rev. & ed. by Oliver R. Willis. New York and Chicago: A. S. Barnes & Co. vi+220 pp., wood-eng. illus.

Wood, Alphonso. [1895.] How to Study Plants: An Illustrated Flora for Teachers' Reading Circles. New York: American Book. Illus.

Wood, Alphonso and J. Dorman Steele. 1879. How to Study Plants. Fourteen Weeks in Botany: Being an Illustrated Flora. New York: A. S. Barnes & Co. xii+318 pp., illus. [Steele's Series in the Natural Sciences.]

Wood, Horatio Curtis. 1872 or 1874? A contribution to the history of fresh-water algae of North America. Washington. 21 chromolith. pls. [Smithsonian Contributions to Knowledge, vol. 29.]

Woodworth, Francis Channing, see Thinker, Theodore.

Wright, Mrs. Julia McNair. 1891. Sea-Side and Way-Side. Boston: D. C. Heath. Illus. [Nature Readers; Seaside and Wayside, no. 3.] {Also, Boston, 1903.}

Wright, Mrs. Julia McNair. 1898. Botany: The Story of Plant Life. Philadelphia: The Penn Publishing Co. 208 pp., illus.

Youmans, Eliza Ann. 1870. The First Book on Botany. Designed to Cultivate the Observing Powers of Children. New York: D. Appleton & Co. 183 pp., wood-eng. illus. {New & enl. ed., New York: D. Appleton, 1876. New ed., thoroughly rev. The First Book on Botany: A Practical Guide in Self-Teaching [etc.]. New York [etc.], 1883. 158 pp., wood-eng. illus.}

Youmans, Eliza Ann. 1873. The Second Book on Botany. A Practical Guide to the Observation and Study of Plants. New York: D. Appleton & Co. 310 pp., wood-eng. illus.

Youmans, Eliza Ann. 1885. Descriptive Botany. New York: D. Appleton & Co. xxvi+336 pp., illus. {New ed. New York, Cincinnati, [etc.]: American Book Co., [c1898]. 158 pp., illus.}

Young, C. S. 1895. All of Nature's Fashions in Lady's Slippers for the Northern and Eastern Parts of the United States. With photogravures from the living plant. Boston: Bradlee Whidden. [20] pp. & 6 pls.

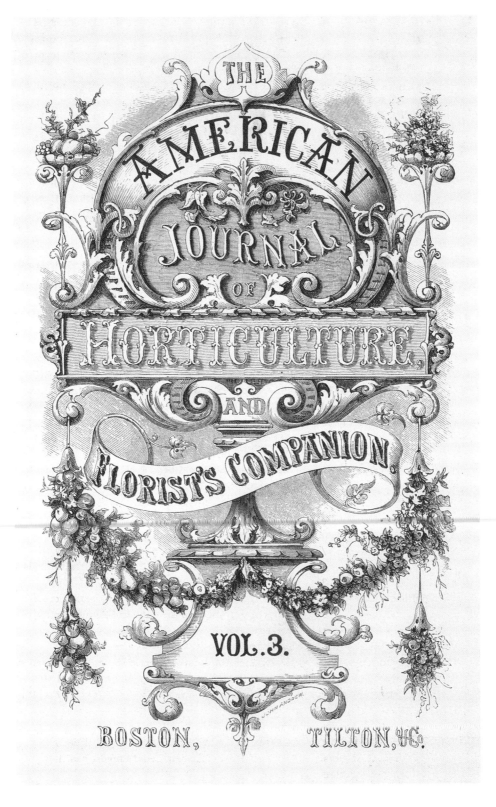

THE AMERICAN JOURNAL OF HORTICULTURE AND FLORIST'S COMPANION.

VOL. 3.

BOSTON, TILTON, &Co.

Title page of *The American Journal of Horticulture and Florist's Companion,* 1868.

Some
periodicals
with
botanical or
other plant
illustrations

American Agriculturist; for the Farm, Garden, and Household [subtitle varies]. New York: Geo. A. Peters, vols. 1–10, April 1842–1851; New York: Orange Judd Co., n.s., vols. 1–89(20), 1852–1912. Illus. {Over several years incorporated more than 30 other agricultural journals.}

The American Chrysanthemum Annual 1895. Michael Barker, ed. Floral Park: Mayflower Publishing Co., [1895?]. Frontis. & 44 pp., pls. & illus.

The American Garden; a Monthly Illustrated Journal Devoted to the Gardening Interests of America. James Hogg, ed. (later F. M. Hexamer). Brooklyn, New York , n.s., 1874–1877; ser. 2, 1878–1879; [ser. 3] vols. 1–12, 1880–1891. Preceded by: The Flower Garden; a Quarterly Magazine of Floral Progress. Nos. 1–7, 1872–1874. Not entered. Superseded by: American Gardening; a Weekly Illustrated Journal of Horticulture. F. M. Hexamer, ed. (later E. H. Libbey and L. H. Bailey). New York: A. T. De La Mare Ptg. & Pub. Co., Ltd., vols. 13–25(509), 1892–1904. Illus.

American Gardener's Magazine, and Register of Useful Discoveries and Improvements in Horticulture and Rural Affairs. Conducted by C. M. Hovey and P. B. Hovey, Jr. Boston, vols. 1–2, 1835–1836. Few illus. Superseded by: The Magazine of Horticulture, Botany and All Useful Discoveries and Improvements in Rural Affairs. C. M. Hovey, ed. Boston: Hovey & Co.; New York, vols. 3–10, 1837–1844; n.s., vols. 1(11)–10(20), 1845–1854; ser. 3, vols. 1(21)–5(25), 1855–1859; ser. 4, vols. 1(26)–4(29), 1860–1863; ser. 5, vols. 1(30)–4(34), 1864–1868. Illus.

American Journal of Horticulture and Florists' Companion. Boston: Tilton & Co., vols. 1–4, 1867–1868. Illus. Superseded by: Tilton's Journal of Horticulture. Boston [etc.], vols. 5–9, 1869–1871. Illus.

American Journal of Science; More Especially of Mineralogy, Geology, and the Other Branches of Natural History. New York: J. Eastburn & Co.; New Haven: Howe & Spalding, vol. 1, 1818–1819; ed. 2, vol. 1, 1819. Superseded by: American Journal of Science and Arts. New Haven. 1820–1879. Not entered.

The American Pomologist; Containing Finely Colored Drawings, Accompanied by Letter-Press Descriptions of Fruits of American Origin. Alfred Hoffy and William Draper Brincklé, eds. Philadelphia, vol. 1, 1861. 10 pls.

Annals of the Lyceum of Natural History of New York. New York, vols. 1–11, (1824/25–1874/76), 1824–1877. Pls. {E.g., Schweinitz, Lewis David von. 1825. Monograph of the North American species of the genus *Carex*. Annals [etc.] 1(2): 283–374. 9 pls.}

Baltimore Cactus Journal; a Monthly Publication Devoted to the Culture of Cacti, Succulent and Other Plants Closely Allied to the Cacti [etc.]. Baltimore: Baltimore Cactus Society, vols. 1–2, Jul. 1894–Apr. 1896. Illus.

Botanical Bulletin; a Paper of Botanical Notes. John M. Coulter, ed. Crawfordsville, Hanover [Indiana], vol. 1, (1874/75), 1875–1876. Superseded by: Botanical Gazette; Paper of Botanical Notes. John M. Coulter and M. S. Coulter, eds. Hanover [Indiana], Chicago, vols. 2–152(4), (1875+), 1878+. Pls., illus.

Botanical Gazette see Botanical Bulletin.

Bulletin from the Botanical Department of the State Agricultural College, Ames, Iowa. C. E. Bessey, ed. (later Byron D. Halsted). Cedar Rapids, nos. 1–3, 1884–1888. Illus.

Bulletin of the Botanical Division, Department of Agriculture. Washington, nos. 1–8, 1886–1889. Superseded by: Bulletin of the Section of Vegetable Pathology, Department of Agriculture. Washington, nos. 9–10, 1888–1889. Superseded by: Bulletin of the Division of Botany, U.S. Department of Agriculture. Washington, nos. 12–29, 1890–1901. {E.g., Scribner, Frank Lamson-. 1886. Report on the fungus diseases of the grape vine. Bulletin no. 2. 136 pp. & 7 pls. (col.).; and Scribner, Frank Lamson-. 1888. Report on the experiments made in 1887 in the treatment of the downy mildew and the black-rot of the grape vine, [etc.]. Bulletin no. 5. 113 pp., illus.}

Bulletin of the Division of Agrostology, U.S. Department of Agriculture. Washington, nos. 1–24, 1895–1901. {E.g., Smith, Jared Gage. 1896. Fodder and forage plants, exclusive of grasses. Bulletin no. 2. 58 pp., illus.; Scribner, Frank Lamson- (& Elmer Drew Merrill). 1897–1900. American grasses. (Illustrated.) 3 pts. Bulletins no. 7, no. 17, & no. 20; and Bentley, Henry Lewis. 1898. A report upon the grasses and forage plants of central Texas. Bulletin no. 10. 38 pp., illus.}

Bulletin of the Division of Botany, U.S. Department of Agriculture see Bulletin of the Botanical Division, Department of Agriculture.

Bulletin of the Division of Pomology, U.S. Department of Agriculture. Washington, nos. 1–10, 1888–1901. {E.g., Taylor, William Alton. 1898. The fruit industry, and substitution of domestic for foreign-grown fruits, with historical and descriptive notes on ten varieties of apple suitable for the export trade. Bulletin no. 7, viii+[58] pp. & 5 pls. (col.).}

Bulletin of the Section of Vegetable Pathology, Department of Agriculture see Bulletin of the Botanical Division, Department of Agriculture.

Bulletin of the Torrey Botanical Club. New York: Torrey Botanical Club, vol. 1+, 1870+. Pls., illus.

Bulletin, United States Department of Agriculture. Washington, D.C., nos. 1–25, 1895–1901. {E.g., Smith, Jared Gage. 1899. Studies on American grasses. A synopsis of the genus *Sitanion*. Bulletin no. 18. 21 pp. & 4 pls.; and Scribner, Frank Lamson- and Elmer Drew Merrill. 1900. The North American species of *Chaetochloa*. Bulletin no. 21. 44 pp., illus.}

Contributions from the United States National Herbarium, Division of Botany, U.S. Department of Agriculture. Washington, vols. 1–7, 1890–1902.

Floral Magazine and Botanical Repository. Philadelphia: D. & C. Landreth, vol. 1, nos. 1–5, 1832–1834. 31 lith. pls. (col.).

The Florist and Horticultural Journal see Philadelphia Florist and Horticultural Journal. Philadelphia.

Garden and Forest; a Journal of Horticulture, Landscape Art and Forestry. Conducted by Charles S. Sargent. New York: Garden & Forest Publishing Co., vols. 1–10, 1888–1897. 285 line illus. (by Charles Edward Faxon).

The Gardener's Monthly and Horticultural Advertiser. T. Meehan, ed. Philadelphia: W. G. P. Brinkloe, vols. 1–17, 1859–1875. Wood-eng. illus. Superseded by: The Gardener's Monthly and Horticulturist. T. Meehan, ed. Philadelphia, vols. 18–30, 1876–1888. Pls. United with Horticulturist and Journal of Rural Art and Rural Taste.

The Gardener's Monthly and Horticulturist see Gardener's Monthly and Horticultural Advertiser.

Hoffy's Orchardist's Companion see Orchardist's Companion

Horticultural Register, and Gardener's Magazine. Boston: G. C. Barrett [etc.], vols. 1–4, Jan. 1835–Dec. 1839. Lith. pls. (col.).

The Horticulturist and Journal of Rural Art and Rural Taste; Devoted to Horticulture, Landscape Gardening, Rural Architecture, Botany, Pomology, Entomology, Rural Economy, etc. A. J. Downing, ed. (later Henry T. Williams). Albany and Rochester: Luther Tucker, James Vick, vols. 1(1)–30(354) [vols. 8–30 also styled as ser. 2, vols. 1–23], 1846–1875. Pls. (col.). Merged with Gardener's Monthly and Horticultural Advertiser, to form Gardener's Monthly and Horticulturist.

How to Grow Flowers; an Illustrated Monthly Magazine Devoted to Successful Floriculture. [Ella V. Baines, ed.] Springfield [Ohio], 1896–1900.

Journal of Mycology; Devoted to the Study of Fungi. Washington and Columbus [Ohio], vols. 1–14, Jan. 1885–Apr. 1908. Pls., illus.

L B Case's Botanical Index; an Illustrated Quarterly Botanical Magazine. Richmond [Indiana], vols. 1–4(2), 1877–1881. Wood-eng. illus.

Ladies' Floral Cabinet; a Magazine of Floriculture and Domestic Arts. New York, vols. 1–16(1), 1872–1887. Merged with: American Garden, later American Gardening. Some pls., many illus.

Ladies' Wreath and Parlor Annual. Mrs. Sarah Towne, ed. New York: J. H. Martyn (later Martyn & Miller; Martyn & Burdick; J. C. Burdick; Burdick, Reed & Roberts; Burdick & Scovill; John F. Scovill), vols. 1–16?, 1847?–1861? {Issued as monthly publications which were collected and reissued as "annuals." 12 (flower) lith. pls. (col.), per vol. The text does not relate to plants and includes other unrelated "remainder" plates, views, portraits, etc.}

Magazine of Horticulture, Botany and All Useful Discoveries and Improvements in Rural Affairs see American Gardener's Magazine

The Mayflower; an Illustrated Monthly Magazine. Devoted to the Cultivation of Flowers and Plants, Gardening and Home Adornment in General. John L. Childs, ed. Hempstead and Floral Park: J. L. Childs, vols. 1–22, 1885–1906. Pls. (col.), many illus.

Meehans' Monthly: A Magazine of Horticulture, Botany, and Kindred Subjects. Conducted by Thomas Meehan. Illustrated with colored lithographs by L. Prang & Co. and numerous copper and wood engravings. Germantown: Thomas Meehan & Sons, 1891–1902. 12 vols. Pls. (col.).

Monthly Flora, or Botanical Magazine, Comprising the History, Description, and Colored Engravings of 24 Exotic Flowers, 24 Wild Flowers of America, and 12 Trees with Fruits. With an Introduction on the Physiology of Plants and a Tabular View of the Linnaean System. Illustrated with engravings. New York: Lewis & Brown, vol. 1, 1846. Pls. (col.).

Orchardists Companion, or Fruits of the United States: A Quarterly Journal, Devoted to the History, Character, Properties, Modes of Cultivation, and All Other Matters Appertaining to the Fruits of the United States. Embellished with richly colored designs of the natural size, painted from actual fruits when in their finest condition, and represented appended to a portion of the branch, with leaves and other characteristics, as seen on the tree. Also the flowers, cut fruits and stones. Alfred Hoffy,

Proprietor, ed. Philadelphia: A. Hoffy, vol. 1(1–4), 1841. 48 pls. (col.). Superseded by: Hoffy's Orchardist's Companion; or, Fruits of the United States [etc.]. Philadelphia: A. Hoffy, vol. 2(1), 1843. 12 lith. pls. (col.).

The Philadelphia Florist and Horticultural Journal. H. C. Hanson, ed., "Conducted by a committee of practical gardeners." Philadelphia, vol. 1, 1852. Pls. (col.). Superseded by: The Florist and Horticultural Journal; a Monthly Magazine of Horticulture, Agriculture, Botany, Agricultural Chemistry, Entomology, etc. H. C. Hanson, ed. Philadelphia, vols. 2–4(1–9), 1853–1855. Pls. (col.).

The Plant World; a Monthly Journal of Popular (General) Botany. F. H. Knowlton and Charles Louis Pollard, eds. Binghamton, N.Y.: The Plant World Co., vols. 1–22, 1897/98–1919.

Popular Gardening for Town and Country (later Popular Gardening and Fruit Growing); an Illustrated Periodical Devoted to Horticulture in All Its Branches. E. A. Long, ed., [etc.]. Buffalo: Popular Gardening Publishing Co., vols. 1–6, 1885–1891. Merged with: American Garden. Illus.

Proceedings of The Academy of Natural Sciences of Philadelphia. Philadelphia, vol. 1+, 1841+. Pls., illus. {E.g., Meehan, Thomas. Contributions to the life-histories of plants. [Nos. 1–16.] Proceedings, 1887–1894, 1897, 1899, & 1900–1902. 48 pls.}

Report of the Botanist, Department of Agriculture Washington, D.C.: United States of America – Department of Agriculture, Botanist. (1872–1900), 1872–1900. Pls. {Reports for 1872–1887 are reprinted from: Report of the Commissioner of Agriculture [of the United States of America]. Washington, D.C.; reports for 1888–1900 are reprinted, without change of pagination, from: Yearbook of the United States Department of Agriculture. Washington, D.C.}

Report of the Commissioner of Agriculture. Washington, 1862–1888. Superseded by: Report of the Secretary of Agriculture. Washington, 1889–1893. Pls. (some col.), illus.

Report of the Missouri Botanic Garden. St. Louis, no. 1+, 1890+. Pls., illus. {E.g., Trelease, William. A revision of the American species of *Epilobium* occurring north of Mexico. Report 1891. 48 pls.; Mulford, A. Isabel. A study of the

Agaves of the United States. Report 1896. 38 pls.; and Scribner, Frank Lamson-. Notes on the grasses in the Bernhardi Herbarium [etc.]. Report 1899. 54 pls.}

Report of the Pomologist, U.S. Department of Agriculture. Washington. 1886–1901. Pls. (several col. in each vol.).

Report of the United States National Museum. Washington, 1881+. Pls., incl. heliotypes.

Transactions of the Academy of Science of St. Louis. St. Louis, vol. 1+ (1856–1860+), 1860+. Pls. {E.g., Engelmann, George. 1880. Revision of

the genus *Pinus*, and description of *Pinus elliottii*. Transactions [etc.] 4(1): 161–189. 2 pls.}

Transactions of the Massachusetts Horticultural Society. Boston: For the Society by William D. Ticknor, vol. 1, no. 1–3, 1847[–1851]. 15 pls. (lith. & chromolith.).

Woodward's Record of Horticulture for 1866 (–67). New York: Geo. E. & F.W. Woodward, 1867–1868. 2 vols. Wood-eng. illus.

Yearbook of the United States Department of Agriculture. Washington, D.C., (1894+), 1895+. Pls., (some chromolith.), illus.

238

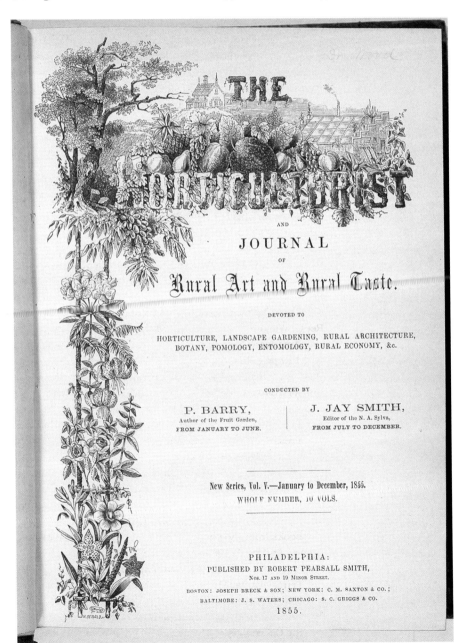

Title page of *The Horticulturist and Journal of Rural Art and Rural Taste*, January–December 1855.

Various library catalogues were consulted in making this list including Library of Congress, University of California, New York Botanical Garden, Arnold Arboretum, the Hunt Botanical Library, etc. Other sources included:

Bennett, Whitman. 1949. A Practical Guide to American Nineteenth Century Color Plate Books. New York, N.Y.: Bennett Book Studios, Inc. xxii+133 pp.

Childs, John Lewis. 1917. Catalogue of the North American Natural History Library of John Lewis Childs. Floral Park, N.Y.: Privately published. [v]+150 pp.

Cooper, Gayle et al. 1972–1989. A Checklist of American Imprints for 1830 (–39). 13 vols. Metuchen, N.J.: The Scarecrow Press.

MacPhail, Ian. 1981. The Sterling Morton Library Bibliographies in Botany and Horticulture, I: André and François Michaux. Lisle, Ill.: Morton Arboretum. [vi]+35 pp.; 1983. ... II: Thomas Nuttall. Lisle [etc.]. [vi]+35 pp.; 1986. ... III: Benjamin Smith Barton and William Paul Crillon Barton. Lisle [etc.]. [ix]+39 pp.; 1992. ... IV: John Torrey. Lisle [etc.]. [vi]+40 pp.

Meisel, Max. 1924–1929. A Bibliography of American Natural History, the Pioneer Century, 1769–1865: The Rôle Played by the Scientific Societies, Scientific Journals; Natural History Museums and Botanic Gardens; State Geological and Natural History Surveys; Federal Exploring Expeditions in the Rise and Progress of American Botany, Geology, Mineralogy, Paleontology and Zoology. 3 vols. Brooklyn, N.Y.: Premier Publishing Co. (Republished, New York: Hafner, 1967; Mansfield, Conn.: Maurizio Martino, [1994].)

Morton Arboretum; The Newberry Library. 1997. From Forest to Park: America's Heritage of Trees. The Morton Arboretum. The Newberry Library. 10 December 1997–14 March 1998. Chicago, Ill. 124 pp., illus. {Checklist of exhibit artifacts, pp. 112–121.}

Nissen, Claus. 1966. Die Botanische Buchillustration: Ihre Geschichte und Bibliographie. 2. Aufl. Stuttgart: Hiersemann. 3 vols. in 1.

Pennsylvania Horticultural Society. 1976. From Seed to Flower: Philadelphia, 1681–1876. A Horticultural Point of View. Philadelphia. 126 pp.

Reese, William S. 1999. Stamped with National Character: Nineteenth Century American Color Plate Books: An Exhibition. New York: The Grolier Club. 120 pp., illus. (col.).

Rinderknecht, Carol and Scott Bruntjen. 1964+. A Checklist of American Imprints for 1840 (+). Metuchen, N.J.: The Scarecrow Press. In progress.

Shaw, Ralph R. and Richard H. Shoemaker. 1958–1966. American Bibliography: A Preliminary Checklist for 1801 (–1819). 22 vols. New York: The Scarecrow Press.

Shoemaker, Richard H. and Gayle Cooper. 1964–1973. A Checklist of American Imprints for 1820 (–29). 12 vols. New York (later Metuchen, N.J.): The Scarecrow Press.

Sotheby's, firm. 1999. Sale 7332. Fine Books and Manuscripts Including Americana. ... Auction: ... June 22, 1999. New York. 377 pp. ["A selection of fruit books from the pomological library of Robert A. Nitschke," lots #197–246.]

Tucher, Andrea J. 1984. Agriculture in America, 1622–1860: Printed Works in the Collections of The American Philosophical Society, The Historical Society of Pennsylvania, The Library Company of Philadelphia. New York and London: Garland Publishing. xix+212 pp. [Americana to 1860 [etc.]. 2.]

Tucher, Andrea J. 1985. Natural History in America, 1609–1860: Printed Works in the Collections of The American Philosophical Society, The Historical Society of Pennsylvania, The Library Company of Philadelphia. New York and London: Garland Publishing. xix+287 pp. [Americana to 1860 [etc.]. 4.]

Some sources of information